'YOU'RE SO FAT!'
EXPLORING OJIBWE DISCOURSE:

'You're so fat!' was the greeting extended to the author's wife on her return to the Algonquin community of Pikogan in northwestern Quebec. The Anishnaabe elder was in fact complimenting her for looking robust and healthy.

Non-Natives have much to learn in order to understand Native experience and culture. Spielmann sets out to show how one might use the techniques of conversation analysis and discourse analysis to accomplish this. Ultimately, he seeks to capture the essence of Native experience by exploring how Native people talk about that experience, an approach that is missing in existing books about Aboriginal people.

'You're So Fat!' will be of interest to linguists, anthropologists, sociologists, and others interested in exploring issues in conversation analysis, ethnography, and Native studies.

ROGER SPIELMANN is an associate professor in the Department of Native Studies at the University of Sudbury.

ROGER SPIELMANN

'You're So Fat!'
Exploring Ojibwe Discourse

UNIVERSITY OF TORONTO PRESS
Toronto Buffalo London

© University of Toronto Press Incorporated 1998
Toronto Buffalo London
Printed in Canada

ISBN 0-8020-4112-4 (cloth)
ISBN 0-8020-7958-X (paper)

Printed on acid-free paper

Canadian Cataloguing in Publication Data

Spielmann, Roger Willson, 1951–
  'You're so fat!' : exploring Ojibwe discourse

Includes index.
ISBN 0-8020-4112-4 (bound)   ISBN 0-8020-7958-X (pbk.)

1. Ojibwa language – Discourse analysis.   2. Ojibwa Indians.   I. Title.

PM851.S64 1998   497'.3   C98-930076-5

University of Toronto Press acknowledges the financial assistance to its
publishing program of the Canada Council for the Arts and the Ontario Arts
Council.

This book has been published with the help of a grant from the Humanities
and Social Sciences Federation of Canada, using funds provided by the Social
Sciences and Humanities Research Council of Canada.

Contents

Part Four: Conclusion

Preface

'You're So Fat!' is designed to meet a painfully felt need in the discipline of Native Studies. In most of our courses in the Department of Native Studies at the University of Sudbury, there is still a scarcity of material, both textbooks and articles, that reflects what we refer to in our discipline as the Native perspective. Writing books is a long and arduous task, and 'You're So Fat!' is but one attempt to contribute to one of the crucial areas in the discipline of Native Studies: the teaching of language in all its richness and complexity. We see it as essential that both Native and non-Native scholars have access to a variety of research tools and perspectives in order to understand and represent Native experience accurately. 'You're So Fat!' seeks to provide these perspectives and techniques of conversation analysis and linguistic discourse analysis in order to lay the groundwork for understanding Aboriginal experience based on naturally occurring conversations, legends, stories, and traditional teachings. My hope is that this book will not only be beneficial for students in the disciplines of Native Studies, anthropology, and linguistics, but will also be engaging for anyone interested in coming to a deeper understanding of what it means to be an Aboriginal person in Canada as we head into the twenty-first century. In that sense, 'You're So Fat!' is, in the words of Bruce Krajewski, 'an invitation to a labyrinth ... [to] a place that can teach you how to make your way in the dark' (1992: 96).

There is no question that Ojibwe culture and the cultures of other First Nations traditions differ substantially from those of non-Native society in Canada. Few would argue that there are considerable differences in customs, languages, beliefs, traditions, ideals, and aspirations between First Nations people and non-Natives. Further, cultural differences which lead to tension in Native/non-Native interaction are not limited to the 'average' Canadian. During the Oka crisis in 1990, for example, the prime minister of Canada brought this tension into the national arena when he referred to Mohawk claims for sovereignty as 'bizarre.' What is it about First Nations people in Canada that evoke such strong feelings in non-Natives? What are some of the major cultural differences which lead to cross-cultural misunderstandings? Certainly there are no easy answers, but I am convinced that a basic understanding of some of the cultural differences would go a long way towards establishing mutual respect and a sense of 'different yet equal' between Native people and non-Natives.

In 'You're So Fat!', I will be talking about some of the basic differences in thinking between Native people and non-Natives, with a focus on Ojibwe-specific ways of speaking and interacting. One premise of this book is that Aboriginal world views can best be understood by paying careful attention to how people *talk* about the world around them: relationships, the environment, family, community, spirituality, and so on. That is where the techniques of conversation analysis and linguistic discourse analysis come in. By the end of the book you should feel that you have developed at least a mini-expertise in these research methods, and learned a lot about Ojibwe people in the process. I am convinced that many cross-cultural misunderstandings between people indigenous to this land now known as Canada and people with European ancestry arise from not knowing how to interpret properly the thinking and behaviour of someone from a different culture. Further, I believe that the best way to begin to understand Ojibwe ways of thinking is by exploring Ojibwe discourse and interaction patterns as they are reflected in naturally occurring talk. By exploring how Ojibwe people talk about their world, we can begin to come to a mutual understanding and respect for each other. The techniques of conversation analysis and linguistic discourse analysis are employed to begin to provide some answers to the twofold question in which this book is grounded: What are some of the basic cultural differences which so often lead to misunderstandings between Native people and non-Natives in Canada? And how can these vast stretches of misunderstanding be bridged?

The answer to that question requires you to set aside your preconceived notions about Native people and enter into a new realm. Ojibwe World awaits you.

Acknowledgments

Writing 'You're So Fat!' has reminded me of how much Anishnaabe people have transformed my life and thinking, and how that transformation has shaped this book. The people in the communities of Pikogan and Winneway, in particular, have added a dimension to my life that continues to this day. The years I have spent with Anishnaabe people have been among the most rewarding of my life. They taught me about themselves, but also about myself. It would be impossible to thank all of them here, but I want to express my deepest gratitude to some. My friendship with Gordon Polson and Louise Lahache has enriched my life in ways they may never know. They taught me to laugh in the darkest moments and they stayed with me through thick and thin. For that I will be forever grateful. Equally important in my life have been Albert and Anna Mowatt and their whole extended family at Pikogan. They took my family under their wings and taught us not only to speak their language but to love life and the Creator. Hector and Dorothy Polson, too, opened their hearts and home to us and were an integral part of my own transformation. Major Kistabish and Normand Mowatt have been special people in my life over the years, as have been Alfred Polson and his brother Raymond. They've all taught me more than they realize. I would be remiss not to mention Tom Rankin, Richard Kistabish, and Bishop Vincent Cadieux from the community of Pikogan, and Lena and Louis Polson, Walter Polson, Lisa McMartin and Bertha Chief from the community of Winneway for their help and encouragement over the years. To all in the communities of Pikogan and Winneway I wish a heart-felt *Gichi Miigwech!* Please forgive me for not mentioning you all by name; you know who you are.

I also wish to thank all of the Anishnaabe people who have been so helpful and encouraging to me in Sudbury as well. Special thanks go to Mary Ann Corbiere for her support and helpful discussions about language over the years. Her intuitive insights and linguistic expertise have had a great influence on my own thinking. I also wish to thank James Dumont for both his presence and profundity; Herb Nabigon, Schuyler Webster, and Barb Waterfall for their healing laughter; and all of my colleagues in Native Studies at the University of Sudbury. I want to thank my students in the courses I have taught at the university. They put up with a lot of my early thinking on discourse analysis. I only hope that I didn't cause any permanent damage.

Many others offered a great deal of support for this book: Dr Lawrence Steven (director, MA humanities) for granting me a graduate research assistant while I was on sabbatical; Alice Dickson (the aforementioned assistant) not only for spending hours reading the manuscript and offering valuable suggestions for making it better, but for her warm spirit and friendship. She helped to make the manuscript stronger and more reader-friendly. Julie Mallon spent many hours keyboarding parts of this manuscript and Mary Recollet was an angel in helping me to get the final manuscript ready. I also wish to thank Zorica Benkovic for giving me much kind encouragement as a fellow traveller on this journey of discovery. Other university colleagues offered helpful hints and encouragement along the way, in particular Dr John Sahadat of the Department of Religious Studies at the University of Sudbury. I also wish to thank the Laurentian University Native Education Council (LUNEC) for their support of my research for 'You're So Fat!'

Others outside of the University of Sudbury context have been of invaluable help and support to me, most notably Dr Lisa Philips Valentine of the University of Western Ontario (anthropology) and Dr Rand Valentine of the University of Wisconsin-Madison (linguistics). Their friendship as well as their expertise in linguistic and cultural matters have taught me much which is reflected in this book. I learned a great deal from Lisa Valentine's book *Making It Their Own: Severn Ojibwe Communicative Practices* (1995) and I remain extremely indebted to her work. Rand Valentine gave me much encouragement in the writing of this manuscript and his insights into Ojibwe discourse and culture-specific ways of thinking and doing things are greatly appreciated. I truly believe that he knows more about the Ojibwe language than anyone in the world (although he disagrees). Virgil Duff, executive editor at the University of Toronto Press, and his editorial assistant, Margaret Williams, continually encouraged me throughout the whole process. Their patience knows no bounds.

Finally, I wish to thank my family, to whom this book is dedicated. I have the three loveliest daughters in the world, Jennifer, Melissa, and Stephanie, whose sense of wonder at the world around us is a constant encouragement to me. And, of course, the person who did more than anyone else in encouraging, listening, rewriting, hand-holding, and in general just being there, Ruth Spielmann, my one true love. Perhaps we'll have more time to spend together now that 'the book' is finished.

'YOU'RE SO FAT!'

PART ONE
LANGUAGE AND CULTURAL VALUES

1

'That's What They Tell Me': Introduction and Overview

Much has been written in recent and not-so-recent years about Anishnaabe (Ojibwe and Algonquin) people, mostly by non-cultural members interested in studying them so as to better 'understand' them.[1] But what of the Anishnaabe perspective? Who, really, speaks for cultural authenticity? Few people living in Canada today would disagree with the fact that there still exists a great deal of misunderstanding and tension between Aboriginal and non-Aboriginal people. One of our primary concerns in the discipline of Native Studies is to create awareness and foster understanding between Aboriginal and non-Aboriginal people in order to continue the process of building bridges of understanding. I believe that Aboriginal traditions and values have a lot to offer non-Aboriginal people in Canada: a different way of looking at the world around us, the environment, material possessions, relationships with other people and, perhaps most importantly, our relationship with nature and the Creator. Should we not be listening to the words, thoughts, dreams, and visions of the Aboriginal people themselves as we seek to explore Aboriginal ways of seeing the world around us?

In the legends, stories, teachings and conversations that constitute the heart and soul of *'You're So Fat!'* we find a love of sharing and a passion for connecting with others. In their own way, everyone with whom I talked over the years has taught me something: I feel as if I've stumbled into a gold mine of thought, rich in insights relevant to all human beings. The value of listening to Anishnaabe people has had a profound affect on me ever since I first sat at the feet of these caring teachers. I found that the joy of learning, of coming away from each person with a richer vision of the times we live in, carries with it a responsibility, an expectation, to act upon what I am learning and to understand how such action informs the choices I make in life.

This book seeks to bring you into the heart of Aboriginal experience as a departure point for exploring Ojibwe discourse. It is assumed that the majority of readers will be generally uninformed about Aboriginal history and culture-specific ways of thinking and doing things. Few would argue that First Nations existed and survived for millennia with their own ways of living and thinking, forms of governance, and ways of relating to each other as individuals and kin, other First Nations, the environment, and the spirit world. This chapter intends to dispel the notion that Indian people are all the same. While there certainly are common cultural themes and concerns which are shared across First Nation traditions, there also exists great diversity in Aboriginal thought, practice, and experience. The chapter is designed to lay the necessary foundation for exploring Ojibwe cosmology, ethnomethods, ethnography of speaking, and interaction patterns via analysing naturally occurring discourse and talk.[2]

Setting the Context

In one sense, this entire book is a methodological mélange. There is no ideal reader and my approach is associative and interdisciplinary in many respects. I do not write to exhaust the reader with academic gibberish, but to stimulate interactive dialogues about the lives and thinking of real people. It is a recurring theme that careful attention to the features of spoken discourse and naturally occurring talk by Ojibwe people themselves sheds light on what at first appears to be common knowledge about Ojibwe ways of thinking and looking at the world around us, but in the final analysis reveals something previously unexplored about the nature of Ojibwe experience. When these discourse and interactional features are explored in the context of traditional teachings, stories, legends, and naturally occurring talk, we enter a world where we are better able to understand the relationships between performative features of Ojibwe discourse, culture-specific techniques of transmitting cultural knowledge, and Ojibwe cosmology.

I have included personal experiences because I consider them as important as the socio-cultural scaffolding of naturally occurring talk in which these experiences are grounded. I take it as a given that some readers will be exasperated by the lack of systematic tidiness. So be it. My main purpose is not to co-opt the richness and complexity of Ojibwe ways of thinking and doing things, but to provide a forum for the people themselves to breath life into what appear to be mere words

on dead, dry leaves. Thus the analyses presented in this book presume
no closure. In fact, I see it as a virtue of this kind of exploration that
much will be revised, reversed, or reinvented, particularly by Anishnaabe readers themselves. Further, one ought to keep in mind when
reading that the straightest passage into Anishnaabe ways of thinking
and doing things leads through family, kinship, community, stories,
and face-to-face interaction. Thus, in the beginning my observations
were uncritically 'etic' (from a cultural outsider's perspective).[3] As I
became more and more 'emic' (from a cultural insider's perspective) so,
too, does the analysis I present in this book rely more and more on the
'Living Voice' – that is, face-to-face interaction, recounted stories, and
the teachings of people who are not merely speakers of an Aboriginal
language but masters of it.

Where the Teachings Originate

The teachings, legends, and stories explored in *'You're So Fat!'* come primarily from the Algonquin communities of Pikogan and Winneway
(located in what is now the province of Quebec), and the Odawa community of Wikwemikong, Ontario. The Algonquin teachings were
recorded from 1979 through 1990. Pikogan and Winneway are two of
nine Algonquin communities in northwestern Quebec. Most of the community of Pikogan originates from the Abitibi region of Quebec, with a
few members from the Temiskamingue area. In the village of Pikogan
(which means 'teepee'), the Algonquin language is still widely used
among the 550 people living there, although French (and some English)
is being used more and more, particularly among the younger generation. The majority of families live in their reserve homes, making frequent trips to their trapping grounds throughout the year. There are
approximately 370 Algonquins living in the community of Winneway.
The people were originally located at Old Long Point on the shore of the
Ottawa River. In the 1920s the people moved to Sand Point and in the
late 1940s the community relocated to its present site at Winneway. The
native language is Algonquin, although English is understood by
almost everyone in the community. Algonquin is linguistically considered to be a northern dialect of Ojibwe (hence my use of Ojibwe in this
book to refer to both Ojibwe and Algonquin linguistic traditions). It is
common for linguists to refer to Algonquin as 'the Algonquin dialect of
Ojibwe,' although Algonquins generally distinguish their language and
culture from the Ojibwe. The second languages spoken throughout

Algonquin territory are French and English, depending on the specific community.

The interviews and recordings of naturally occurring talk from Wikwemikong were collected during the period of 1991 through 1996. The community of Wikwemikong is situated on the eastern peninsula of Manitoulin island in Ontario. It is the largest of the five Ojibwe/Odawa reserves on the island. Wikwemikong is considered to be an unceded reserve with a population of around 5,000 (2,400 living on the reserve itself and 2,600 living off-reserve). While the majority of the people at Wikwemikong over the age of thirty-five speak Ojibwe fluently (as well as English), most of the younger members of the community speak English exclusively.

A Personal Note

Some of my most memorable times during the eleven years we lived in Pikogan were spent sitting with the elders in their homes on the reserve or in their cabins in the bush. I would listen to them tell stories and talk: about life, about hunting and fishing, the spirit world, non-Native people and, in particular, about the one in their midst, often accompanied by much laughter. I never felt left out, though, or in any way put down. They always had a way of making me feel welcome and a part of their conversations. Being able to speak the language has a way of ensuring one's acceptance in another culture. The more time I spent with the community elders the more comfortable I became and the more I learned to respect their way of life and way of thinking.

I should make it clear from the outset that I am in no position to speak on *behalf* of First Nations people. They are certainly capable of speaking for themselves and do so quite articulately. What I have to offer is the immigrant's perspective on Anishnaabe culture. But I do believe this perspective is of value. In many instances, and for many reasons, the immigrant into another culture is forced to develop a cross-cultural perspective in order to learn how to interact appropriately. This helps one to see the differences between two cultures. On the flip side of the coin, the history of Native/non-Native relations in Canada has been dominated by non-Native people speaking on behalf of First Nations people. As one Native woman, Lenore Keeshig-Tobias, recently wrote in *Saturday Night* 'I am automatically on guard whenever white people speak or write about Indians. What do they want this time? I ask. What are they looking for – adventure, danger, material wealth, spiritual power, a cause, a book, or maybe just a story? It matters not if this person is invited; the history of the relations between European Canadians and Natives ... allows no kinder response' (1990:67). I believe she's right. So what I have to offer is my own learning experience as an immigrant into one Native community and the opportunity to listen to the 'Native Voice' as we take a close look at conversational interaction, legends, stories, and myths.[4]

Yet I still feel quite awkward writing this book.[5] It is out of that sense of awkwardness that *'You're So Fat!'* has a dual purpose: to act as a forum for listening to, learning from, and coming to appreciate traditional Anishnaabe stories and teachings; and to provide an introduction to exploring the richness and complexity of the Anishnaabe language and culture-specific interactional features of language-in-use. As such, I share Linda Akan's research directive:

My only role in this process is to try in the best way that I know to make the message of the Elders understandable to the westerner. It was necessary for me to take my translation of the text back to the Elder and ask for verification of the translation and validation of the implications that I had drawn from the discourse. Having done this, I feel that most of what is written here is related directly to the knowledge of the Elders unless I have stated otherwise. (1992:194)

A Note on Terminology

A related issue has to do with terminology. Much has been written over the years about what sociolinguists commonly refer to as 'in-group' language and 'out-group' language (Crystal, 1987; Hymes, 1981). That is, a specific term of reference used by a people who share a common cultural heritage may be considered derogatory when used by a cultural outsider, but acceptable when used by cultural members themselves. In many First Nations communities, for example, it is common to hear members refer to themselves as 'Indians,' or even as 'savages' or 'redskins.' Such terms are commonly used for joking, teasing and, perhaps most importantly, for expressing in-group solidarity. When I worked with African-American youth one summer in Dallas, Texas, the use of the term 'nigger' was commonplace among the youth themselves, as in: 'Hey, he's one bad nigger' (a compliment!), or 'Hey, nigger, what it is?' But if a white person were to refer to a black person by calling him a nigger, that person risked being killed. It is the same with 'maudit sauvage' (goddam savage) in Quebec. It can be (and is) used in jest between

Native people themselves, but when used by French people to refer to a Native person, it most often results in hostility and fighting.

Drew Hayden Taylor, well-known Ojibwe playwright and author, in his essay 'Oh, Just Call Me an Indian,' writes in light-hearted fashion about the confusion as to what term to use to refer to himself and his people: 'While we were growing up we were all proud to be *Indians*. The word had a certain power to it that set as apart from the white kids. Somehow the cry of "Proud to be Indigenous!" just doesn't have the same ring' (1996:13).

After going through a dozen or so different terms commonly used to refer to Aboriginal people (Native, Aboriginal, Indigenous, First Nation, Bill C-31 Indian, on-reserve Indian, off-reserve Indian, Treaty Indian), he concludes: 'Even I get confused sometimes. That's why I usually use the term "Indian." I'm just too busy or too lazy to find out which way the political wind is blowing. By the time I go through all the categories, I've missed my deadline. Then I become an *unemployed* Indian' (p. 14).

It should be noted, too, that not all members of a particular 'in-group' agree. As Lenore Keeshig-Tobias recently wrote: 'How I loathe the term *Indian*. And not because of a negative self-image. It's because of a deep pride in my heritage and culture, and knowledge of my history. *Indian* is a term used to sell things – movies, books, cars, gasoline, etc. *Indian* is a figment of the white man's imagination' (1990:67).

Strong stuff, for sure, but it pays to keep in mind that not all Aboriginal people agree with her. In responding to her comments, Solomon Ratt, a Cree from Manitoba, writes: 'I am Cree. I for one do not mind being called *Indian* because in using the term most people know one is referring to North American Indians. Referring to me by the euphemism *Native* belittles my Indian heritage, since a native to a country by definition is one who was born in that country. Hence Native refers to all those born here in Canada regardless of their ethnic background.' The point to remember is that every cultural group uses and responds to in-group language which those outside the culture are not invited to use.

One final comment on the issue. I recently did an informal survey and asked a few of my Native friends which term they prefer and which they use to refer to themselves. They were unanimous in preferring cultural outsiders to refer to them as Aboriginal people, Native people, or First Nations people. But most of them thought of themselves almost exclusively as Anishnaabe. Another popular in-group term currently in use around here is 'Neechee,' as in, 'Hey, are there any Neechees down in the lounge?' The term comes from the word *Niijikiiwe*, which in many

Anishnaabe dialects means, 'My brother/sister.' We can begin to grasp how in-group terms usually spring from somewhere deep inside cultural members. For me, I think it is important to keep in mind this distinction when thinking about how people refer to themselves and how they wish to be referred to by outsiders. At the very least, it is a sign of respect to use terms for a people that they themselves prefer.[6]

What Is Meant by Discourse?

I use the word 'discourse' often in this book, and it is important for the reader to understand how I am using that term. Michael McCarthy provides us with a starting point for that understanding when he suggests that 'Discourse analysis is concerned with the study of the relationships between language and the contexts in which it is used' (1991:5). Ruth Finnegan claims that '"Discourse" is often used as an umbrella term to cover *all* forms of verbal communication,' and she applies the term to 'all kinds of active verbal communication' (1992:14). John Gumperz was one of the first to articulate the nature of discourse in the context of contemporary discourse studies: 'Communication is a social activity requiring the coordinated efforts of two or more individuals. Mere talk to produce sentences, no matter how well formed or elegant the outcome, does not in itself constitute communication. To create and sustain conversational involvement, we require knowledge and abilities which go considerably beyond the grammatical competence we need to decode short isolated messages' (1982:1).

Emphasizing this relationship, Joel Sherzer helps us to gain a better grasp of what is meant by discourse: 'In my view, discourse is a level or component of language use, related to but distinct from grammar. It can be oral or written and can be approached in textual or socio-cultural and socio-interactional terms ... Discourse is an elusive area, an imprecise and constantly emerging and emergent interface between language and culture, created by actual instances of language in use and best defined specifically in terms of such instances' (1987:296). He claims that much of the work being done in contemporary linguistic anthropology is grounded in discourse and that discourse is 'not only worthy of investigation in its own right, but as an embodiment of the essence of culture and as constitutive of what the language-culture-society relationship is all about' (p. 297).

Bruce Krajewski provides us with another clue to the distinctly social nature of discourse when he writes about dialogue as 'the give and take between two, the question and the response, the circular movement. That dialogue is primary to understanding shows that understanding is a social, not a private, act, nor a mental operation' (1992:8). Crystal suggests that the study of discourse 'focuses on the structure of naturally-occurring spoken language, as found in such "discourses" as conversations, interviews, commentaries and speeches' (1987:116).

In her book *Relevance Relations in Discourse* Regina Blass expands on the notion of discourse by showing how features of naturally occurring talk are pragmatic rather than purely semantic matters. She goes on to suggest that discourse is not purely a linguistic notion; it is an *interactional* one as well: 'What is crucial to discourse comprehension is the recognition of relevance relations, which are *relations between the content of an utterance and its context*' (1990:24–5, emphasis mine).

Wallace Chafe, in *Discourse, Consciousness and Time*, pictures discourse is an index of reality or 'consciousness.' He urges those interested in the study of discourse to 'restore conscious experience to the central role it enjoyed in the human sciences a hundred years ago' (1994:4). Chafe makes the point that the study of discourse, how people use language in naturally occurring interaction, can tell us much about how people think and view the world around them.

In *Narrating Our Pasts: The Social Construction of Oral History*, Elizabeth Tonkin describes how oral histories are constructed and how they should be interpreted. She raises the issue of genre and its importance in understanding discourse (a concept to which we will return in chapter 8). She writes: 'The different conventions of discourse through which speakers tell [their stories] and listeners understand them can be called *genres*. A genre signals that a certain kind of interpretation is called for ... Genres provide a "horizon of expectation" to an audience that cannot be derived from the semantic content of discourse alone' (1992:2).

Tonkin helps us to understand that representations of reality are constructed and sustained by people in everyday talk and situated in real time and space. And that, basically, is how I am using the term discourse in *'You're So Fat!'*: as verbal interaction, language-in-use, naturally occurring talk, whenever words come out of one's mouth in virtually any social situation.

The study of discourse most often relies on written transcriptions of naturally occurring conversations, legends, stories and the like – what discourse linguists commonly refer to as texts. Some may argue that reducing actual talk to written form takes away the power of what is being spoken. Even written transcriptions, however, carry a power of their own. As Regna Darnell attests, texts in the Amerindian tradition help to make what is said accessible to anyone interested in coming to a deeper understanding of culture-specific ways of thinking and perceiving. She writes:

Texts provide evidence which cannot be falsified by the preconceptions of the observer ... They can be analyzed and re-analyzed if necessary or they can be valued for their own sake – as distilled records in the words of particular individuals of the knowledge systems of their cultures ... [expressing] the best that had been known and thought and expressed in human history. By contemporary standards, there is certainly an arrogance in the privileging of information written down; but it coexists with respect for the words so written and for the knowledge of their speakers. (1996:167)

Teun van Dijk recently edited *Discourse Studies: A Multidisciplinary Introduction* (1997), a two-volume set which provides a comprehensive introduction to discourse studies. He considers the study of discourse to encompass the analysis of the linguistic, social, cultural and cognitive properties of text and talk in their various contexts. The books make the claim that discourse is not merely form and meaning but also action. Whether in informal, everyday conversations or professional dialogues, the contributors to *Discourse Studies* emphasize how people *do* things while they are speaking or writing. These books stress that both discourse and its mental processing have a social basis and can only be fully understood in relation to social interaction.

Algonquian Discourse Studies

Perhaps the most significant book to date on Ojibwe-specific discourse and interaction patterns has been Lisa Philips Valentine's, *Making It Their Own: Severn Ojibwe Communicative Practices*. While Valentine's analysis is confined to one Ojibwe community at Lynx Lake, Ontario, she provides an excellent overview of the development of discourse analysis. Her portrayal of the Severn Ojibwe perspective on life, as accessed via talk, plays with the boundaries, delights in contraries, and shows how people talking to and about themselves reinforce social norms in the Lynx Lake community. She writes: 'Discourse is the universe through which sociocultural relationships are most actively created, reinforced, negotiated, changed, and disseminated ... For the most part, the discourse of other peoples has been translated, interpreted, and reported through the words of the anthropologist. In much of this study, however, the words of Severn Ojibwe people are presented so that they may speak for themselves' (1995:4).

According to Valentine, discourse analysis is concerned with how people produce and interpret language-in-context. Discourse analysts discover and describe the linguistic structures of conversational sequences, speech activities, oral and literate registers, and stance (among other constructions) and seek to relate these constructions to social and cultural norms, preferences and interactional expectations. In broad terms, the field articulates how lexico-grammar and discourse systematically vary across social situations and at the same time help to define those situations.

Nikotwâsik iskwâhtêm, pâskihtêpayih! Studies in Honour of H.C. Wolfart, edited by John Nichols and Arden Ogg (1996), is another valuable book rich in insights into Algonquian languages and cultures. The volume is impressive in bringing together scholarly work on Algonquian languages and cultural themes which runs the gamut from detailed phonological and morphological studies to higher-level discourse analyses.

In 'Amik Anicinaabewigoban: Rhetorical Structures in Albert Mowatt's Telling of an Algonquin Tale', Rand Valentine invites us to enter the world of a monolingual-speaking Algonquin elder by listening to Albert Mowatt's rendering of a traditional Algonquin legend, the same legend we'll be exploring in great detail in chapter 10. Of the distinct discourse features which both occur in and interact with the telling of this legend, Valentine claims that: 'Overarching all components is the category of genre. For example, form-content parallelism is often most salient in genres associated with traditional tales ... [and] form-content parallelism pervades all discourse components in Mr. Mowatt's rendering' (1996:394–5).

Much of Valentine's exploration of rhetorical structures in Algonquin is laced with fascinating details, particularly in his treatment of syntax and larger discourse structures. While the reader only catches a glimpse of the dynamics of a monolingual-speaking elder recounting a traditional tale in a real-life context, Valentine's analysis provides us with a window on the inner workings of the Algonquin mind and, as such, helps us to better appreciate the uniqueness and complexity of Algonquin-specific ways of thinking and doing things.

Amy Dahlstrom's article, 'Narrative Structure of a Fox Text,' explores the salient features of narrative structure in Fox, an Algonquian language, including the rhetorical development of the story, changed conjunct clauses, the use of anaphoric temporal adverbs, and obviation.

This last feature constitutes a unique feature of Algonquian discourse. As Dahlstrom writes, 'Algonquian languages are famous for having a grammatical opposition within third person known as OBVIATION. In clauses involving more than one third person argument, the third person most central to the discourse is singled out as PROXIMATE and the referred to by unmarked third person forms, while the more peripheral third persons are referred to by marked OBVIATIVE forms' (1996:121).

Kevin Russell pursues the feature of obviation in Algonquian discourse in his article 'Does Obviation Mark Point of View?' He does this by exploring the pattern of proximate choice in 'The Story of the Skirt,' originally told by Simon Mimikwas and included in Bloomfield's (1934) collection of texts. He writes: 'Stripping away the basic layers of retelling, the basic narrative will either be a first-person narrative ... or a third-person narrative whose distribution of proximate and obviative referents still remains to be explained ... If the concept of point of view is to have any relevance in explaining the ... distribution of proximates and obviatives, it must be in answering the question "Who sees?" rather than "Who speaks?"' (1996:370).

Russell employs an interesting analytical technique in parts of his analysis, that of the cinematographer: 'If the proximate referent is indeed a focalizer ... the cinematic equivalent would be a film shot with the camera being carried around by the proximate character. Since obviation status can change in the course of a narrative, the camera will occasionally be tossed from character to character' (p. 371).

I employ a similar analytical technique in my discourse analysis of the Algonquin dialect of Ojibwe (in chapter 10), and I think Russell's exploration of proximate-obviative switching in a narrative text helps to clarify what such switching can perform for the narrator. As he suggests, 'Proximate choice and the various kinds of point of view are resources that can be manipulated independently of each other in order to give structure and texture to a narrative' (p. 379).

Previous Studies on Native Discourse and Interaction Patterns

A number of other studies in the past few years have provided us with some clues as to what constitute some of the main cultural differences between Native people and non-Natives in Canada, most of which are best accessed by exploring discourse. James Dumont, Anishnaabe healer and professor of Native Studies at the University of Sudbury, provides us with a solid foundation for beginning to understand the profundity of these cultural differences in his article 'Justice and

Aboriginal People' (1993). He begins by exploring the principal tradi-tional values of Aboriginal people and then proceeds to compare and contrast fundamental values, behaviour and interaction patterns between Aboriginal and non-Aboriginal people. Dumont goes on to present a table of value differences leading to contemporary conflict in ways of thinking and doing things between Native people and non-Natives. While he relates his insights to the conflicts arising between Aboriginal people and the Canadian judicial system, his exploration of these values, along with the meaning of each value and the resulting behaviour, helps us to gain a better grasp of what those basic value dif-ferences are between Native people and non-Natives in Canada today.

Scollon and Scollon (1981), too, laid some important groundwork for exploring the relationship between cultural differences between Native people and non-Natives, when they examined how the differences between Native and non-Native discourse systems may produce conflict and confusion in inter-ethnic communication. Richard Rhodes (1988) writes about Ojibwe politeness and social structure and suggests that conventional ways of being polite among the Ojibwe may be considered to be conventionally rude to most non-Natives. Clare Brant (1990), the late Mohawk psychologist, pointed out a number of potential areas of misunderstanding between Native and non-Native people based on value differences such as non-interference, emotional restraint, sharing, the Native concept of time, and Native protocol, among others. Brant's cultural-member observations have been criticized by some Aboriginal people, however, particularly for some of its over-generalizations.

One of the more insightful students of Aboriginal languages in the Iroquoian and Algonquian traditions over the past decade has been John Steckley. Steckley uses morphological analysis of select mor-phemes in the Huron language to present evidence that flies in the face of two commonly held stereotypes of Aboriginal languages: first, that they contain relatively few words, and secondly, that they cannot express philosophically abstract concepts. In 'More than Eight Million Words: Huron Language Productivity' (1994d), we are presented with a single Huron verb root that has the capacity to be used to develop 8,258 words. As there are around one thousand verb roots in the Huron lan-guage, Steckley arrives at the figure of more than eight million words. In 'Verbs and Nouns' (1994b) Steckley shows how verbs and nouns can play very different roles in Aboriginal languages in comparison to English and French. Verbs dominate the former, with nouns decidedly playing a secondary role. The opposite applies with the latter. He also introduces us to the key notion of morphology (structure of words), so important in understanding the complex nature of many Aboriginal languages (1994c). Further, we see how morphology works through looking at one type of word part and how it operates in three Aboriginal languages. We also see that there are ways of categorizing pronouns that are different in some Aboriginal languages from those of English and French (1994a).

Other recent books and articles continue this attempt to build bridges of understanding between Native discourse and interaction patterns compared to Euro-Canadian ones, but in non-academic terms that are designed to reach a wider, non-academic audience. Three that strike me as being especially informative, and which relate to discourse and interactional differences between Native people and non-Natives, are the writings of Drew Hayden Taylor, a well-known Ojibwe playwright, author, and humorist, and Rupert Ross, a non-Native assistant crown attorney for the District of Kenora. In *Dancing with a Ghost: Exploring Indian Reality* (1992) and *Returning to the Teachings* (1996), Ross dispels the stereotypical notion that Aboriginal people in Canada are 'just like white people.' His observations are based upon years of experience working with Ojibwe and Cree people. His audience is primarily non-Native and he goes a long way in delineating some of the unique ways of thinking, communicating, and perceiving the world around us that distinguish Aboriginal values, ethos, and behaviour from Euro-Canadian ones. Many of his observations revolve around the Canadian legal system and its impact on the lives of Aboriginal people. He concludes that the Canadian legal system fails Aboriginal people because it does not recognize Native-specific values, thinking, and cultural practices.

When his first book came out, we used it quite extensively in our introductory course in the Department of Native Studies at the University of Sudbury. His personal anecdotes relating to his experiences and friendships with Aboriginal people are particularly revealing. A number of my Native friends and colleagues are of the opinion that the book helps to facilitate a better understanding of how Native ways of thinking and behaving are grounded in culture-specific discourse. Most of them, however, also commented on the danger of Ross, as a cultural outsider, exploring 'Indian reality,' the phrase itself suggesting that First Nations people constitute one homogeneous group. A few people suggested that Ross is overly romantic about 'Indian people' in both books, and that his writing, at times, comes across as patronizing. Still, in broad strokes, Ross's books do provide a glimpse into the differences in values, beliefs, thinking, and behaving that continue to baffle most non-Native people today.

The musings of Drew Hayden Taylor are of a different nature. Where Ross is dark and intense, Taylor is playful and profound, perhaps because he is a cultural member himself and is thus able to explore differences in thinking and discourse between Native people and non-Natives from an insider's point of view. I have had the privilege of getting to know Drew personally over the past few years; he has taught me much through his writings and our conversations together, which are always fuelled by humour and laughter. Taylor has a way of seeing things with a kind of Native *Far Side* perspective which helps both Native people and non-Natives see the differences between Native and non-Native ways of perceiving the world around us, but also getting us to laugh along with him as he explores such topics as 'Missionary Positions,' 'North of Sixty, South of Accurate,' 'An Aboriginal Name Claim,' and 'Why the Natives Are Restless,' among others. Taylor relies upon Native intuition, a keen eye for observation, and a bizarre sense of humour to educate non-Native people about the richness and complexity of Native-specific ways of thinking and interacting, and in so doing plays an important part in the bridge-building literature.[7]

Overview of the Book

'You're So Fat!' is designed for those who do not necessarily share a common stock of knowledge about Aboriginal history, values, ethos, and culture-specific ways of perceiving the world. It is an exploration of Aboriginal ethnomethods, the value systems which motivate Aboriginal-specific ways of thinking and doing things, and how those ethnomethods and the values which underlie them can be understood by examining Aboriginal discourse. A key component of the text is the examination and analysis of Aboriginal ethnohistories, values, ethos, and traditional teachings using a discourse-centred approach. Finally, it is hoped the book will be accessible to a wide audience, both Native and non-Native. It aims to contribute to the bridge-building literature currently being produced which strives to bring non-Native people to a deeper and more representative and authentic understanding of what it means to be an Aboriginal person in Canada as we head into the twenty-first century.

Chapter 2 is designed to bring the reader into the heart and soul of the Ojibwe experience by exploring interaction patterns, naturally occurring conversation, and the underlying values which motivate Ojibwe peoples. It focuses on face-to-face interaction in Ojibwe communities and relies heavily on politeness protocol, culturally appropriate interaction patterns, and learning how to fit into a Native context or community. The chapter also seeks to ground the reader in cross-cultural realities and to enable both Native people and non-Natives to come away with a deeper understanding of and appreciation for Aboriginal experience.[8] It uses Native community experiences, anecdotes, humorous stories, and teachings from the elders to get across the point that we are dealing with substantively different ways of thinking and doing things between Native people and non-Native. By relying on Native intuition and observation, it is suggested that an understanding of those value differences is essential for decreasing the tension, misunderstanding, confusion, and stereotypes which have evolved since the first contact between European-based peoples and Aboriginal peoples.

Chapter 3 looks at some of the basic differences between Algonquian languages and Indo-European languages such as English and French. It is based on the belief that an understanding of the distinctive features of any language can tell one a great deal about the psyche of a people. For example, Ojibwe is a non-sexist language in that its pronouns are not gender-specific; one can only determine whether one is referring to male or female by context. The chapter also discusses a number of distinctive language features designed to show the richness and complexity of the Ojibwe language and demonstrate how language truly acts as a window on a people. Other language-related areas discussed include language revitalization and maintenance, language and identity, and language preservation in relation to self-determination.

Chapter 4 explores the everyday life experience of Ojibwe people by examining naturally occurring talk and natural, everyday interactions relating to how Ojibwe reality is socially constructed. Emphasis is placed on discovering and describing performative features of talk: storytelling, joking/teasing, providing accounts, making requests, complimenting, and so on. The chapter is designed to lay the foundation for understanding the relationships between performative features of talk and everyday conversation, ethnomethods, and world view by presenting the basic methodology involved in doing conversation analysis. The chapter guides the reader through the basic methods of analysing performative features of language as it occurs in natural contexts. Our interest in this chapter, then, is with interactional strategies and reflections of ethos and values in naturally occurring talk. Some of the other areas explored include preferred and dispreferred conversational responses, the organization of conversational sequences, and membership categories.

Chapter 5 proposes that legends and stories told in conversation are elaborately designed to display potentially related topical orientation. The storyteller serves as a principal character in the story, directing the listeners to attend to certain features of the story in subtle but specific ways, concealing some of the ways a story works from those listeners, making a moral point or illustrating a maxim, and so forth. When stories are told in conversation, the storytellers display their artfulness and competence as storytellers. The Ojibwe people are capable of employing some rather complex and intricate interactional devices with the listeners in mind. In this chapter we concentrate on one such device, that of verb tense organization, by examining some short stories told in conversation in English and comparing them with two Ojibwe legends.

Chapter 6 shows how the methods of conversation analysis can be of tremendous value in understanding some of the methods that people engaged in ongoing conversation use to initiate, sustain, and terminate a series of topically related utterances in the context of humorous talk. This chapter explores not only some ways in which laughter and humour are managed in Ojibwe conversation, but also some of the culturally defined humorous themes at stake in Ojibwe.

Chapter 7 examines how one common conversational activity, complaints, is made in Ojibwe. Complaints are normally generated either to seek a remedy for a perceived problem in the social reality of the one making the complaint, and/or to seek some form of sympathy or solidarity. In looking at complaints in naturally occurring conversation, we find that Ojibwe complainants try to preserve anonymity when possible. Another feature of the complaint structures we examine in this chapter is that occasions for complaints in Ojibwe seem to provide legitimate grounds for transmitting and reinforcing cultural values.

Chapter 8 explores some of the salient features of hortatory and expository discourse by monolingual speakers of the Algonquin dialect of Ojibwe. In particular, discourse features and cultural themes from one elder's teaching on 'What Happens in Life' are examined and compared with another teaching on prayer. This chapter is intended to provide an introduction to linguistic discourse analysis by taking a detailed look at contemporary teachings. The value of understanding these higher-level features of Ojibwe is presented in relation to issues such as recovering and maintaining Native-community oral histories, understanding how stories, legends, and myths are generated and transmitted, and language revitalization and maintenance programs in Aboriginal contexts. What such teaching tells us, according to the elders, goes beyond human relationships to the very nature of our relationship with the Creator. In this chapter we see how Ojibwe people create and sustain their social world by talking about it, and how that talk opens up a window on the psyche and thinking of a people.

Chapter 9 analyses teachings about bear dreams and lucky dreams, with the objective of discovering and describing some of the features of Ojibwe narrative and expository discourse. The main contention in this chapter is that careful attention to the features of spoken discourse sheds light on what at first appears to be common knowledge about Ojibwe discourse, but in the final analysis reveals something previously unexplored about the nature of Ojibwe ethnography of speaking. When these discourse features are explored in the context of teachings about bear dreams and lucky dreams in one dialect and then compared with teachings about warning animals and dream visitors in a related dialect (Odawa), these teachings enable us to understand better the relationships between performative features of Algonquian discourse, culture-specific techniques of transmitting cultural knowledge, and Ojibwe cosmology.

Chapter 10 looks at the role that stories, legends, and myths play in the lives of Anishnaabe people in the contemporary scene. While the strength of the oral tradition has certainly diminished with the introduction of literacy and the advent of the tape-recorder and videotape, the oral tradition is still strong in the minds of Ojibwe people, both young and old. The chapter takes a twofold approach to understanding Ojibwe discourse: to introduce the reader to the oral tradition and its place in contemporary Aboriginal experience; and, on an academic level, to understand how linguistic discourse analysis can lead to deeper understandings of the Ojibwe language and the competency of Ojibwe speakers. This section should be valuable to Ojibwe language instructors and both Native and non-Native linguists, anthropologists, and educators interested in exploring some of the complex features of Ojibwe discourse. While the non-academic reader may be put off by some of the technical analysis, this and other chapters are designed also for the non-academic reader who is interested in learning about some of the stories, legends, myths and traditional teachings in the Algonquian tradition.

Chapter 11 presents instances where people telling stories in naturally occurring conversation recount things that did not happen (termed collateral information in the linguistic discourse literature). We first take a look at a linguistic discourse analysis treatment of collateral as found in the linguistic literature relating to narrative and then examine the same phenomenon from the perspective of conversation analysis. This is intended not merely to extend a linguistic discourse analysis treatment of the issues, but to show how the issues get transformed in theoretically interesting ways.

Finally, chapter 12 ties together the various strands of the book. Suggestions are made as to how the methods and techniques presented here can be used to understand better Anishnaabe ways of thinking and doing things with an interest in contributing to the bridge-building literature in a practical and accessible manner. Ultimately, 'You're So Fat!' seeks to capture the essence of Aboriginal experience by exploring how Anishnaabe people talk about that experience – an experience that is saturated with a wisdom, humour, and joyfulness that is painfully missing from existing books about Aboriginal people. The 'Living Voice' is at the heart and soul of the book, that is, listening to the Native voice with the invitation to join in on a journey of discovery and exploration. The journey for Native people lies in the process of recovering traditional teachings and ways of thinking. For non-Natives it relates to understanding Native ways of thinking and perceiving the world around us. Finally, this chapter offers Aboriginal language teachers, educators, ethnographers, applied linguists, and virtually anyone interested in culture-specific ways of thinking and doing things a fundamentally different way of looking at language.

2

'You're So Fat!': Exploring Value Differences between Native and Non-Native People in Canada

In this chapter I want to probe a bit more deeply into what many non-Native people in Canada consider to be the strange world of Aboriginal people; in particular, what it means to 'act appropriately' in an Aboriginal context. My two oldest daughters attended a band-run school in the Algonquin community of Pikogan in northwestern Quebec. It was an experience they will never forget and one that has given them a bicultural outlook on life. I remember when my oldest daughter was in Grade 1 she came home one day and announced, 'I'm an Indian. My teacher said so.' In fact, her teacher had encouraged the students to be proud that they were Anishnaabe and my daughter figured she was included too. It took a few months for my wife and I to convince her that she was really a little white kid and not an Indian! Our lives were essentially transformed in many ways by living in that community and developing relationships with Anishnaabe people. When we moved to Sudbury, where I began teaching in the Department of Native Studies at the University of Sudbury, all three of my daughters began attending a non-Native school and making friends with non-Native kids for the first time in their lives. We wondered how we would adjust and, believe me, it was tough for all of us at first to move back into a primarily non-Native cultural milieu. It wasn't just the language differences that threw us off, it was something deeper – something having to do with the core of our being and the adopted values that now fuel our own way of living and perceiving the world around us.

This chapter, then, explores some of the cultural differences between Native and non-Native interaction from our own experience living in an Algonquin community. The current state of our knowledge of Ojibwe ways puts us in a good position to elucidate some of these cultural differences and culture-specific interactional strategies between Native people and non-Natives in this country. When explored in the context of Native/non-Native relations and the tension that often exists when members of two different cultures come into social contact, these observations enable members of both traditions to come to terms with the underlying cultural assumptions in operation.

Listening to the Aboriginal Voice

In many Aboriginal communities it is common to hear the elders express the following concerns when approached by non-Natives: 'Why do your people keep trying to tell us who we are? Why can't you accept us for who we are?' Non-Aboriginal people do too often write off Aboriginal people as 'assimilated' or 'just like white people.' One can easily fall into the trap of failing to really listen to what one is being told and thus miss the wealth and richness of Native cultures, languages, and traditions. A people's stories and texts may be approached as cultural settings, and the concept of culture itself offers one a kind of 'living document' which describes culture-specific ways of thinking and doing things.

What were things like for the people indigenous to Canada before the Europeans arrived and how have Native cultures changed since then? As Rich Rhodes (1988) has suggested, while many Aboriginal people are interested in traditional medicines, few would be willing to forsake the white man's medicine altogether. While many love to hunt, trap, and fish, not that many seem anxious to return to a semi-nomadic life living off the land. For most Aboriginal people, questions of tradition depend much more on the examples set by living people, most notably the elders, than on the content of written records. The truth about the traditional values and ways of life of Aboriginal people are to be found in what the elders do, think and say today, rather than what has been written in books and academic articles by non-Native people.

So perhaps the best way to try to understand what we refer to as the Native perspective on life is to take a look at some of the basic values and traditions which continue to fuel Aboriginal thinking and behaviour. Traditional values are still very strong in most Aboriginal communities today, but the way these values operate in daily life tends to be confusing to many non-Natives. This chapter explores some of those basic differences with a view to creating understandings about traditional indigenous values and traditions which still exist today.

Despite the growing number of culture-specific ethnographies, books and various descriptions of Anishnaabe people written by both Native people and non-Natives, their values and ways of thinking remain a mystery to most non-Native Canadians; some I know would consider 'Anishnaabe values' to be an oxymoron: 'You're writing a book on what?' people reply when I tell them I'm writing a book on Ojibwe ways of speaking, thinking and interacting. One of the key people who influenced me to write this book, Gordon Polson of the Algonquin First Nation, has taught me much about Aboriginal ways of thinking and doing things. Gordon reminds me of what the anthropologist Clifford Geertz once wrote: 'Understanding the form and pressure of ... Natives' inner lives is like grasping a proverb, catching an allusion, seeing a joke or reading a poem' (1987:70).

I am amazed at how resilient the Anishnaabe spirit is; after all, First Nations people in North America have endured a few hundred years of assault on their cultures. They have not survived by casting themselves as victims or lamenting the dispossession of their lands, languages, and forms of spirituality. Nor do I run across many First Nations people who live in self-pity. The humourless stereotypes perpetuated by non-Native Canadians over the years, while ludicrous from a Native perspective, continue to permeate Canadian culture to this day and have been invented by non-Natives for a variety of self-serving reasons, mostly based on ignorance of First Nations' cultures. From the 'noble savage' to the 'poor Indian,' the 'stoic warrior,' the 'every Indian is a drunk,' and even as the 'saviours' of modern society, First Nations people themselves have responded to these stereotypes most often with sharp humour, resigned laughter, and a good dose of sarcasm. After living with First Nations people for a number of years I am sad that so many non-Natives continue to see First Nations people as humourless, stoic, and a bunch of drunks. I never laughed so hard and so often as I did when living in the community of Pikogan. Everyday life on the reserve is fuelled by laughter, joking, and other forms of humour, even amidst tragedy, and mostly directed towards the common enemy of cultural ignorance.

First Nations in North America have defined themselves by using variations of the term 'the People' for millennia. The European practice of lumping all people indigenous to North America as 'Indians,' thereby glossing over the tremendous diversity of Aboriginal experience, languages, forms of worship, patterns of governance, and culture-specific ways of thinking and doing things, continues to this day. Of course, nothing could be further from the truth, as attested by the political differences which surface regularly in the Canadian media among different First Nations and their differing ways of viewing the world. The First Nations people are only asking for the same privileges and respect that are taken for granted by the majority of Canadians: the right to manage their own affairs in their own communities and territories and to have some say in the destiny of their respective nations. Ethnicity and a sense of identity come through the doorway of cultural self-definition and collective epistemologies and histories. And perhaps the best way to come truly to understand these epistemologies and histories is to listen carefully to how Native people talk about them.

Towards an Ojibwe Ethnography of Speaking

Recently there have been some important studies on the ethnography of speaking among non-Indo-European languages, such as Aboriginal languages in North America. Lisa Valentine, in her recent book on the ethnography of speaking among the Severn Ojibwe of Lynx Lake, *Making It Their Own*, writes: 'The ethnography of speaking is not a field or a discipline; rather, it is a perspective, an orientation towards the relationships among language, culture, and society' (1995:4). In the context of language-in-use, Valentine characterizes the ethnography of speaking, then, as being based on the following set of assumptions:

1. All speech communities are heterogeneous, meaning that all sorts of different speaking styles are found in every speech community, from conversational styles to dialects and beyond.

2. Speech communities overlap and intersect with one another. There really is no such thing as a homogeneous speech community.

3. It is important to understand the overlapping and intersecting functions of language and language-in-use.

4. Languages and language usage include a variety of related components, such as the linguistic levels of phonetics, phonology, morphology and syntax, as well as components at the discourse (beyond the sentence unit) level (1995:6).

Recent studies in the ethnography of speaking suggest that this perspective on language and culture is going through a redefinition, similar to the movement we saw in the field of linguistics during the 1960s and 1970s with the advent of sociolinguistics, conversation analysis, and discourse analysis. Earlier on, however, the European missionaries, both Catholic and Protestant, were the ones who first attempted to analyse and understand the Aboriginal languages they encountered in the so-called new world in order to preach the Christian gospel. Steeped in the tradition of analysing Indo-European languages, these early missionaries cum linguists tried to analyse these non-Indo-European Aboriginal languages using the existing linguistic categories derived from Indo-European ones, often with disastrous consequences. As a result, the early linguistic descriptions are sometimes fundamentally flawed and give a skewed picture of the richness and complexity of these languages.

As the field of linguistics began to develop in the Americas in the early part of the twentieth century, linguists began to realize that one cannot *a priori* depend upon Indo-European linguistic structures and categories to analyse and understand the structures of non-Indo-European languages. Leonard Bloomfield was one of the first American linguists to begin to study Aboriginal languages with reference to non-Indo-European language-specific forms and patterns. His book *Language* (1933) became the standard for those interested in studying Aboriginal languages in the Americas and has become a classic in its field. Still, much of this early linguistic analysis by Bloomfield and others seemed foreign to the speakers for whom these languages were their mother tongue, and many linguistic descriptions of Aboriginal languages in the Americas, even to this day, are replete with misconceptions and large categories somewhat comically referred to as analytical 'residue.' The best linguistic studies coming out in recent years have been done by Aboriginal members themselves, who have been trained in linguistic analysis (Christensen, 1993; Corbiere, 1997).

OJIBWE WAYS OF SPEAKING AND INTERACTING

How does the study of naturally occurring discourse help us to understand culture-specific ways of thinking, doing things, and perceiving the world around us? I remember an experience I had shortly after entering the Native community which began to clue me in to some of the basic cultural differences which exist between Native people and non-Natives and how those differences can begin to be understood by paying attention to culture-specific ways of speaking and interacting. I was new to the community and just beginning to learn the Native language. One day my car broke down and I had it towed to the nearby town to have it repaired. Not wanting to stay at the garage all day, I decided to call one of my friends from the reserve, an elder who was teaching me his language and his way of life. I called him on the phone and asked him, in what I thought was a polite way of making a request, '*Gigaagii biinda naajiwiizhinan naa?*' ('Could you come and pick me up?'). He hesitated and then said, '*Ehe*' 'Yes.' When he arrived, I jumped into his truck. He turned to me and, as only a friend could, said, 'Don't say, *Gigaagii biinda naajiwiizhinan naa?*, just say, *Biindaa naajiwishin!*' ('Come and get me!'). I was trying to be polite by using the technique that I learned in my culture. But to his ears, the way I asked him was rude. It was as if I was questioning his ability to drive or something. Yet his way of asking for a favour sounded rude to my ears. The difference is that, in Ojibwe culture, cooperation is assumed, whereas in my culture, people seem more comfortable when cooperation is negotiated.

Perhaps the best way to begin to gain an understanding of how studies in the ethnography of speaking can lead to deeper cross-cultural understanding is to look at some of the teachings of the elders in the community where we lived. One teaching (to which I will return in chapter 8) I heard from one of the elders is this:

Bimaadiziwin Ezhiseg.
This is what happens in life.

Maawaji niitam ge-doodaman.
Here's the most important thing to do.

Giga-manaajihaag giniigihigoog giishpin ginwezh wii-bimaadiziyan.
You will respect your parents if you want to live a long life.

Gaawin wiikaad giga-ashidamaasiwag gegoon wiidamawikwaa.
You will never turn away from what they tell you.

Misawaaj gikenimadwaa banahaagewaaj mii bezhigwan wewenda giga-doodawaag.
Even if you think they're off the path, still you will carefully do what you are told.

Miinawaj godag gegoon.
So then another thing.

Gaawin wiikaad giga-majenimaasii awiyag.
You will never treat someone badly.

Giga-gichi-inenimaa moozhag.
You will always think highly of her/him.

Giishpin majenimaj awiyag, gagwe-waniiken gaa-majenimaj.
If someone treats you badly, try and forget it.

This principle of respect for nature, the Creator and other people can be seen operating in a variety of cultural ways of doing things, and these different ways often lead to confusion and misunderstanding between non-Natives and Native people. Living in one Native community, I had many opportunities to observe non-Natives entering the community in order to work together with community members on one project or another. More often than not, the project would be undermined by underlying tension between the Native and non-Native researchers. I think that one key reason for this is that non-Natives are not willing to relinquish control of a project. I remember working on a community survey at Pikogan with another non-Native. Since I had been involved with the community for a number of years, community members would invariably bring their complaints about other non-Native researchers to me, the white guy. It was sometimes awkward to hear Native people talking about how white people always want to be the bosses of these projects.

On the other hand, I have listened to non-Natives involved in teaching and research in the Native community express frustration about how difficult it is to work with Native people. They would say things like: 'These people are so rude. They're never on time and they're always laughing at me.' I usually answer something along these lines: 'In any cross-cultural situation, it's important to learn how to interact appropriately, because what is considered to be rude behaviour in one's own culture is often conventionally polite in another, and vice versa. So it's important to pay attention to appropriate ways of interacting and the values underlying these culture-specific ways of doing things.'

In thinking about politeness techniques and appropriate interaction in the community where we lived, we saw that most contacts between Native people and non-Natives got off to a bad start simply because most non-Native people were not aware of how to interact appropriately in face-to-face situations in the community. It can be as simple as how people say good-bye to each other. In non-Native interaction, for example, it is assumed that a certain formula will be followed when people are done talking with each other, something like:

A: Well, I better get going.
B: Yeah, me, too. See you later.
A: Okay, see you.

In the community of Pikogan, however, more often than not, leave-taking is done by turning and walking away when one is finished speaking. This would certainly be considered very rude in non-Native society, but it is considered a polite way of saying good-bye in many Ojibwe communities. The same holds true for telephone conversations. I remember talking with one of the elders on the telephone and, all of a sudden, he hung up. At first I thought that I must have said something to offend him. As this pattern kept repeating itself, though, I began to realize that I was the one expecting some kind of formulaic leave-taking at the end of the conversation. In the minds of many of my Ojibwe friends, however, when the conversation is over they hang up. What need is there to say more?

Traditional values are still very strong in the community where we lived and the way these values operate in daily life tend to be confusing to many non-Natives. When my wife's father passed away and she had been away from the community for a month, one of the elders, a woman, came up to my wife when we returned and said with a big smile (and in front of a lot of other people), '*Oh, gigichi aajiboonan!*' which means 'Oh, you're so fat!' In non-Native culture that's not much of a compliment. In fact, one would rarely, if ever, say something like that to someone unless you were trying to hurt that person's feelings. But in this instance it was offered as a compliment. The elder had been concerned that my wife would not be eating enough while mourning and would return to the community looking thin and unhealthy. In the community of Pikogan, someone who has plenty of meat on their bones is considered healthy and strong. Part of the reason for this goes back to when people were living in the bush, as most of the elders at Pikogan had done for over half of their lives. It was always important to have plenty of flesh on your bones to tide you through the time when game was scarce. Such a value remains strong even though most people don't live exclusively in the bush any more. Of course, after my wife received this compliment she immediately went on a diet!

Another area which seems to cause many non-Natives considerable stress when interacting with Native people is how people in the Native community are frequently borrowing, lending, and requesting favours. In the community of Pikogan, for example, when someone asks to borrow something, it is rare that anyone will directly say no. There are cultural ways of letting someone know that you would prefer not to lend them the requested item which are examined in a later chapter. One of our friends who lived in another Native community told me about the time when one of the men in the community bought a power lawn-mower. Almost immediately he was bombarded with requests from others to borrow it. Soon it broke down because so many people were using it. When he got it fixed, the same thing happened. So he did the cultural thing; he got rid of it. He sold the power mower and bought a push mower. Of course, no one wanted to borrow that! While it meant a little more work for him, he maintained harmony in his social relationships by getting rid of the thing that was causing disharmony. It should be kept in mind here, however, that in community life the person being asked is usually expected to loan the item, and usually does. If not, at least a substitute is given, such as tobacco or food or some other item. These guidelines are especially true within kinship relations. There, things can be taken (or borrowed) without directly asking. The Native cultural concept of ownership is quite contrary to the commonly held non-Native notion, where possessions tend to be hoarded and protected. This conceptual difference can be seen in many dialects of the Ojibwe language, where no term exists for 'personal ownership.' I think a good deal of misunderstanding between Native people and non-Natives in the areas of lending, borrowing, and making requests has to do with the Native view of possessions. Basically, things are just things. That is not to say that greed and envy are absent in the Native community. But there seems to be an understanding that relationships with people are far more important than things, and maintaining the harmony of the moment is more important than creating tension by refusing a request or putting more value on things than on people. These are the kinds of areas where studies in discourse analysis can help us better to understand Ojibwe cosmology and ways of thinking and doing things.

HARMONY IN SOCIAL RELATIONS

In my experience in Pikogan, personal confrontations are avoided whenever possible. Maintaining harmony in one's relationships is the important thing. Among adults especially, anyone who tries to control or coerce another person to act in a certain way is viewed as doing something intrinsically bad. One of the main complaints that I heard from my friends about non-Native people was, 'They're so *pushy*. They're always telling you what to do and they're always trying to get you to do things their way.' We saw this same attitude expressed on television during the Oka crisis in 1990. The mayor of the town of Oka said, 'Why don't those Mohawks build an authentic Indian village to attract tourists?' In other words, 'Why don't those Indians do things our way?'

Another example of this harmony principle can be seen in how people ask for money and lend it in the community. It is interesting to see the techniques that people in the community use to borrow money from one another compared to how it works in Native/non-Native interaction. When we first came to Pikogan we were often asked to lend people money. Usually people would say, 'I'll pay you back tomorrow.' Of course, we took it literally and were disappointed when we didn't get paid back the next day! Eventually we caught on that tomorrow meant sometime in the future. We almost always got paid back eventually, though it was not always with money but with gifts of moosemeat or beaver or someone doing us a favour.

In situations in which a non-Native had lent money to a Native person, the non-Native would invariably put some pressure on the Native person to get paid back. More than a few times I was in a position to observe what happened. When faced with such direct confrontation, my friends from Pikogan would usually say something like, 'I'll pay you back next week,' or 'I'll bring you your money tomorrow.' Again, the important thing was that a tense moment or a confrontation had been avoided and the harmony of the relationship maintained, at least temporarily. Inevitably, when non-Natives would come to my wife and myself to ask how they could get their money back they would be angry and upset because they believed that they had been lied to. From my Anishnaabe friends' point of view, though, they didn't lie. The harmony of the moment had been maintained when there was potential for real tension. Whether they intended to pay the person back the next day or the next week is not clear, but a confrontation had been avoided and interactional harmony had been maintained.

These kinds of cultural differences often lead non-Native people to the mistaken conclusion that Aboriginal people are dishonest or unreliable. Most non-Native people don't understand the extreme importance of maintaining harmony in the moment rather than allowing any kind of tension to develop by having to refuse a request. These Native values are completely contrary to the non-Native way of obtaining commitments and promises for future events as in, for example, 'When are you going to pay me back?', a question I never heard in the community where we lived.

Avoiding personal confrontation helps to prevent any embarrassment that a member of the community might feel in a potentially tense situation. I began to appreciate the value of maintaining harmony in face-to-face interaction when I saw how effectively the principle worked in Pikogan. I remember being at a friend's house one day when his cousin, a band councillor, came by with a petition. My friend read the petition and then signed it. Later that day another relative came around with another petition exactly the opposite of the first one. After chatting together for a while my friend then signed the second petition. When I saw him sign the second one I thought, 'What the hell is he doing?' When I asked him about it he just shrugged. The important thing in his mind was to maintain the harmony of the relationship at that moment. The fact that he had signed two opposing petitions was no big deal compared to the importance of avoiding tension and maintaining harmony in his kinship relationships.

The value of maintaining the harmony of the moment is difficult for many non-Natives to understand. Native students in a non-Native school system, for example, will often be seen as apathetic or lazy because they are not as willing to raise their hand or blurt out the answer to a teacher's question as many non-Native students are. To do so might be interpreted as putting yourself in a superior position to your friends and bring on the risk of teasing or ostracism. We non-Natives often do not understand the strong cultural values at work in everyday life, particularly the extreme importance of maintaining harmony in the moment rather than allowing any kind of tension to develop by having to refuse a request or engage in face-to-face confrontation.

A corollary of maintaining harmony in all social relations is that of sharing. Certainly every culture has some sense that it is good to share things. In fact, before entering the community of Pikogan, I felt that I was a very generous person and one who was quite willing to share. I quickly realized that I was really quite a stingy person by Native standards. It took me a long time to come to the place where I was willing to share freely with those around me, especially my car and my money. Giving gifts, money, possessions, and time are an important part of Ojibwe life. Generosity is an important value in the Ojibwe ethos and seems to be rooted in two basic principles. The first is a recognition that all possessions, successes, and honours are from the Creator. Many times I observed people receiving such things respond in gratitude and thanksgiving by sharing with those near to that person. Secondly, generosity is rooted in the philosophy that giving to another furthers the development of relationships; by giving to another one is creating a kind of social security for oneself against possible future need. As one person told me, 'Sharing things and giving things away keeps our community going.'

I come from a society that puts a high value on independence and individuality. The traces of these values are still a part of me and the way I organize my life and thinking. I will always be a *Zhaagnaash* (non-Native). But the people with whom we lived for so many years, and with whom we are still in touch, do not share the value of extreme independence. Over the years the elders I came to know would emphasize that we need the help of others as we go through this life. When my wife and I began living with Anishnaabe people, we slowly learned that dependence and generosity are important investments towards a secure future. Certainly living with a foot in two cultures created some confusing situations for us. The way I understand the values of interdependence and generosity now is quite different than the understanding I had prior to living in an Aboriginal community. The way I see it now, most Anishnaabe people I know are freely willing to share all they have, and to extend hospitality at every opportunity, in order to establish and maintain a tightly knit social network. This network, in turn, ensures that, when one is in need, one can expect reciprocal treatment from others. In that sense, relationships become one's source of security in an uncertain future. The bottom line is: individuals cannot make it by themselves. This value seems to be a far cry from my own strongly entrenched cultural value of looking out for number one.

Another underlying principle in this widespread practice of sharing and giving things away reflects the Ojibwe attitude toward possessions. For one person in the community to outshine another by hoarding wealth or having many more possessions than most others causes that person to be a target for criticism and gossip. Thus sharing and generosity tend to maintain an equilibrium and a harmony in the community, both in terms of economics and relationships. According to many of the elders, one sign of a 'good' Anishnaabe is that he or she shares freely and is always willing to give things away.

It is interesting, too, to keep in mind how the introduction of technology into many Native communities is changing some of these important cultural values, more often than not for the worse. Before electricity came into one Atikamekw community, when somebody killed a moose he would bring the moose back to the village and distribute the meat according to the culturally proper means of distribution in the community. Nobody would dare think of hoarding the meat for themselves. What would happen to those without meat? And how would the meat be preserved anyway? After electricity came into the community one of the first pieces of technology to follow was the freezer. Now when somebody kills a moose, he can just throw the meat in the freezer and it will last all winter. The whole value of sharing meat is changing and, with it, the cultural strength of sharing. Interestingly in the Native language, the term coined for that piece of technology is the 'stingy box,' because now you don't have to share your meat (Tim Stime, Atikamekw linguist, personal communication, 1984).

LEXICAL AND CULTURAL DIFFERENCES

Going beyond culture-specific politeness maxims, non-Natives are more often than not unaware of traditional beliefs which motivate behaviour in the Native community. I remember one summer when an anthropologist came to the community to collect legends and stories from the community elders. While it was a collaborative project in a loose sense, it seemed that the person assigned by the band council to work with the anthropologist was not fully aware of what was going on. In the course of trying to elicit legends from the elders, the non-Native researcher became increasingly frustrated at the lack of legends that people would tell. She did not understand that, in Pikogan, people talked about how the elders only tell legends when there is snow on the ground, when certain spirits are sleeping and thus ought not to be disturbed. Certainly the anthropologist was well trained in elicitation techniques and research methods, but she had never considered inquiring about traditional values and appropriate times and ways of eliciting information. After a few days she left the community under the impression that the people were uncooperative and unwilling to participate in 'her' project.

A phrase I often heard in Pikogan is *Aadidoog*, which means 'I don't know.' That word can mean a lot of different things. Sometimes it is simply a profession of ignorance about what has been asked. At other times it can mean, 'I know what you're asking, but I don't want to deal with it right now.' Or it can mean, 'It's none of your business.' People who asked direct questions were often seen as being very rude in the community where we lived, especially when non-Natives asked questions which suggested doing things the way a non-Native would. I would often hear people use this phrase as an alternative to saying no to a request. I remember one time being at a friend's house at Pikogan when a relative came over and asked my friend, 'Does your wife have any money?' Instead of answering yes or no (after all, he might not, in fact, have known), or going to ask his wife if she had any money, he answered, 'I don't know.' The person who came to borrow money knew how to play by the cultural rules and responded with 'Never mind,' and let the matter drop.

Many of us in non-Native society pride ourselves in being able to carry on a conversation to the point that we are experts at filling the air with words. We can talk and talk and talk, even when there is nothing to talk about. Most of my friends at Pikogan talk only when there's something to say and, while this is but one small area, it illustrates how different ways of doing things, and the values which underlie those ways, can lead to serious cultural misunderstandings. Silence itself can be a specific message. I remember being in the bush one time with a couple of the guys. We started walking through the bush and I asked *'Aadiyezhayak?'* ('Where are we going?'). Silence. Five minutes later I asked again *'Aadiyezhayak?'* Silence. Finally, after my third attempt, one of the guys turned to me and said *'Gigaa-giigendaan aapiich oditamaak'* ('You'll know when we get there'). Now that makes sense. I would find out when we got there (although now I forget where we were going!).

It goes back to different ways of doing things and different ways of thinking. In non-Native society, for example, we like to introduce ourselves to each other by name, we shake hands, we look each other directly in the face, we ask direct questions, we insist on using the word 'please.' Yet all these things could be insulting and downright rude in the village where we lived. Even the first question we usually ask in non-Native culture gives us a clue as to some of these cultural differences in the use of language. 'What do you do?' is a common thing to ask somebody in my culture. Status is somehow attached to what someone *does* rather than to who someone *is*. The common question I heard in Pikogan when there was a visitor was *'Aadiwejiyan?'* ('Where are you from?') or 'What First Nation do you belong to?'

Ojibwe Values at Work in Everyday Life

I want to build upon and depart from some observations made by Clare Brant, the late Mohawk psychologist, to whom I have already referred. Brant (1990) lists a number of behavioural differences between Native people and non-Natives which, when not properly understood, he believes leads to much confusion, tension, and stereotyping among non-Native people. Some of Brant's distinctive cultural characteristics are presented in simplified forms which can contribute to that confusion and tension. At this juncture I want to use Brant's list of distinctive characteristics as a model for exploring Ojibwe-specific differences in thinking and behaving in order to present you with a realistic picture of these

cultural characteristics as they are grounded in everyday life and interaction in the community where we lived.

We try to dispel quite early on in our Native Studies courses the idea
that Aboriginal experience is homogeneous. Nothing could be further
from the truth. There are tremendous differences in Native thinking,
perceiving, relating, and behaving which are grounded in different
Aboriginal traditions, and anyone attempting to grasp the richness and
complexity of those traditions, regardless if one is Native or non-Native
must acknowledge that heterogeneity. But it needs to be noted, too, that
there are certainly commonly shared indigenous themes which can be
found in all First Nations traditions. What I would like to do here is to
present these common themes as they play themselves out in everyday
life in the community of Pikogan.[1]

Brant claims that one shared cultural theme for Aboriginal people is
that of *non-interference*. I think the term has taken on a life of its own, one
which tends to distort what is really going on in relationships between
Aboriginal people. In the community of Pikogan, for example, I noticed
quite early on that people don't force their thinking on you. In my non-
Native tradition it seems common to hear people telling others what
they should or ought to do. I remember being in the bush with one of
the men from the reserve. His family had a small cabin on their traditional hunting and trapping grounds, far from the beaten path, and situated on a beautiful lake. At one point I decided to go fishing from the
shore of the lake with a borrowed fishing rod. He watched me as I
became more and more frustrated; I wasn't even getting a nibble. After a
while he said to me, 'One time my uncle tried fishing there. He didn't
catch anything. Then he moved over to where the rocks are. He caught
lots of fish there.' I thought about that and finally decided to go over
and fish by the rocks. But it got me thinking. In my experience, the common thing to say would be something like: 'Hey, man, you aren't gonna
catch any fish there! It's too shallow. You should go over where those
rocks are to fish.' In other words, 'Don't be stupid. Do what I tell you to
do and you'll catch fish.' But the way my Native friend got the message
across was by telling me a story about his uncle. Whether I got up and
moved to another spot was my decision, and he respected that.

I believe the underlying value for not forcing your thinking on others
is one of *respect* for individual autonomy. That kind of respect certainly
helps to promote positive interpersonal relationships in a small community or extended family setting. After I began to catch on to that value, I
began to see it at work almost every day in the community. The same

principle could be seen in how people raised their children in the community. When we first moved to Pikogan, we observed that the kids on the reserve seemed to run around with no supervision. The parents seemed to take a hands-off approach to child-rearing, at the very least. After a while, though, we realized that the children were being looked after very carefully. All of the adults in the community shared a sense of guardianship for them.[2] In time, we too began to feel more at ease letting our own children run free in the community. We knew that they were being watched by others on the reserve and we began to take on that responsibility, too, when there were youngsters playing in our 'space.' From a cultural outsider's perspective, it appeared that the children were running around wild (to use an expression we heard more than once). This is no small matter, because there are non-Native people who are in positions of authority with respect to Aboriginal families and communities, and judgments based on ignorance have had (and continue to have) devastating affects on families and communities. Horror stories abound of how non-Native workers with agencies such as the Children's Aid Society (CAS) would conclude that children were being neglected and take them away from their families and communities in order to 'protect' them. I remember one Native woman working with CAS bemoaning the damage that is so often done out of 'good intentions' by non-Natives ignorant of culture-specific ways of doing things and the deeply entrenched values which underlie them. She commented to me on how she wished non-Natives would at least be required to take some courses in Native Studies (or some equivalent training) before being put in decision-making positions vis-à-vis Aboriginal families and communities. Sadly, most agencies still do not require their employees to educate themselves about Aboriginal ways. Thus the damaging consequences continue.

Another illustration of this principle of not forcing your thinking on others can be seen in the way in which a person would inform another person in the community about an upcoming event. Very rarely would someone try to solicit a definite *commitment* from somebody to attend the event as one would in non-Native culture. People would relay information about an upcoming meeting but rarely try to force a commitment by saying, 'Will you be there?' or 'Oh, you've just *got* to come to the meeting!' Most often, a person would simply convey the information that a meeting had been called or an event was to take place and the person being addressed would know that he or she was invited to come. Rarely, if ever, would you see someone create a tense moment or disrupt the harmony of a relationship by trying to force someone to make a commitment.

Through this principle each individual is seen as having a sacred purpose for being. To intrude upon an individual's development and destiny would be rude and inappropriate. Thus in Pikogan parents rarely spanked or severely reprimanded their children. Children are disciplined, for sure, but in subtle ways. They are encouraged to learn by experience and observation. Sometimes this was seen by non-Natives living nearby in stereotypical fashion. I have heard non-Native people say, for example, 'Those Indians just let their kids run wild,' and we've all heard the expression, 'They're acting like a bunch of wild Indians.' In fact, the underlying principle of not forcing one's way of thinking on another is at work here. In the minds of the Native people I know, each individual is placed on this earth by the Creator to fulfil his or her own destiny. So Native parents respect their children's freedom of choice and let their children *be* as much as possible, unless there exists the threat of direct physical danger. After all, in the Native view of things, the development of an individual's will to do right is of greater importance than coercing that person to behave in a certain way.[3]

Another value which I saw operating in everyday life in the community of Pikogan had to do with how people teach and learn. I was used to being *told how* to do things and I learned primarily via didactic means and reading. Most of what I learned in the community of Pikogan I learned by being *shown*. From learning to interact appropriately in the community setting to learning how to set a rabbit snare, the elders would show me, with great patience, how to do things. At first such a teaching method seemed incongruent with my own experience, where learners are rewarded for successive approximations of the behaviour that they have been instructed to carry out.

It is in respect for another culture that people of my culture so often fail. Not because we are racists, but simply because we remain ignorant of how other people think and do things and view the world. And what a shame that is. We miss knowing about the richness of a culture which has no unwanted children and where the old people are not put away in institutions but have a valuable role to play in the community. One of my non-Native attitudes which changed drastically was that of *respect*. Living in Pikogan, I found that my friends there had a deeper sense of what respect means than I did. For them, there is a strong feeling that one's life and experience is, in a very real sense, meant to be just the way it is. The way it was expressed to me many times and in many different ways over the years is that the Great Spirit has a purpose for each individual, each creature, each natural phenomenon, and each event and nothing happens apart from that design.

My two oldest daughters attended a Native school in the community of Pikogan until we moved to Sudbury in 1990. We wondered how they would adjust to attending a non-Native school for the first time in their lives and, believe me, it was tough for them at first. For one thing, they had learn to what to call their teachers and others in positions of authority. At Pikogan everyone in the community is on a first-name or nickname basis – elders, parents, the chief, children, dogs, everyone. And, of course, all the teachers in the community school are called by their first names by the students. In most non-Native schools, though, the policy is to call teachers and other school officials by their formal titles or Mr and Mrs. For our girls, learning to call their teachers 'Mr and Mrs so-and-so' was often quite confusing. After all, when you've gone through Grade 6 calling your teachers Julie or Molly, it takes some time to learn that calling teachers by their first names is just not acceptable any more.

'Wait-time' is something else that really seems to baffle non-Natives. Wait-time refers to the length of time people in a conversation are willing to wait for a reply. When Native children attend non-Native schools, for example, the classroom climate seems to be too pressured and teachers don't give enough time for students to respond to a question. The usual reaction from a non-Native teacher is that the Native student is either unwilling or unable to answer. As a consequence, Native students are often seen to be slow or uncooperative when they fail to respond according to non-Native cultural standards. The non-Native teacher is usually not aware of the different *timing expectations* at work in Native interaction. As a teacher with both Native and non-Native students in my classes, I have noticed that Native students like to think about questions posed in class before rushing to answer. It is interesting to see the frustration from both sides. While the non-Native students are puzzled by what they consider to be a slow response time, the Native students comment on how pushy non-Native people are with language, how they're always in a hurry to fill the air with words, and how they like to interrupt people.

I remember hearing Ovide Mercredi, the former national chief of the Assembly of First Nations, when he spoke at Laurentian University. The audience was a mixture of Native people and non-Natives and when he finished his presentation he invited people to ask questions. After two or three questions a non-Native woman stood up and said, 'Look, I've noticed that the first few questions have been asked by non-Natives. I think we need to give the Indians a chance to ask questions, too!' After a bit of a pause Chief Mercredi said very diplomatically to her, 'You don't need to worry about the Native people here. Just because they're not talking doesn't mean they're not thinking about what is being said. When any of the Native people here are ready to ask a question, they will. You don't have to worry about us or feel that you have to stand up for us. We're perfectly capable of doing that for ourselves.' Eventually, when the time was right, a number of Native people began to ask questions. To me, it goes back to different ways of doing things, different timing expectations, and a different perspective on what it means to interact with people in a Native kind of way.

The truth is that most Native people already know which non-Native ways are worth learning and which ones are not, and they will quickly take advantage of them. But it is generally not a two-way street. Most Native people I know are quite knowledgeable about non-Native ways and are conversant in a 'foreign' language, either English or French. Most Native people have gone through the Canadian educational system and know about Canadian history from a distinctly non-Native perspective. But it is rare to meet a non-Native person in Canada who is knowledgeable about the Native way of life, who speaks a Native language, or is knowledgeable about Canadian history from a Native perspective. When you think about it, whose way of thinking and doing things, those of Native people or non-Natives, has more to offer in terms of coping with life as we enter the twenty-first century? The question presses.

I was often invited to go to the bush for hunting and trapping with some of the elders in the community where we lived. One elder in particular, Okinawe, taught me many things over the years about his language, his people, and his way of life. He was always patient with me. One night, as we waited quietly in the cool breeze listening for the sound of the moose, he reached down and put his hand on the ground beneath us. He spoke in his Native language and said, 'The earth is our mother. I can feel her in my very being. We depend on the earth and on each other. So we share what we have with one another.' I was struck with the irony of how the Aboriginal people in Canada seem to be the very ones possessing the central insights into the land and the environment. The elder that night told me how the land is essential to his way of life. Without it, he said, his people could not survive. His observation was strikingly revealed during the Oka crisis in 1990. The contrast between this elder and the prime minister of Canada at that time could not have been more stark. One, a Native elder, who speaks of our harmony with the earth and community with one another, the other committing human life and tanks to use against First Nations peoples in his own country. And, you know, I really believe that the vision each represents is fundamental to the kind of future we will have in this country we call Canada.

Conclusion

It is easy for non-Natives to become upset, to throw up their arms and say 'What the hell do these people want?' or 'Why can't they just accept the fact that they live in Canada and be like us?' The result is often confusion, misunderstanding, and impatience. So we miss the fascinating adventure of discovering a different way of life and a different way of looking at the world. There are other areas which I don't go into in this chapter, such as attitudes towards approval and gratitude, the all-pervasiveness of spirituality and the spirit world, Native epistemology, the concept of time, and the Native perspective on the land and Mother Earth.[4] Some of these areas will be explored in later chapters as we begin to take a detailed look at Ojibwe discourse and naturally occurring talk. The examples in this chapter are merely the tip of the iceberg when it comes to cultural differences between Native people and non-Natives in this country. But they help to show how cultural misunderstandings arise when people of different cultures are ignorant of the other's way of life. Many times over the years I have been surprised by how very different Ojibwe values are from my own, and all these different ways of thinking and doing things tend to erect barriers between people when they are not understood. It is hoped that the insights gained in this kind of study may lead to better relations between Native people and non-Natives as we enter the twenty-first century.

3

'My Ass Is Frozen!': Exploring Language as a Window on a People

In this chapter I want to explore some of the basic differences between Algonquian languages (of which Ojibwe is a member) and Indo-European languages such as English and French. We will also look at the deeply rooted nature of the oral tradition which continues to exist in Aboriginal cultures and explore the language/identity issues at stake in many Aboriginal communities. Our starting point is the belief that an understanding of the distinctive features of Ojibwe (or any language) can tell us a great deal about the psyche of a people. But first, I want to set the tone for what we will be exploring by recounting a story told by a friend of mine, Louise Lahache, which appeared in her article 'What Language Does Mother Earth Speak?'

A few years ago, when he was seven, my youngest son asked me one of those kid questions. You know, the kind that are really hard to answer because there is something there that we rarely stop to contemplate. Having four children, I've handled many kid questions, even the one about where the white goes when the snow melts, but I'm still trying to formulate an answer for this question: 'Mom, what language does Mother Earth speak?' For me, the really difficult thing is not in figuring out what language Mother Earth speaks. Being a Mohawk woman, I am witness to a tradition of long Thanksgivings that address the earth, water, skies, winds, the creatures that live there and all of creation in the Mohawk language. I know that the proper way for Mohawk people to address Mother Earth is through the Mohawk language, just as Algonquin people address Mother Earth in Algonquin. I have also learned that Mother Earth responds best to the languages of the people who have sprang from her and then returned their bodies to nurture her. Now here is my difficulty in answering my son's question. I know that wherever he will be, the indigenous language of that part of the world is the language Mother Earth speaks. The proper way of respecting and relating to her will be found in the language of the land and in its people. That's the easy part of the answer, but how do I explain to my child that those languages are disappearing all over the world? Two years have passed and I'm still examining the possible answers. (1994:2)

In this chapter I want to try to answer some of the basic questions I have heard over the years from both Native people and non-Natives about Aboriginal languages. Perhaps the first and most important question is: How difficult is it to learn to speak a Native language? I usually try to have some fun with people when they ask me this by telling them: 'From personal experience learning to speak a language like Ojibwe is pretty damn near impossible. Ojibwe has more than a million words and stems and morphemes and stuff that linguists call by names that they must have gotten by reading science fiction books. So the most important thing to remember about learning to speak an Aboriginal language such as Ojibwe is this: *Forget it!*' The real answer, though, is that Ojibwe, like most Aboriginal languages in Canada, is such a difficult language to learn that you either have to make a lifetime commitment to learn it or realize that, while you might never really learn how to speak it fluently, at least you can learn a lot about it.[1]

The next question we want to tackle is: What are some of the distinctive features of Ojibwe that differentiate it from Indo-European languages such as English and French? As a corollary to that, we will explore what the relationship is between knowing one's Aboriginal language and one's sense of identity.

Linguistic Concepts and Cultural Differences

Some of the more glaring examples of cultural differences which lead to tension in Native/non-Native interaction have to do with language differences. Ojibwe is a very rich and complex language and even minor changes in the pronunciation (or spelling) can completely change the meaning of a word. When I was first learning the language I remember standing with some of the elders watching a hockey game. At one point, one of them turned to me and politely asked *'Gigaawajinan naa?'* which means 'Are you cold?' I wanted to answer her with a nifty phrase that I had learned recently from another elder, *'Ehe, nigichi maashkaawidiye,'* which means 'Yes, my ass is frozen!' But I forgot the exact phrase and what came out of my mouth was, *'Ehe, nigichi minokwidiye,'* which means 'Yes, I have a really nice ass.' The elder immediately went into fits of laughter and turned to her friends and said, 'I asked him if he was cold and he says he has a real nice ass!' Only then did I realize my mistake. People still remind me of that incident years later.

Ojibwe belongs to the great Algonquian family of languages in North America. Other Algonquian languages include Cree, Algonquin, Montagnais, Atikamekw, Blackfoot, Kickapoo, and Micmac, to name but a few. Like many North American Indian languages, the verb is the heart of the language. Ojibwe has a complex set of prefixes and suffixes that can be attached to words to indicate all sorts of things. Also, word order within sentences is much freer than in English. To a speaker of English, the hundreds and even thousands of different forms of the Ojibwe verb and the elaborate noun-marking system can be quite challenging. One should keep in mind, too, that language differences really reflect differences in ways of thinking, and this is one of the areas that seems to cause much confusion and misunderstanding between Native people and non-Natives.

Ojibwe is, in a very real sense, a non-sexist language. By that I mean that there is no specification of gender in the pronominal system (with the use of pronouns). Whether one is referring to a man or a woman can only be determined by the context of what is being said. So if you say 'Niwaabamaa,' for example, that could mean either 'I see him' or 'I see her.' Only the context of a phrase or utterance gives a clue as to whether one is seeing a man or a woman. While the linguistic evidence is indisputable (no one would or could reasonably argue the fact that there is no specification of gender in the pronominal system of Ojibwe), how that feature of language reflects Ojibwe-specific ways of thinking and perceiving reality is open to discussion. In this case, I believe that this linguistic feature, built into the structure of the language itself, sheds light on traditional male-female relations in many First Nations cultures, where women were considered relatively equal with men (Brizinski, 1993; Medicine, 1983; Ezzo, 1988; Ross, 1996).[2]

Ojibwe is also distinct from English in what is referred to as a *hierarchy of person* which reflects the very basic cultural value of respect. What this means is that the second person, 'you,' always takes grammatical priority. You can say 'Niwaabamaa' ('I see him or her'), but the construction for 'I see you,' *Giwaabamin*, puts the second person pronoun at the beginning of the word and places the first person pronoun at the end, exactly the opposite of the way it is said in English. So the second person, 'you,' always comes first in the language, which reflects a strong cultural preference of considering others – be they individuals, family, or community – as more important than self. This cultural preference can be observed virtually every day in the community of Pikogan when people are making decisions. People I spoke with about it told me that they thought a lot about how what they were deciding would affect their family, extended family, their community and even their First Nation before making a major decision such as to go away to school or to take a job in another location. In some ways, it seemed almost the reverse of my own non-Native decision-making. When making the decision to move away from the community to come to teach at the university, for example, the decision was made by my wife and myself. We really didn't take into account our extended family (our parents, grandparents, and relatives), nor did we share the same sense of community as the people at Pikogan. And we certainly didn't consider (or care) how our decision might affect our nation. Yet the elders would regularly comment on how difficult it must be for my wife to live so far away from her parents (who were in British Columbia), it was so rare for someone from Pikogan to actually move away from their support systems of the extended family and community.

Another major distinction between English and Ojibwe, and again related to different ways of thinking and viewing the world, is in the way the verb is treated. The verb is the heart of the Ojibwe language and how it is put together in the language is extremely complex. There are, in fact, four different categories of verbs in Ojibwe. These are based on whether the subject or object is animate (that is, considered to be a living entity in the culture) or inanimate (that is, considered to be in some sense non-living), and whether the construction of the sentence is transitive (where there is a subject and an object) or intransitive (where there is a subject but no object). The distinction between what is animate and what is inanimate is not always clear to the non-speaker and relates to a distinctly Ojibwe way of perceiving the world. In most dialects of the Ojibwe language (Odawa being the sole exception), a rock is considered to be animate or a living entity. This expresses the traditional Ojibwe view of person-objects which are other-than-human but which have the same ontological status – that is, the same qualities as beings.[3] We'll return to some of these distinctive features when we begin to explore Ojibwe discourse analysis in the chapters to follow.

The four verb categories, then, revolve around these two basic concepts of transitivity and animacy. The four categories are perhaps best understood by examining the following chart.

Verb category	Example
Transitive-Animate (TA)	*'Niwaabamaa'* (I see him/her)
Transitive Inanimate (TI)	*'Niwaabadaan'* (I see it)
Intransitive-Animate (AI)	*'Nibaa'* (He/she is sleeping)
Intransitive-Inanimate (II)	*'Noodin'* (It's windy)

I realize this stuff gets a bit technical here, but it is important to understand some of these basic linguistic concepts as they relate to cultural differences between Ojibwe and non-indigenous ways of thinking and perceiving. On the surface, we can at least grasp the sense that Ojibwe ways of thinking and perceiving are reflected in the language itself. For example, in English we use one word, 'eat,' to express a certain activity. In Ojibwe there are three different words for 'eat.' How those words are used (not to even get into how they came to be!) reflects not only a linguistic difference between Ojibwe and non-Ojibwe people in Canada, but reflects different ways of seeing and thinking. In Ojibwe the word used to express the activity of eating revolves around the concepts of transitivity and animacy. You could say *wiisini* (he/she is eating), *omiijin* (he/she is eating it), or *odamwaan* (he/she is eating him/her). The last one may sound a bit strange to an English-language speaker, but it reflects the fact that what are commonly considered to be objects in English can be considered to be either living or non-living in Ojibwe. If one were to eat a rock (a bizarre example, granted), one would say *Nigii amwaa* (I ate him/her) because rock (*asini*) is considered to be an other-than-human person in most dialects of Ojibwe. How a rock came to be considered in this way is not entirely clear, although there are some interesting ethno-explanations in the literature (Dumont, 1992; Hallowell, 1926). The important fact here is that it illustrates features of Ojibwe that are completely different from English, and that language does, indeed, reflect how people think and perceive the world around us.[4]

Another distinctive feature of Algonquian languages such as Ojibwe is that of *obviation*. While English contains what is commonly referred to as the third person, Ojibwe employs both a third person (termed proximate by linguists) and a fourth person (termed obviative). The proximate is grammatically unmarked, but the obviative is marked. This may seem like a small thing, but in reality it is a nifty grammatical feature which helps to distinguish between people being referred to when one is speaking or telling a story. It is much easier to keep track of who is doing what to whom in Ojibwe, for example, than it is in English. If someone were to say to you, 'Bill saw Ted go into his house,' a natural question arises – which house did Ted go into, his own house or Bill's? In English there is no grammatical marker to let you know this. Because the fourth person is marked grammatically in Ojibwe, however, one immediately knows which house Ted went into. Kevin Russell gives us a clue to understanding this feature of obviation in another Algonquian language, Cree. He writes: 'In any stretch of Cree discourse involving more than one third person referent, only one of these referents can appear in the unmarked grammatical form known as *proximate*; all others must appear in the marked *obviative* form' (1996:367).

The distinction between third and fourth persons in Algonquian languages has implications for how people telling legends and stories structure their narratives (which we explore in more detail in chapter 10). While the feature of obviation also makes it easier to keep track of who is doing what to whom, which is particularly welcome in long, complex narratives such as one often hears in Ojibwe, that is not to say that English is inherently deficient in relation to Algonquian languages. Languages do differ, though, in the kinds of things they are able to do, and the distinctive features of Algonquian languages referred to in this section provide us with some salient examples of how different Ojibwe is from English and what that tells us about different ways of perceiving the world around us.

In the same vein, something which sometimes surprises non-Native people is that there are no words for please, sorry, or apologize in Ojibwe. This can lead non-Native people to make assumptions about Native people which just aren't true. I have heard non-Native people say quite often over the years, 'Indians are so rude, they never say please!' That is not to say that there are not ways of being polite in Ojibwe culture (Rhodes, 1988; Spielmann, 1993a; Darnell, 1993; Ross, 1992, 1996). It does, however, provide us with a clue that those ways of doing things are different between cultures and thus tend to lead to cross-cultural misunderstandings and the reinforcing of stereotypes. The following story illustrates how this can happen even among those who are interested in trying to understand Native ways.

After having lived in the community of Pikogan for a number of years, we went one summer to visit my wife's parents in Victoria, British Columbia. My three daughters had spent their entire lives in the Native community and the oldest two had gone to the band-run school on the reserve. All their friends were Native and they were socialized in politeness protocol according to community standards. The first time we sat around the dinner table together with grandma and grandpa, my oldest daughter, Jennifer, who was six years old at the time, said 'Pass the potatoes.' Grandma, relying on what in her culture constitutes polite behaviour, asked her, 'What's the magic word?' Jennifer looked a bit puzzled and then hazarded the guess, 'Potatoes?' Needless to say, grandma corrected her and later that evening implied to us that our children's behaviour sometimes seemed a bit rude. We tried to explain that politeness behaviour differed from culture to culture and that it was important to try not to judge the behaviour of someone socialized in a different cultural context. Interestingly, that is pretty much the same message I attempt to transmit in my Native Studies courses to non-Native students. The results, as they were with grandma, are often mixed.

Language Revitalization and Maintenance

There is perhaps no greater sense of need in any Aboriginal community than to keep the Aboriginal language strong. Language is the soul of a people and many elders, from a variety of First Nations traditions, maintain that a nation which respects itself speaks, preserves, cultivates, and develops its language. Some elders go so far as to say that, if an individual does not speak his/her Aboriginal language, that person is a not fully Anishnaabe and lacks a deeply-rooted sense of identity. At this point I want to take a look at some of the issues for First Nations people concerning the maintainance and revitalization of Aboriginal languages.

What is it about language which evokes such strong feelings in people? For many living in Canada it is an issue which is never really given much thought. You speak a language and, if you are from a non-Aboriginal tradition, it probably never occurs to you that your language could be dying. But what if your children were forced to learn another language in order to become educated? What if you, as a parent or grandparent, were no longer able to communicate with your own children or grandchildren because you no longer shared a common language? What if people ridiculed your language as primitive and deficient? What if you were told that you could no longer speak your mother tongue or use it to worship God and teach your children your values? All of this happened to generations of First Nations people in Canada.

Is it any wonder that Aboriginal languages are on the decline in First Nations communities? Keep in mind when considering the attempt to revitalize and preserve Aboriginal languages that there is no sense of *retrievability* for these languages. If the last English or French speaker in Canada died, there would still be some place in the world where the language could be found and retrieved. When an Aboriginal language dies, it is gone forever. And with it tremendous amounts of knowledge, insight, and experience are lost for ever. Is it any wonder that First Nations are taking such forceful and drastic steps to revitalize and maintain their languages?

According to the 1993 Declaration on Aboriginal Languages by the Assembly of First Nations, 'Our languages were given to us by the Creator as an integral part of life. Embodied in our languages is our unique relationship to the Creator, our attitudes, beliefs, values and the fundamental notion of what is truth' (1993:2).

Aboriginal languages are of utmost importance to their people's education, both formal and informal. In those communities where the Aboriginal language is still strong, one senses a great pride in the history and culture of the community, in personal identity as beings with a spiritual core, a greater involvement and interest of grandparents and parents in the education and development of their grandchildren and children and a greater respect for the elders: 'Language is the principle means by which culture is accumulated, shared and transmitted from generation to generation. The key to identity and retention of culture is one's ancestral language.'

I believe it is important to listen carefully to the 'Living Voice' as expressed by the elders in all Aboriginal traditions in order to gain a sense of the passion of language. These elders are not merely speakers of their languages but masters of them. In many Aboriginal communities across North America Aboriginal languages are still used as the everyday means of communication, and there are still people who speak their Aboriginal languages exclusively and who speak neither of the so-called official languages of Canada. One wonders at the beauty and complexity of their languages and how they seem to embody culture-specific ways of thinking, interacting, praying, teasing, storytelling, and, well, just about everything. The sad thing is that most of us, in our lifetimes, will witness the end of a tradition which has existed for millennia in this country, the last of the monolingual speakers of Aboriginal languages.

Granted, there will continue to be speakers of Aboriginal languages for generations to come. Most linguists predict that, of the fifty-three existing Aboriginal languages in the eleven language families in Canada, three, Ojibwe, Cree, and Inuktitut, have a good chance for long-term survival. But will there be a continuation of monolingual speakers of the language? Probably not. There is just too much non-Native presence, influence, and media penetration in Aboriginal communities for that tradition to continue, and that's a damn shame. Such a situation provides even more of a reason to listen to these elders talk about the importance of Aboriginal language preservation. As one Mohawk elder puts it:

A history of Canadian government suppression and oppression of Native languages has created an attitude of apathy and fatalism about the need and utility of Native languages by the Native people themselves. The heart and soul of Native identity – language – must be nursed back to health, rejuvenated and restored to the status of *official languages* in Native Communities. (Norton, 1990:ii)

But there is reason to be optimistic. First Nations across North America are working hard to reverse the trend by implementing culturally appropriate curricula and teaching methods to combat this vandalization. The essence of Aboriginal identity and value transmission begins with knowing one's Aboriginal language and is based on a holistic approach to communicating and learning. The lifeblood of Aboriginal people, according to the elders, is embodied in their languages.

Our Native language embodies a value system about how we ought to live and relate to each other. It gives a name to relations among kin, to roles and responsibilities among family members, to ties with the broader clan group. If you destroy our language, you not only break down these relationships, but other aspects of our Indian way of life and culture are destroyed, especially those which describe our connection with nature, the Great Spirit, and the order of things. Without language we will cease to exist as a people. (Eli Taylor, Sioux Nation)

When we talk about language, we understand language to be in many sounds and many voices. Language is in your eye. The language is in your voice. The language is in how you walk. The language is in how you sing. We have the ear to understand and that's the language of our people. (Eva McKay, Sioux Nation)

The young people are beginning to speak our language less and less. When we lose our language, then we will no longer exist as the Creator intended. We will be a different people. (Albert Mowatt, Algonquin Nation)[5]

It is this recognition of the vital role of language in maintaining one's identity that motivates the efforts of instructors such as Ojibwe language professor Mary Ann Corbiere. Language ensures continuity in an ever-changing world. As Corbiere writes in 'Teaching Native Languages So That They Will Survive':

It is the contemporary context that needs to be emphasized. The goal of teaching a Native language is not simply to preserve the language, but to preserve it as a functioning language – one that can be used in the many varied contexts Native people find themselves in now: at home, in ceremonies, at hockey or baseball games, in the Band office, in the schools, at the shopping centre, and at the bingo hall or the casino. While many of these activities might not be thought of as traditional Native activities, they are very much a part of Native lives today. (1997:219)

Verna Kirkness, director of the First Nations House of Learning at the University of British Columbia, writes with passion about the need to revive and maintain ways of living and thinking and to revitalize and preserve Aboriginal languages. In her article, 'Aboriginal Languages in Canada: From Confusion to Certainty' (1989), she offers some suggestions for designing effective language-learning programs in Aboriginal communities and implores both Aboriginal and non-Aboriginal people in Canada to work together to keep Aboriginal languages strong. Basil Johnston, an Anishnaabe elder, also addresses the urgent need to revitalize and preserve Aboriginal languages. He argues that Aboriginal languages need to regain their place of prominence in Aboriginal communities as languages which embody the ways of thinking, living, behaving, and relating to others as equal to any other language and he stresses the importance of these languages (1991). Robert Leavitt (1992) provides us with some substantive clues as to how language decline leads to loss of one's Aboriginal identity. He suggests a series of recommendations as to how universities, in particular, can contribute to the strengthening and preservation of this invaluable resource.

Before exploring the relationship between language and identity, I want to close this discussion by returning to my initial question: Why is it important to support the renewal and preservation of Aboriginal languages? First, the studying, preserving, and teaching of Aboriginal languages is a personal and powerful statement of respect. Further, understanding the importance of Aboriginal languages to First Nations people, and the reasons for revitalizing and preserving them as languages used in everyday interaction, provides non-Native people in Canada with some resources for exploring and understanding alternative ways of thinking, behaving, and perceiving the world around us. Mono-cultural perspectives in today's world can be dangerous in that they encourage only one way of thinking and looking at the world. Further, Aboriginal languages are important keys to the survival of distinct and thriving cultures and world views. Perhaps these languages can teach us about different ways of thinking about justice, the environment, human relations, spirituality, and resource management. The Ojibwe language can teach us much about basic human values such as generosity, honesty, relationships and physical/emotional needs. In *First Nations Family Justice* (Awasis Agency of Northern Manitoba), George Muswagon writes: 'Language is the medium through which history, culture and world view are transmitted; therefore the best connection to historical roots are First Nations languages ... It is their particular way of viewing the world, and their place in it, that sets First Nations people apart from non-First Nations people. This world view has never really been lost; it remains intact in the languages' (1997:40).

The battle is far from over and I trust that this brief discussion helps you to grasp a sense of the importance and urgency of preserving and revitalizing Aboriginal languages today as the foundation for preserving and strengthening Aboriginal nationhood and identity.[6]

Language and Identity

One of the more pressing concerns in many Aboriginal communities as we head into the twenty-first century is how to preserve their language. Robert Bunge, a Lakota Sioux, ventured that 'A people who lose their language and the view of the universe expressed by that language, can no longer survive as a people, although they can survive as rootless individuals' (1987:19). If Bunge is right, then the need for Aboriginal language revitalization and preservation lies at the root of the continued existence of First Nations in Canada. Bunge is certainly not alone in making this claim. Most of the elders in the community where we lived believed that to be considered fully Anishnaabe a person must speak his/her Aboriginal language. Further, many Aboriginal writers side with Bunge's notion that, without maintaining the Aboriginal language, a First Nation can no longer survive as a distinct people (Johnston, 1991; Akan, 1992; Christensen, 1993).

When coupled with the notion that language is one of the central features that distinguishes one group of people from another, language becomes the ultimate symbol of identity (Bunge, 1987). Peggy Brizinski concurs, suggesting that, 'if a group's language is suppressed, the culture begins to be lost' (1993:67). Blondin claims that 'speaking your Native language strengthens your identity, and in that way strengthens and maintains the collective culture' (1989:15). The recent Royal Commission on Aboriginal Peoples seems to agree that language is essential to one's sense of identity: 'Language is the principal instrument by which culture is transmitted from one generation to another, by which members of a culture communicate meaning and make sense of their shared experience. Because language defines the world and experience in cultural terms, it literally shapes our way of perceiving – our world view' (1996, vol. 3:602).

There are many references in the commission's report to the importance of reviving and maintaining Aboriginal languages in Canada and which support Bunge's claim that language is crucial to Aboriginal identity. Bunge writes, 'Language is not just another thing we do as humans – it is *the* thing we do. It is a total environment; we live in language as a fish lives in water. It is the audible and visible manifestation of the soul of a people' (p. 13). A person from any tradition should be able to look to their own intuition about language in order to get a grasp of the issue. For example, for mother-tongue English speakers, how important is speaking English to one's sense of 'Who I am'? For Aboriginal people, one might ask, 'How important is it that I speak my traditional language? If I don't, does it somehow make me a "rootless individual," thus lacking the "soul" of my people? If I do, does that somehow make me more fully Anishinaabe? Why or why not?'

At one point Bunge writes: 'The first thing a victorious people does to a vanquished people is to disarm them – take away their weapons and take over their lands. This is bad enough, but then there follows something even worse – the theft of the psyche of the people. The English knew the Highlands of Scotland would never be pacified until the Gaelic language was destroyed' (p. 13). Certainly there are parallels here with the Canadian government's dealings with First Nations over the years. Many people are aware that Aboriginal people in residential schools were often punished for speaking their languages and that other overt assimilation policies were designed to stop Aboriginal people from speaking their languages. It surely seems that the Canadian government figured that one of the key elements that needed to be eliminated in order to 'tame' and 'civilize' these people was language.

A number of other points made by Bunge deserve to be explored in more depth. He writes, for example, that 'Among the Sioux there is a saying: "The white man ... sees with only one eye." This is because the white man is taught to see only with the mind – facts – and he forgets to combine or add that imaginative and moral aspect of nature which alone makes facts meaningful and beautiful to human beings' (p. 14). But is this true? Is Bunge talking here about something inherent in the nature and structure of the English language or is he confusing the issue by referring to a western perspective on the world, a perspective which just happens to be commonly shared by English-speakers? And what about Aboriginal people who are mother-tongue speakers of English? Can they, too, only see with one eye and thus lack the 'imaginative' and 'moral' aspect of nature?

At another point Bunge writes: 'Language is a spiritual experience. [Our Aboriginal language] is not only the language of the sweat lodge, but is an everyday sacred way of perceiving and expressing these perceptions. The universe of discourse of the dominant European tongues is that of an impersonal, inanimate mechanistic and amoral state of affairs while the universe of discourse of Lakota and other Aboriginal languages is one of a personal, animate and moral state of being' (p. 17). For those who might argue against Bunge's position, a number of points should be addressed. One key element that one might argue is that, while language is important to one's identity, there are other important factors as well. For example, is one following some kind of traditional teachings or way of life? Are traditional values, teaching, stories, and ceremonies being passed down to those who no longer speak the language? How has one been brought up and taught in relation to the language issue? All of these can feed into one's sense of identity to the point that, while one wishes he/she spoke his/her Aboriginal language, it is only one factor of many which relates to one's sense of identity. This is not to say that language is not important to cultural maintenance and a sense of identity, but it suggests that one is required to take a hard look at the tenacity of other factors that play a role in what constitutes identity.

Few would argue that knowing how to speak one's Aboriginal language is a key component to one's sense of identity, but is it the sole determinant? Many Aboriginal people claim, instead, that culture is more than merely an expression of language. Culture comprises the values and traditions of a community as well as the social and political formation of a group of people who define themselves as unique. Though most would agree that Aboriginal people have suffered severe cultural loss through unilaterally enforced policies of assimilation in Canada, it is equally evident that Aboriginal people have demonstrated a tremendous capacity and volition to adapt to change. In fact, my sense is that assimilative policies failed because the Canadian government consistently underestimated the resiliency of spirit of Aboriginal elders. The legacy of the history of Native/non-Native relations in Canada demonstrates quite clearly that Aboriginal people have been able to withstand assimilation policies. They have been able to come up with innovative ways of circumventing these policies and thus have managed to maintain unique identities. As Morrison and Wilson suggest, 'Social behaviour has changed, [but] the cultural rules generating behaviour have not' (1986:529). The natural conclusion, based on the fact that First Nations had managed their own affairs for millennia prior to the arrival of European peoples, is that the identity of the Aboriginal person can also be found in his/her cultural values and in the perception of how one sees oneself. In other words, traditional values continue to exist and inform Aboriginal attitudes, beliefs, and behaviours, which in turn continue to provide the foundation for their sense of identity.

One of the more interesting researchers of Ojibwe cosmology and ontology was Irving Hallowell. Although not Ojibwe himself, some well-respected Ojibwe scholars refer to his writings as containing some authoritative insights (e.g., Dumont, 1992; 1994). Responding to Bunge's thesis that one is a 'rootless individual' if one does not speak one's own Aboriginal language, Hallowell suggests that there are psychological characteristics that are Aboriginal in origin and persist in Aboriginal people living in post-contact times. James Dumont, a third-degree Midewewin healer and professor of Native Studies at the University of Sudbury, concurs that Hallowell often had his finger on the pulse of Ojibwe identity (Dumont, 1994). Hallowell claims that changes can and have occurred within Aboriginal cultures since contact with European-based peoples, but such changes have not substantively changed or destroyed Aboriginal identity (1960).

My own observations and experience with Ojibwe people in the 1990s confirm that his analysis remains authentic. Identity can (and does) persist even among Aboriginal people who no longer speak their Aboriginal language. Such a view is not new, and while it may be considered somewhat idealistic in the contemporary context, I would certainly argue otherwise. Spindler and Spindler claim that Aboriginal cultures can be best understood as surviving, perhaps in a fragmentary fashion, as well as any other culture on the global scene, including Canadians' own continuing struggle with identity. As such, it seems quite natural for people to strive to merge these fragments into an operational system.

As Spindler and Spindler suggest, 'Only cultures that remain pristine ... remain in hostile isolation from all outside cultural encounters' (1984:13).

Dumont (1994) has wisely suggested that, even though a Native person may appear to be losing his/her language, and even culture, that person's value system remains amazingly intact. In my own relationships with Aboriginal people, I cannot help but agree with Dumont when he says that most Aboriginal people in contemporary times feel almost as comfortable within their environment and their being as they did in more traditional, pre-contact times. There certainly is strong support and empirical evidence that today deeply entrenched traditional values, and not merely language, are the main factors which influence a Native person's sense of identity, of who one is deep down.

Language Preservation in Relation to Self-determination

While First Nations peoples have made great strides in the past fifteen years in reclaiming their linguistic identity and heritage, the crux of the matter is that most negotiations, dialogue, arrangements, agreements, and misunderstandings between First Nations and the Canadian government today are still grounded in English and French. The necessity of thinking through the implications of liberating Aboriginal languages is a first step, I believe, in creating a more equitable relationship between First Nations and Canada. By drawing from indigenous writers representing a more global framework, I want to put the issue of linguistic hegemony into understandable terms. More often than not, the revitalization and maintenance of Aboriginal languages in Canada is almost an afterthought in the quest for self-determination and self-government, whereas it is in fact a fundamental issue for First Nations people. The conditions that have supported linguistic hegemony in the past, media penetration into Aboriginal communities and the change in traditional methods of language and culture transference in the communities have just begun to be recognized.

Does it not strike the average Canadian as odd that, while Canada has prided itself as being a defender of human rights in the international community, the country's own Human Rights Commission has condemned its treatment of Aboriginal peoples? Why is it that Canadian service providers routinely translate educational and health-related materials into the languages of the people with whom they are sent to serve in other parts of the world, but educational and health-related information is not routinely translated into Aboriginal languages in its own country? Is it any wonder that most Aboriginal peoples consider the Canadian government to be operating by a double standard? These and other questions are at the heart of the matter of the liberation of Aboriginal languages in Canada.

Soon after the arrival of Europeans, missionaries and government agencies purposefully and systematically attacked the use of Aboriginal languages, and the effects of these actions are still evident today. Many parents and elders were and still are reluctant to teach their children and grandchildren their Aboriginal language out of fear that they, too, may suffer for it the way many of them did (Kirkness, 1989). First Nations are now working to reverse these attitudes and trends. Aboriginal peoples are seeking to define and implement culturally appropriate curricula and teaching methods to combat illiteracy, both in Aboriginal languages and the two other official languages in Canada (Royal Commission on Aboriginal Peoples, 1996). Research has shown conclusively that mother-tongue language development enhances second-language acquisition (Kirkness, 1989) and the development of a national First Nations' languages policy ought to be vigorously pursued by the Canadian government.

Decisions about developing a national policy for revitalizing and preserving Aboriginal languages cannot be made solely on economic factors (Is it worth it? How much will it cost? What contributions do these languages make to the economy?). From a First Nations perspective, it is a moral issue, an issue of respecting human dignity. Aboriginal peoples did not willingly abandon their languages; it was, more often than not, a violent process and a matter of government policy. What began in the residential schools continues through the generations today, much like a hereditary illness.

Aboriginal languages have a unique status; they are the only languages originating in this country. Aboriginal languages contain knowledge and concepts that no other language can express and there is no other sanctuary from which they can be retrieved. When Aboriginal languages in Canada are lost, they are lost to the world and the knowledge and insights they contain are lost with them.

DECOLONIZING LANGUAGE

The Assembly of First Nations (AFN) report titled *Towards Rebirth of First Nations Languages* (1993) established a five-part system for 171

Aboriginal communities with an analysis of speakers in each age group for the first four conditions (i.e., flourishing, enduring, declining and endangered), and absolute numbers (i.e., fewer than ten speakers) for the fifth. One of the benefits of doing this analysis is to be able to see that although a language may seem to be doing well generally (flourishing and enduring), it might be in a bad state locally (declining, endangered, or critical). This distinction is important, for each language lives or dies mostly by what is being done at the local level. Two good illustrations of this fact come from the examples of the Ojibwe and Cree languages. Foster presented them as being two of the three strongest languages, ones having excellent chances of survival. However, in another part of the AFN publication we can see that communities with Ojibwe and Cree speakers fall into all five conditions: flourishing, enduring, declining, endangered, and critical. It is disturbing to find that slightly less than one-third (30 per cent) claimed their community language to be in the relatively secure conditions of either flourishing or enduring, the same percentage that are endangered, while more than two-thirds (about 69 per cent) are in the much less secure conditions of declining, endangered, and critical.

Some Aboriginal leaders in Canada talk about 'decolonizing' Aboriginal languages, and one tends to get a negative impression about the task ahead for First Nations peoples in Canada. I prefer to think in terms of 'liberating' Aboriginal languages. Linguistic hegemony, the institutionalized dominance of language, thinking, abstractions, and conceptualizations, of the kind currently and historically experienced by First Nations people, is perhaps the most subtle form of hegemony. At this point I want to pursue some thoughts by Paulo Freire from his well-known book *Pedagogy of the Oppressed* (1970) with an interest in building upon and departing from some of his seminal ideas as we relate his thinking from a South American perspective to the current situation in Canada between Native people and non-Natives.

PAULO FREIRE AND DECOLONIZATION

One of the basic components of the relationship between those in positions of power in Canada and the relatively powerless status of the First Nations as represented by the major Native organizations is what Freire refers to as 'prescription': 'Every prescription represents the imposition of one [person's] choice upon another, transforming the consciousness of the [person] prescribed into one that conforms with the prescriber's consciousness. Thus, the behavior of the oppressed is a prescribed behavior, following as it does the guidelines of the oppressor' (1970:31).

Nowhere is this more relevant than in the area of linguistic hegemony which continues to exist today in Canada. In terms of liberating Aboriginal languages in Canada, Freire, quoting José Luiz Fiori, provides us with a clue as to the dimension of the struggle: 'Liberating action necessarily involves a moment of perception and volition. This action both precedes and follows that moment, to which it first acts as a prologue and which it subsequently serves to effect and continue within history. The action of domination, however, does not necessarily imply this dimension; for the structure of domination is maintained by its own mechanical and unconscious functionality' (p. 36).

The liberation of Aboriginal languages in Canada has, in a sense, already begun. The realization that already some First Nations languages have been lost forever is a daunting reflection and a challenge to First Nations' leaders to put an end to the ongoing linguistic hegemony. I am convinced the moment of perception and volition has arrived. As Freire states, the first stage must deal with 'the problem of the oppressed consciousness and the oppressor consciousness, the problem of who oppress and who suffer oppression. It must take into account their behavior, their view of the world, and their ethics. A particular problem is the duality of the oppressed: they are contradictory, divided beings, shaped by and existing in a concrete situation of oppression and violence' (p. 40).

Such a duality is diametrically opposed to the cultural sensibility of First Nations peoples, at least traditionally. While some cultural themes and values are in a state of flux as the process of acculturation continues to unfold, other traditional and cultural values, such as dialectic thinking as opposed to dualistic thinking, are still very much entrenched in the Native mind-set (Rhodes, 1988; Polson and Spielmann, 1990; Dumont, 1994). Freire suggests that dualistic thinking, either-or thinking, is conceptualized in the dominant society thinking in Canada: 'The oppressors do not perceive their monopoly on *having more* as a privilege which dehumanizes others and themselves. They cannot see that, in the egoistic pursuit of *having* as a possessing class, they suffocate in their own possessions and no longer *are*; they merely *have*. For them, having more is an inalienable right, a right they acquired through their own "effort"' (p. 45).

What better description of the mind-set of the government of Canada vis-à-vis First Nations people? In relation to linguistic hegemony, for example, whose fault is it that First Nations languages have been lost or diminished? The Aboriginal voice has been, until quite recently, relatively subdued on the matter. And that is understandable. As Freire suggests, 'when [people] are already dehumanized, due to the oppression they suffer, the process of their liberation must not employ the methods of dehumanization' (p. 53).

But I do not wish the discussion to sound like mere political rhetoric. In a recent conversation with a member of the James Bay Cree First Nation, he talked about a key concept in the liberation of language for his people. He told me: 'The next time we enter into treaty negotiations with the government, or if we ever renegotiate an existing treaty, we will insist that the treaty document be in the Cree language. Then *we* will be the ones in charge of the primary task of interpreting the contents of the treaty' (personal communication, 1994). He presents a position that is integral to the whole concept of liberating Aboriginal languages, towards the decolonization of language among the First Nations. The issues of treaty language, language of instruction in relation to the education of Aboriginal youth, and the language of preference among First Nations peoples are issues that must be brought to the forefront in the battle to dismantle linguistic hegemony. Many First Nations leaders take the position that linguistic liberation is vital to the struggle against social, political, economic and religious hegemony in the 1990s (Erasmus, 1989; Norton, 1990, 1992; Mawhiney, 1993).

NGUGI WA THIONG'O: THE POLITICS OF LANGUAGE

The current focus on Aboriginal languages and all that linguistic liberation implies cannot be meaningfully discussed outside the context of those social, political, cultural, and spiritual forces that have made it both an issue demanding the attention of First Nations peoples in Canada and a problem to be resolved. Some elders say that language revitalization and protection must be ensured before any significant progress can be made in the areas of land claims, self-determination, and the reclaiming of distinctively Native ways of life (Fox, 1991).

Ngugi Wa Thiong'o is regarded as a 'Living Voice' in the minds of many Africans. While he wrote his first novels in English, he resolved to put his stories into his own idiom, Kikuyu, so as to communicate primarily with his own people as well as to express himself in his Native tongue. He provides us with a starting point in relation to integrating his thinking with the current state of the liberation of First Nations languages in Canada.[7] 'The choice of language and the use to which language is put is central to a peoples' definition of themselves in relation to their natural and social environment, indeed in relation to the entire universe' (1986:4).

Ngugi cuts to the heart of the matter, not from a 'mainstream' perspective, but from a distinctly African one. First, he writes of the tripartite nature of language:

Language, any language, has a dual character: it is both a means of communication and a carrier of culture ... Language has three aspects of elements. There is first ... the language of real life, the element basic to the whole notion of language, its origins and development: that is, the relations people enter into with one another ..., the links they necessarily establish among themselves in the acts of people, a community of human beings. (p. 13)

Certainly Ngugi is touching on a crucial area of language which is more often than not glossed over. A person's stock of knowledge, in any culture, is a major factor in determining how a person thinks; a shared way of thinking about life and looking at life is, really, what culture is all about. If we assume, for example, that the Native perception of power is related to the acquisition of direct, experiential knowledge, and that knowledge is gained via language, what can we learn about when Ngugi writes, 'the relations people enter into with one another ..., the links they necessarily establish among themselves in the acts of people, a community of human beings'? These considerations take us back to Ngugi's first observation about the language of real life, 'the element basic to the whole notion of language, its origins and development: that is, the relations people enter into with one another ..., the links they necessarily establish among themselves in the acts of people, a community of human beings' (p. 13).

Ngugi continues: 'Is it right that a man should abandon his mother tongue for someone else's? It looks like a dreadful portrayal and produces a guilty feeling.' Certainly this is the state of feeling, of perception, for many Aboriginal people who have been constrained, for a variety of reasons, to abandon their own mother tongue for a foreign language. As Ngugi writes, 'See the paradox: the possibility of using mother tongues provokes a tone of levity ... but that of foreign languages produces a categorial ... embrace [of] "this fatalistic logic of the unassailable position of English".' He concludes: 'The fact is that all of us who opted for European languages ... accepted that fatalistic logic to a greater or lesser degree' (p. 7).

Returning to Ngugi's third observation about language, which I see as the strongest link in the chain of linguistic hegemony over First Nations people, he writes of a situation very much like the one of the First Nations peoples of Canada: 'But since the new, imposed language could never completely break the native languages as spoken, their most effective area of domination was the third aspect of language as communication, the written ... The language of his conceptualization was foreign' (p. 17).

The most devastating aspect of this form of linguistic hegemony is that it became, in many ways and forms, official dominant society policy in Canada in relation to First Nation languages, particularly in relation to the residential school system which was in place in Canada for 150 years. The situation described by Ngugi hits close to home for First Nations people in Canada. He writes:

So the written language of a child's upbringing in the school (even his spoken language within the school compound) became divorced from his spoken language at home. There was often not the slightest relationship between the child's written world ... and the world of his immediate environment in the family and in the community. For a colonial child, the harmony existing between the three aspects of language as communication was irrevocably broken. This resulted in the disassociation of the sensibility of that child from his natural and social environment, what we might call colonial alienation. (p. 17)

It is easy to appreciate, then, the reasons for my affinity with the writings of Ngugi. Extrapolating from his writings, we can see the strength of the linguistic chains that continue to bind First Nations people. While they continue to use 'foreign' languages in talking and writing about the liberation of Aboriginal languages in Canada, and will continue to do so for a long time to come, the real strength and depth of Aboriginal identity as distinct peoples will ultimately depend on the ability of First Nations people to revitalize and reinstate the idiom of their cultures in their own languages. Training and development means, in my mind, the releasing of the dammed-up creative powers in First Nations people. Such a step is already under way with the training of Aboriginal language teachers and the development of band-run schools among First Nation peoples in Canada today.

Today the importance of language among First Nations people as a means of maintaining and transmitting the uniqueness of Native culture is being increasingly understood and stressed. Within Aboriginal language themselves one has access to our relationship with the Creator, traditional beliefs and values, and a fundamental notion of what is truth for First Nations people. Thus I take the view that the development and growth of First Nations languages in Canada today is the essential element in the development and growth of self-governing First Nations. These languages do not merely describe traditional systems of government but define who First Nations people are. Certainly no one would disagree with such a fundamental statement, but it is my position that agreement is one thing and placing priority on decolonizing or liberating language is another, something more fundamental and, until recognized as foremost and foundational in First Nations' struggle for liberation, will only lead to more rhetoric and the strengthening of the colonial bond which continues to exist between the nation of Canada and the First Nations living within Canada.

Conclusion

In this chapter I have tried to establish the context for the rest of *'You're So Fat!'* by showing how one can begin to understand Ojibwe reality through talk and come to grasp the relationship between language, identity, and self-determination. Since early contact with the Europeans, Aboriginal people have attempted to retain and regain control over their languages and ways of thinking and doing things. Many non-Natives still believe that Native people will eventually assimilate into mainstream society and that their languages, customs, and beliefs are, for the most part, unimportant. Nothing could be further from the truth from a Native perspective. Governmental policies in the 1990s continue to promote the misconception that First Nations people will eventually assimilate and both past and present policies have targeted Aboriginal languages as one way of achieving this. There is, however, a great deal of optimism within the Native community at large that First Nations people will continue to retain their languages and identities in spite of such policies. While grand chief of the Assembly of First Nations, in 1989 George Erasmus described how First Nations people have survived contact with European-based peoples: 'Our people have retained ... extraordinary tenacity, the central core of their beliefs, values and cultures. We have no doubt of our continued survival, far into the future. We have always been here. We are not going anywhere' (p. 295).

PART TWO
INTRODUCTION TO CONVERSATION ANALYSIS

4

'When Yes Means No': An Introduction to Conversation Analysis in Ojibwe

When I began teaching in the Department of Native Studies at the University of Sudbury I noticed an interactional phenomenon which, in retrospect, I remember having encountered many times over the years spent hanging out with Anishnaabe (Ojibwe and Algonquin) people. I was talking with one of my students, Clem Nabigon, and I happened to ask him about one of his assignments that was due. I asked him, 'Did you finish your essay yet?' He responded, 'Yeah.' I then asked, 'Oh, good. Did you turn it in?' He said, 'Well, I'll have it finished by Tuesday.' I couldn't help having some fun with him, nor could I stop myself from engaging in some analysis of that particular interaction. My analysis went something like this: The real answer to my initial question was no. So really his yes meant no. Being a close friend as well as one of my students, we had some fun with what had happened, but I think we also began to get deeper into what was going on in his Anishnaabe mind by analysing it a bit. The best place to start, I figured, would be with his own ethno-analysis of the interaction; in other words, how does *he* explain it? He thought about it for a minute, then offered this analysis: 'I guess I was thinking that I'm *almost* finished with the essay in the sense you were asking about, so in my mind it *is* finished.' What he is pointing to here is that the boundaries between past and present, finished and ongoing, product and process, are much fuzzier in Ojibwe thinking than in my own non-Native way of conceptualizing projects. On the other hand, he may have merely been trying to get off the hook for having been caught! But I am inclined to accept his ethno-explanation as reflecting a different way of thinking than is conventionalized in non-Native people, generally speaking. Consider the following interaction:

A: Yeah, I quit smoking.
B: Oh, yeah? When?
A: Well, I haven't really quit yet, but I'm thinking about it.

I was standing around having a smoke outside the university with some of the Native students when A came up, chatted a bit, and then the conversational sequence above took place. Of course, as he was uttering the comment that he was thinking about it, A pulled out a pack of cigarettes and lit one up! Everyone laughed along with him, but part of the humour of the situation had to do, I believe, with the commonly shared thinking between process and product, ongoing and finished.[1]

Another time, I was with two of my Native friends, and I asked one of them if he stayed in touch with John, a close friend who had moved away a few years earlier. He responded, 'Oh, yeah. Well, I haven't spoken to him since he left, but ...' Again, much laughter ensued! As we were all friends (and academics, for better or for worse), we engaged in some mini-analysis of how he had responded. His explanation was. 'Well, I guess I answered like that because in my mind John will always be my friend, whether or not I ever see him or talk to him again.'

Rupert Ross offers support for this difference in thinking and categorizing between Native people and non-Natives, a difference reflected in the very structure of Algonquian languages. He writes: 'Aboriginal people have regularly spoken to me about their verb-based languages. They describe their "verb-world" as one where each person's primary focus is not on each separate thing but on all the movements and relationships *between* things. The ... verb focus is on the many *processes* in which we all participate, at every instant in every day' (1996:239).

The purpose of this chapter is to examine the everyday life experience of Ojibwe people by exploring naturally occurring talk and natural, everyday conversational interactions. These interactions tell us, I believe, something of how Ojibwe people think and how Ojibwe reality is socially constructed. Emphasis is placed on discovering and describing performative features found in conversational interaction: storytelling, joking/teasing, requesting favours, greetings and leave-takings, and so on, with the aim of understanding the relationships between performative features of talk and everyday conversation, ethnomethods, and world view (Schenkein, 1978; Spielmann, 1980; Beach, 1991; Watson, 1992; Watson and Seiler, 1992; Norrick, 1994). The chapter is designed to lead you through the basic methods of analysing conversational interaction as it is in naturally occurring contexts and to introduce you to the basic principles of conversation analysis and how those principles can be applied to the understanding of Ojibwe-specific ways of thinking and doing things. The focus of this chapter is on the 'Living Voice' in Ojibwe communities and what we can learn about politeness protocol, culturally appropriate interaction patterns, and learning how to 'fit into' a Native context or community by observing Ojibwe people engaged in face-to-face conversational interaction. As Michael Pomedli tells us, 'Unrehearsed conversational language houses a marvelous genius. Conversation is expressive, voicing immediate sensations, feelings and ideas, whether on the individual or on the community level. Conversation is admirably flexible, mobile, spontaneous and momentary' (1992:341).

There is no question that the values which underlie Aboriginal interaction patterns are qualitatively different from the values which motivate, generally speaking, non-Native interaction patterns and behaviours. It is the thesis of this book that a deeper understanding of these differences will go a long way towards bringing Native and non-Native together as allies within the context of the nation of Canada. This chapter relies heavily on Native community experiences, anecdotes, humorous stories, and teachings from the elders to get across the point that we are dealing with substantively different ways of thinking and doing things between Native people and non-Natives. By relying on conversation analysis and ethnographic methods, it is suggested that we can come to an understanding of those differences, which is essential to decreasing the tension, misunderstanding, confusion, and stereotypes which have evolved since the first contact between Europeans and Aboriginal peoples.[2]

An Introduction to Conversation Analysis

The field known as conversation analysis (CA) comes from a distinctly sociological background. It was born from the discipline of ethnomethodology, which had been pioneered in the 1960s by Harold Garfinkel. At the time, some sociologists had become fed up with typical sociological treatments of social reality with its emphasis on 'social facts' and causal explanations. Ethnomethodology, and subsequently CA, explores how social structures and realities are *achieved*, *sustained*, and *displayed* in the everyday interaction of human beings.

The interest in CA arose when ethnomethodologists began to realize that natural conversation, when properly understood, is a terrific research site for exploring different versions of reality. After all, naturally occurring talk is accessible and recordable and, while we can't read people's mind, we can listen to how people talk about their reality. Certainly talk exhibits numerous orderly features which, upon analysis, turn out not to be merely features of language but also of interaction. Using tapes and transcripts of naturally occurring talk, conversation analysts proceed in three basic steps: a particular interactional technique or method is located and its orderly features described; the orderliness of the technique is then accounted for by an interactional organization (commonly called a machinery); and its ideal version allows us to access what is commonly available to competent cultural members (mother-tongue speakers of any language) as a 'simplest systematics.' As Sacks et al. write, 'Herein lies a central methodological resource for the investigation of conversation ... a resource provided by the thoroughly interactional character of conversation. It is a systematic consequence of the turn-taking organization of conversation that obliges its participants to display to each other, in a turn's talk, their understanding of other turns' talk' (1978:44).

The studies initiated by Garfinkel give primacy to locating and describing the competence and knowledge of social members, the taken-for-granted assumptions which delimit a member's interpretation of experience. He writes: 'The activities whereby members produce and manage settings of organized everyday affairs are identical with members' procedures for making those scenes "account-able"' (1967:1).

Garfinkel makes the point that people do not necessarily separate the circumstances of social events from their descriptions of those events. Here we touch upon a fundamental concept. When Garfinkel talks about reflexivity, he is referring to this embedding of circumstances in descriptions or accounts, and of accounts coming from within circumstances of social events and arrangements. We may say, then, that the methods under examination are part of all sense-making so that an attempt to locate and describe them is itself a new waiting-to-be-analysed instance or procedure. For the most part, though, people use these procedures or methods in assumed, unformulated, and unexamined ways. The social world is out there somewhere for most people, something objective. It is rarely viewed as a concerted accomplishment, a product, or an outcome of the use of commonly used member's methods. It is the task of the ethnomethodologist to locate and describe these methods.

Language provides us with a vehicle for understanding and dealing with the complexities of human life. It is our primary medium for communicating with one another. We use it to settle our differences and ventilate our feelings, to tell about our experiences, and to pass on our culture's stories. As such, language can become a complicated and elaborate tool. One of the basic considerations in the study of practical reasoning revolves around people's use of everyday talk. Building upon Garfinkel's notion of language, Michael Moermann makes the claim that 'anything ever said is said by someone, to someone, at a particular moment of some specific socially organized and culturally informed occasion. Casual everyday conversation is the most common, frequent, and pervasive way in which speech is socially organized' (1988:x).

What studies in ethnomethodology are really trying to get at is cultural know-how – what people must know in order to act appropriately in a culture.[3] No matter what our own personal cultural background, we all share a sense of the usual and the normal against which we are able to judge the unusual and the abnormal. One kind of cultural know-how that we assume that others share is a stock of knowledge about people, places, what constitutes appropriate behaviour in a variety of interactional settings, and so on. Granted, individuals within the same cultural tradition also have their own elements of knowledge which is not necessarily shared by all cultural members. But a person's stock of knowledge and experience, in any culture, is a major factor in determining how a person thinks. And a shared way of thinking about life and looking at life is, really, what culture is all about. What ethnomethodologists are exploring, then, is a social reality that is visible and accessible to participants and analysts alike.[4] If we assume, for example, that the Native perception of power is related to the acquiring of direct, experiential knowledge, what can we learn about Native social reality by observing and understanding the way in which cultural members interact?

Before we try to answer this question, let us examine some of the techniques available to people for interacting appropriately and the cultural values which underlie those techniques. Certainly face-to-face interaction occurs in a somewhat orderly fashion; it is not usually a haphazard stringing together of words and utterances. I take it that an understanding of appropriate interaction is the key to understanding how people in any culture think and do things. And how people think is understandable only in relation to their own understanding of appropriate interaction. Michael Moerman writes in *Talking Culture: Ethnography and Conversation Analysis*: 'Conversation analysis studies the organization of everyday talk, of language as actually used in social interaction ... [It] provides a component that has been critically missing from the realistic examination of such issues as how language relates to thinking' (1988:10).

Conversation analysis seeks to locate and describe interactional structures in discourse by constructing machineries or simplest systematics, which provide for how it is that discourse activities get accomplished. Social interaction is to a large extent verbal interaction and orderly features of discourse may be located and described, not merely linguistic features but interactional ones. We are not, after all, dealing with a deterministic unfolding of conversation. It is not, for example, like pulling the trigger on a gun and noting the whole predictable unfolding that takes place. Most conversation analysts would agree that there are orderly and conventional relations between utterance types and that the task of the analyst is to discover those relations and elucidate them.[5]

That task includes finding when these relations are ignored, rejected, thrown back on the speaker, and so on. For example, one common feature of conversational discourse is that questions deserve answers. When we recognize this, however, we have to remember that many times questions are not followed by answers, and even this simple conversational maxim can be constrained by culture-specific ways of thinking and doing things. Nevertheless, the structures located in conversational interaction should be able to take care of that as well. In one sense the task of the conversation analyst is not to predict that, for example, 95 per cent of the time questions will be followed by answers, but to discover and describe what becomes available in conversation for whatever can happen.

Furthermore, CA does not try to predict what persons can say, or what kinds of moods they are in. No constraints can be put on what a person can or cannot say. One may request a story, for example, with the expectation that the person being asked will respond with a story. But there are no guarantees nor constraints which would actually require anyone to tell the story (Spielmann, 1988). Anything can happen (and does) in everyday conversation, and a person being requested to tell a story could respond with something like, 'I don't have time right now, I'm off to the disco,' or whatever. As Sacks and Schegloff remind us, 'Finding an utterance to be an answer, to be accomplishing answering, cannot be achieved by reference to phonological, syntactic, semantic, or logical features of the utterance itself, but only by consulting its sequential placement, e.g. its placement after a question' (1974:299).

Further, the aim of CA is not to give one an expertise in 'understanding' a discourse or to find out 'what was really meant' in a conversation. CA is intended to do *provings of possibilities*, to show that what seems to be going on in a discourse is a possibility, and where that takes some

kind of observational evidence. CA attends to the analysis of understandings of talk by attempting to demonstrate how these understandings may be located in the talk itself. In effect, no additional information
is needed. As Roy Turner (1972, 1976) demonstrated in the early days of
the development of CA, every utterance in conversation has social organizational features and what goes on in people's minds gets realized, to
a large extent, through conversation or talk, even though this realization
might not be recognized by the people themselves.[6] Harvey Sacks (1970,
1972) understood with great clarity that we live in a world of talk. As
Moerman suggests, 'In every moment of talk, people are experiencing
and producing their cultures, their roles, their personalities. Conversation analysis has some promise of precisely locating and describing how
that world of talk works, how the experienced moments of social life are
constructed, how the ongoing operation of the social order is organized'
(1988:11).

It pays, too, to note the scope and limitations of conversation analysis.
CA is not, after all, trying to construct a methodology for figuring out
what was meant in a particular conversation. It is not interested in locating and describing formal cognitive features of language or in contributing to purely linguistic grammars or engaging in macro-level language
debates (Nelson, 1994). CA seeks to provide insight into the interactional character of talk, which is beginning to be recognized as important and recommended for further study (Longacre, 1983; Jones, 1983;
Pickering, 1979). To illustrate this, I like to have fun with my students by
asking them to try and make sense of the following exchange without
recourse to context.

A: I have a fourteen-year-old son.
B: Well, that's all right.
A: I also have a dog.
B: Oh, I'm sorry.

Such remarks and responses seem strange when taken in isolation, but
quite natural when taken in the context of the actual conversation in
which A is raising a series of possible disqualifications for apartment
rental with the landlord, B (Sacks, 1992).

Two basic methods are used by those engaged in analysing naturally
occurring conversation or talk: The first method examines conversational
transcripts in order to discover recurring patterns and describes the systematic properties of those patterns. Conversation analysis attempts to

locate some particular organization and isolate its systematic features by demonstrating participants' orientation to those features. The second method seeks to discover what problem(s) the explicated organization solves, what problem(s) it raises, and what implication(s) it has for the existence of further solutions to further problems. The methodology involves listening to and transcribing conversational tapes, searching transcripts for recurring patterns, locating a particular discourse organization, discovering the systematic features of that organization, and describing its formal properties by demonstrating the participants' orientation to those properties.

To reiterate, CA builds upon Garfinkel's initial formulation of ethnomethodology by holding to the view that social structures are achieved, sustained, and displayed in and through interaction.[7] Conversation analysts are interested in how language is employed to accomplish social order as a feature of social reality. In a narrower sense, this interest has to do with how people continually and consistently account for what they do and how they display their activities as rational and ordinary. This accounting relates to talk in that people do many things by talking about them.

Upon analysis it is claimed that discourse exhibits many orderly features, not so much features of language as of interaction.[8] Moerman sums it up succinctly when he writes: 'Conversation analysis is a methodic practice for describing and making sense of the organization of face-to-face interaction, for discovering what participants orient to, enforce, and accomplish in making their interactions orderly and meaningful, for learning how they build the structured integrity of experienced social life' (1991:176).

CONVERSATION ANALYSIS AND ETHNOGRAPHY

The field of conversation analysis keeps extending itself across disciplinary boundaries, and one of the disciplines beginning to take a specialized interest in CA is anthropology. Michael Moerman in his book *Talking Culture: Conversation Analysis and Ethnography* (1988) shows how CA issues can get transformed in theoretically interesting ways when combined with ethnographic principles. He does this by engaging in both ethnography and conversation analysis and shows how ethnography describes contextual features intrinsic to everyday interaction while CA is able to generate accurate non-contexted descriptions of talk. He ends up with what Mandelbaum refers to as 'culturally contexted conversation analysis' (1991:334).[9] Moerman appears to be proposing a synthesis of ethnography and CA in order to address things such as the 'roles, passions ... and strategies' of everyday life (1988:xi). On the other hand, he suggests that, in exploring other cultures and ways of thinking, our findings must necessarily be grounded in naturally occurring talk. In other words, in listening to and trying to understand a particular piece of speech, what do we need to know about the culture and about culture-specific ways of thinking in order to understand it? For Moerman, conversation analysts ask about the social activities that are being conducted in and through talk, where context resides.[10]

Anita Pomerantz (1978, 1984) addresses some of the same concerns by claiming that one must pay attention to local details to provide the context for a specific conversational interaction. Her analysis of compliments and compliment responses among English-speaking North Americans (1978) is provocative and shows how the preference for agreement and for avoiding self-praise are not limited to compliment-giving and responding to compliments, but are the conversational preferences in those environments. Pomerantz was one of the first to make it clear that CA seeks to describe both structure (practices *of* conversation) and interaction (practices *in* conversation). The methodological implications of what Pomerantz is promoting are, I believe, important. If we take it that language is inextricably situated in place and time, then the analysis of language ought to focus on local practices and particular acts.[11] This takes us back to CA's grounding in ethnomethodology. CA begins with the notion that language is a situated, time-bound activity, the study of which should begin with naturally occurring conversational interaction and viewed from the perspective of the people involved in the interacting.[12]

CONVERSATION ANALYSIS AND OJIBWE INTERACTION

In chapter 2 we explored some strongly entrenched values operating in the lives of Ojibwe people today: *respect* as seen in the values of not forcing your thinking on another and the importance of maintaining harmony in all social relations; *spirituality* as seen in its all-pervasive nature and attention paid to sacred power, dreams, visions, and prayer; *generosity* as seen in the recognition that all possessions, successes, and honour in life comes from the Creator; and *helpfulness* as seen in assumed cooperation. At this point I want to take a closer look at appropriate interaction and how the discipline of conversation analysis can enable us to understand better Ojibwe-specific ways of thinking and doing things.

One of our ongoing research projects has involved us in collecting naturally occurring talk in the Algonquin dialect of Ojibwe: conversations, storytellings, legends, and teachings which have been recorded or videotaped by the elders and other community members.[13] In looking for culturally specific ways of doing things, the current state of our knowledge of Ojibwe grammar, lexicon, and dialectology puts us in a good position to discover and describe some of these cultural techniques and strategies. Careful attention to the details of what we commonly call naturally occurring interaction, for example, sheds light on what appears at first blush merely to be how people act in face-to-face conversation, but in the last analysis reveals things previously unreported about the nature of Ojibwe-specific cultural practices.

One activity which kept popping up in natural conversation reflects Ojibwe-specific politeness strategies; specifically, how people make requests in the Algonquin dialect of Ojibwe. By examining some of these conversational sequences, we found that the most common way of getting someone to do something is to tell them to do it using a plain imperative. Note some of the examples we found of people using imperatives to make requests.

Aashkwe bidoon nasema.
Give me a cigarette.
Situation: One friend to another at a pow-wow.

Giiwenishin.
Take me home.
Situation: A visitor at a friend's house with no car or skidoo and the weather is cold.

Ozhitoon niibiishwaaboo.
Make some tea.
Situation: Younger brother to older sister.

To an outsider it may appear that such requests are rude, but to many Ojibwe people the kinds of interaction taking place in these examples is conventionally polite.

In observing Ojibwe interaction in a variety of communities and contexts, we find more often than not that the strategy of being indirect is conventionally polite when making requests for favours which require some substantive effort in order to perform them. Note the following examples, where someone requesting a favour requiring some effort uses a conventionally indirect strategy.

A1: *Aanapiich ge maajaayan?*
    When are you leaving?
B1: *Onaagoshig.*
    Tonight.
A2: *Gidaa dazhiike nimises omigiwaamikaag onaagoshig.*
    You could stay at my sister's house tonight.
B2: Okay.
A3: *Gewiin Jim wii booziiban ashij.*
    Jim wants a ride, too.

In this conversation, utterance A1 is the first move and it seems to do the work of what we might call a pre-request. The request itself actually comes in utterance A2, which is heard as a request for a ride to B's community for Jim the next day. That is evident in utterance A3, which immediately follows B's willingness to stay at A's sister's house for the night. It can be noted from this dialogue that people making requests in Ojibwe can propose and recipients can accept that an implicit request is being made. After all, in this particular conversation there is no explicit request for a ride for Jim. In fact, no mention is made to getting a ride until the request has already been indirectly made by A and oriented to by B. If we were to examine utterances A1 through B2 without taking into consideration utterance A3, our understanding of the topic of the conversation would be quite deficient. As it is, we can see that the topic of the conversation is not, after all, about where B is to spend the night but whether or not B is willing to give Jim a ride the next day.

While most of the examples presented in this book are based upon tape-recorded stories, legends, and conversational interactions, some of the interactions in this chapter are based on memory. Certainly the use of memory for analysing conversational interaction has two disadvantages: memory can be faulty; and relying on memory does not give the interested reader the opportunity to actually listen to the interaction, which is possible with tape-recordings (which anyone is invited to listen to if one so desires). Nevertheless, some conversational interactions I had while living in the community of Pikogan are so deeply etched in my memory that I was taken aback by them as a cultural immigrant. The following interaction sticks with me because it went so much against the grain of acceptable conversational interaction in my own culture.

We first moved into the community Pikogan in the summer of 1979. The use of the Algonquin dialect of Ojibwe was, and is, extremely strong in the community and the elders taught me to speak their language with patience and kindness. Interestingly, when I was becoming conversationally fluent in the language they also figured that I should know how to use the language appropriately in conversational interaction. In our second year in the community, I received a telephone call from one of the men with whom I had become friends. After some small talk, the conversation went like this:

Him: *Anezhitaayan maanigiizhigag e onaagoshig?*
      What are you doing Saturday night?
Me: *Gaa gegoon.*
      Nothing.
      (5 second pause)
Him: Hmmm (hangs up the phone).

I was puzzled by this interaction the first time it happened. At the time, using my non-Native intuition, I assumed that his question, 'What are you doing Saturday night?' was a pre-invitation, so I heard that comments as intending to find out if my wife and I were available to do something with the caller and his wife on Saturday night. Thus, I expected the next remark to be something along the lines of: 'So do you guys want to come over for dinner on Saturday?' Instead he hung up. If the whole thing had stopped there, I might not have caught on to what was happening. However, he called back twice again that day and the conversation proceeded in exactly the same manner! By the third time, I was beginning to get quite irritated. Then he called again. The conversation followed the exact same pattern, except this time, instead of hanging up, he quietly asked *'Gigaagii gaanawenimawaag naa nidabinojizhimag Maanigiizhigag e onaagoshig?'* ('Can you baby-sit for us on Saturday night?') I assured him we would be glad to. Then it hit me. Because I wasn't tuned in to appropriate ways of doing things in the community, such as the appropriate way of making a request for a favour, I had forced him to play the game by my non-Native rules of interaction – to ask me directly for a favour. As it turned out, then, what I initially thought was a pre-invitation utterance was actually a pre-request one. As this pattern kept repeating itself, we came to realize that, in Ojibwe interaction, the strategy of being indirect when making a request for a favour is conventionally polite and requires a collaborative effort.

To my mind this type of conversation supports the view that culture can be viewed as largely methodological in nature.[14] In non-Native society, generally speaking, there does not seem to be such a negative stigma attached to asking someone directly to do something for you. In Ojibwe interaction, there does seem to be a negative flavour related to direct asking. Although we can recall instances where the game is sometimes played in non-Native interaction, it is common in Ojibwe society.

REJECTION TECHNIQUES AND ACTION CHAINS

Another issue which arises from our conversational materials relates to rejections, or refusing a request for a favour without actually having to say no. One of the more revealing methodologies for explicating and understanding culture is by considering the ways in which people make use of the location of a cultural particular – person, event, object, utterance – to decide what it means. By location I mean the placement of a cultural pa ticular in a variety of contexts and settings, and it seems reasonable to think that the most accessible place to start is with sequential positioning in conversation. Our question becomes: how does utterance location and sequential positioning work in the Algonquin dialect of Ojibwe in the context of saying no to a request for a favour? One typical way of indicating rejection of a request is exemplified in the following conversation. My friend B and I were taping a language session when A happened to walk in the door.

A1: *Gidinaataa naa?*
     Are you busy?
B1: *Aadi waa izhaayan?*
     Where do you want to go?
A2: *Odenag niwii izhaanaban.*
     I was wanting to go to town.
B2: *Nichaagamidewiyakizonan nidodaabaan.*
     My car's out of gas.
A3: *Maanooj.*
     Never mind.

In this particular instance I take it that B used a typical evasion device to indicate rejection, or of trying to say no without having to come out and say it directly, thus risking the possibility of A losing face. In examining request responses in Ojibwe we encounter instances where the response provides for the possibility of conversational trouble, where actual performances fall short of preferred performances. By a preferred performance I mean that when someone requests a favour the preferred response is acceptance. The concept of 'preference organization' was designed to describe the characteristic differences which occur in the ways speakers accomplish alternative actions, for example in the acceptance/refusal of invitations (Sacks, 1972; Pomerantz, 1984; Bilmes, 1988). The term does not refer to the personal desires of the individual speakers, but rather to structural features of speaking and sequence structures in which alternative actions are routinely packaged. I use the terms 'preferred' and 'dispreferred,' then, to refer to the seeking/avoidance of alternative courses of action which are reflected in characteristic features in the design of the actions involved. Preference research has shown that for a variety of first actions, such as requests, dispreferred second actions are routinely avoided or delayed. Preferred actions, on the other hand, are usually performed directly with little or no delay.

Most social interaction is, to a large extent, verbal interaction, and I believe that orderly features of talk can be located and described, not merely linguistic features but interactional features. As we noted earlier, the work which has done the most in making talk into a topic for study has been that produced by Harvey Sacks and his students. Two major issues of a sociolinguistic nature have received attention from Sacks: first, membership categories of speaker-hearers, in which the attempt is made to go beyond the surface analysis of talk by proposing a linkage between people's language categories and how people do description and accomplish activities; and secondly, the sequential organization of conversation. According to Sacks, people use social knowledge and practical common sense in three ways: to recognize and make recognizable conversational utterances as possible instances of things like stories, jokes, complaints, and so on; to accomplish conversational activities such as gaining a turn at speaking, closing a conversation, and so forth; and to do a vast number of activities such as promising, criticizing, requesting, and so on. The studies carried out by Sacks in the exploration of the orderliness of conversation suggest that the accomplished character of the organization of talk stands up to formal analysis. Sacks's earliest interest was concerned with the phenomenon of description (Sacks, 1992). He claimed that, in and through their talk, people are continually describing their social world to one another. Anything and everything is describable: things people have done or want to do, events they have seen or not seen, attitudes, motivations, states of minds, feelings. It would not be misleading, according to Sacks, to think of the social world as constituted by its ability to describe itself.

Returning to the conversation above, the role of preference organization in relation to making requests appears to be quite strongly associated with saving face and the avoidance of outright rejection. As Pomerantz (1978) has demonstrated, speakers may revise their utterances-in-progress so as to forestall anticipated rejections. One such device is a pre-sequence utterance such as A asking *'Gidinaataa naa?'* ('Are you busy?'). A's utterance acts as a ground-clearing device directed at establishing the appropriateness of A's subsequent action of making a request. In such a case, the possible rejection of the request may be avoided by the recipient's indication that the activity is not possible. As it turned out in the situation, about half an hour later B hopped in his car, which was allegedly out of gas, and drove to town. It seems, then, that one typical way of avoiding saying no to a request in Ojibwe is by playing the game by offering an excuse, legitimate or not, for not being able to grant the request.

Upon the completion of a request, a slot opens up for a response. Further, responses to requests may be coordinated with an already existing structure in the conversation analysis literature. One kind of structure which connects request responses with a request itself is what Anita Pomerantz (1978) has termed chained actions. She characterizes an action chain as a type of organization in which two related actions, action 1 and action 2, are linked in such a way that the performing of action 1 provided for the possibility of the performance of action 2 as an appropriate next action (hereafter referred to as A1 and A2). Using Pomerantz's example from compliments and compliment responses, we can begin to see how these action chains work. One kind of action chain for compliments is:

A1: A compliments B.
A2: B accepts/rejects the compliment.

another being:

A1: A compliments B
A2: B agrees/disagrees with the compliment.

With an action chain, then, the second part is optional. In the example above we can see that there are two things happening simultaneously: the response slot is being filled, and it is being filled with an A2.

We may now formulate the interactional problems as follows. How does someone who receives a request for a favour in Ojibwe interaction orient to the request so as to transform the results of that orientation into a preferred response? At least two related problems arise, one for the request recipient and one for the person making the request. The recipient's problem has to do with sustaining and protecting the current interaction with a preferred response. The person making the request seeks to avoid giving occasion for a dispreferred response. Our specific concern in this instance is with the preferred response when indicating refusal.

It seems that, in the Algonquin dialect of Ojibwe, upon receipt of a request the recipient who wants or has to offer a rejection still has options available. One of these shows the recipient offering a rejection notice which informs the person making the request of an intent to reject in the recipient's next turn of talk. The person making the request, so informed, ought to do some work in order to provide grounds for the recipient to terminate the rejection action in next turn. Note this three-part structure in the conversation we have been considering above:

A2: *Odenag niwii izhaanaban.*
I was wanting to go to town.
B2: *Nichaagamidewiyakizonan nidodaabaan.*
My car's out of gas.
A3: *Maanooj.*
Never mind.

Technically this sequence can be described as containing two actions beyond the initial request: the rejection notice and the termination of the request. Certainly in Ojibwe society face-to-face interaction is constructed in such a way as to make requesting favours prone to the kind of trouble considered in this chapter. That is, it seems that the generation of requests in ongoing conversation will, at times, give rise to the need for a concerted effort between the person making the request and the recipient in order to sustain and protect ongoing interaction. The following examples follow this same pattern:

A1: *Odaayan na shooniyan gikokomim?*
Does your wife have any money?

B1:   *Aadidoog.*
      I don't know.
A2:   *Maanooj.*
      Never mind.

and

A1:   *Gigaagii izhiiwiizhinan naa?*
      Can you take me somewhere?
B1:   *Nigichi datakadenan.*
      It would really put a strain on me.
A2:   *Gaa nigod.*
      Okay.

Of course, as we noticed in the conversation where A eventually asks B directly if B can make a trip for A that afternoon (above), the person making a request has the option of pursing the matter until a direct yes or no is obtained. This option, however, seems rare in Ojibwe interaction.[15]

Now we can begin to get an idea of how a rejection to a request works in Ojibwe, how it is displayed in everyday talk and how it gives rise to other utterance classes. The concepts of 'face' and 'face-work' are most likely common to every culture, yet the ways in which face is perceived, sustained, and protected are certainly different. Erving Goffman (1959, 1967, 1974) was perhaps the first to describe face-work as the actions taken by a person to maintain his or her image by avoiding or correcting situations which threaten the face that a person wants to project. Goffman claims that face-work is an essential force holding interaction together and he talks about a person having two points of view: a defensive orientation towards saving one's own face, and a protective orientation towards saving the other's face. He writes: 'Some conversational practices will be primarily defensive and others primarily protective, although in general one may expect these two perspectives to be taken at the same time. In trying to save the face' of others, the person must choose a tack that will not lead to loss of his own ... and, he must consider the loss of face that his actions may entail for others' (1967:14).

With Goffman's comments in mind, we can begin to see how a direct rejection of a request in Ojibwe may be considered a dispreferred response. In Ojibwe culture it seems that direct rejection may lead to loss of face and possible interactional trouble. Thus, culture-specific techniques are available to avoid such a possibility, techniques which can be located and described by analysing conversation transcripts. Other cultural features play a part in the development of preferred techniques in Ojibwe culture. In general terms, the preferred procedure for indicating rejection in Ojibwe culture has to do with providing excuses and avoiding direct rejection. The dispreferred procedure relates to direct rejection with the possible loss of face.

Preferred Responses and the Organization of Conversational Sequences

Recall that CA asks how people do things in and through language. How do they accomplish activities and how do they make their accomplishments known to others? In everyday, ordinary interaction people in any culture assume that others will share the same expectations and definitions of the situation they find themselves in. We trust that actions will proceed in familiar ways. When these expectations are violated, one can cause confusion, misunderstanding, and embarrassment.

People do many things. They get along (more or less well) with other people, they tell stories, they joke, they ask questions, they report news, they make promises, they complain, and so on. People regularly do hundreds of things every day in and through language and all of these ordinary activities are treated by conversation analysts as important in their own right. They are practical accomplishments which are deserving of the same kind of attention by social scientists as are more extraordinary phenomena. In CA, people are seen as being concerned to maintain sequential order in conversational interaction. The object of inquiry is not so much language structure as interactional ability in verbal production. This concern can be formulated as follows: conversation analysts study what people say, the accounts they give, in order to see how the structure of the situation is produced and maintained, the manner in which it comes to make sense to the participants. People in any culture make a situation sensible for themselves and for others by talking about it, and it is the procedures of this sense-making which conversation analysts seek to discover and describe.

The methodology used in CA can tell us much about cultural ways of doing things, about preferred and dispreferred practices used in culture-specific interaction, and about how conversational utterances are sequentially organized. While living in Pikogan I had numerous opportunities to notice a kind of sequential object which occurs after a pre-request utterance which displays that the pre-request is not going to do the desired work for the one intent on making the request. Consider the following telephone conversation:

A1: Hello?
B1: *Kwe, giminobimaadiz naa?*
     Hi, how's it going?
A2: *Niminobimaadiz. Giin dash?*
     Fine. How about you?
B2: *Geniin. Giwii-gwagwejimin gegoon. Gaa naa odenag gidizhasii?*
     Me, too. I want to ask you something. You're not going to town, are you?
A3: *Uhhh, aadidoog.*
     Uhhh, I don't know.
B3: *Binimaa godag awiyag nigaa gagwejimaa.*
     First I'm going to ask someone else.
A4: *Gaa naa gidoowesi nogom maanigizhigan?*
     Aren't you playing ball this Saturday?
B4: *Ehe, niwii-doohenaban ...*
     Yeah, I was wanting to play ball ...
     [conversation continues]

What is going on in this conversation? If we take it that utterance B2 is a pre-request for a ride to go to town and A3 the response to that pre-request, then our question becomes: Does A3 provide B with an opportunity to explicitly make the request or is it doing the work of warning B *not* to make the request? As we can see from examining the entire sequence, B hears utterance A3 as constituting what I have characterized as 'notice of intent to reject.' This claim is based upon two quite explicit features: utterance A3, and B's *'Binimaa godag awiyag nigaa gagwejimaa'* ('First I'm going to ask someone else') in B3. It seems reasonable, then, to suggest that B hears A3 as a notice of intent to reject. Then B displays to A that he is orienting to A3 as doing that work. Note, too, that there is never any direct request for a ride to town and that there are no syntactic or semantic resources for hearing either B2 as a request for a ride or A3 as a rejection to a request, nor does A supply any kind of accompanying description to so label it.

Another interesting feature of the above conversation is that A never responds directly to B's comment in B3 but instead changes the topic with a question in A4. Thus, the definitive acceptance or commitment is not obtained by B and A makes good his escape from the potential request by changing the subject. This claim can be supported by noting the possibility of A producing yet another utterance in response to B3. For example, following B3, A could have said, 'Well, I can take you' or something along those lines. As it stands, the conversation changes topics and the possible slot for an acceptance or rejection is sequentially deleted. My point here is that, when an acceptance is not done in the appropriate sequential slot, the one intent on making a request may take this absence as being rejection-implicative, direct rejection being a dispreferred response in Ojibwe interaction for reasons discussed earlier in this chapter. One related point: following this conversation, B didn't call back over the next couple of hours I was visiting with A.

The CA literature has shown quite clearly that talk normally proceeds on a turn-by-turn basis and that conversational participants will generally display understanding and/or appreciation of the prior turn's talk. That is, conversational participants normally understand an utterance-in-progress by reference to the utterance's interactional and sequential location (Sacks, Schegloff, and Jefferson, 1974; Turner, 1976; Pomerantz, 1984). An important conversational maxim can be made in this connection: however a conversational participant analyses an utterance-in-progress, some conclusion ought to be displayed in the recipient's next turn of talk. Atkinson and Heritage write:

Just as a speaker's analysis and treatment of the prior [utterance] is available to the first speaker, so it is also available to the overhearers of the talk. The latter may thus proceed to analyze turns at talk, together with the analyses and treatments of them that are produced by the parties to the talk, and employ methodologies that fully take account of these analyses and treatments. (1984:32)

The analysis of the organization of conversational sequencing in any language and culture will, of course, have linguistic implications. It is possible to make a distinction between the interactional location of an utterance and a conversationalist's turn at speaking because positions in a conversational sequence are linguistically marked. For example, pre-request utterances in Ojibwe generally carry syntactic features usually associated with indirect illocutionary force. Further, we can see the ways in which given versus new information is organized sequentially.

Conclusion

This chapter has introduced some of the basic principles of conversation analysis and has applied some principles from CA to Ojibwe conversation. Simply put, the concern of the conversation analyst is with the methods people use to carry out the activities of everyday life and the practices by which they convey to others that their activities are rational and ordinary. In CA the methodology consists of locating some particular conversational organization, isolating its systematic features by demonstrating participants' orientation to them, and asking: What problems does the organization solve? And what implications does it have for the existence of further solutions to further problems? The crux of the matter is that people do many things by talking about them. By exploring how people go about doing something in and through talk, we may be able to better understand this thing we call culture.

I have drawn from some simple conversational fragments in this chapter, exploring how people in the community of Pikogan go about making requests or asking for favours, and rely on culture-specific ways for saying yes or no to those requests. I also made some preliminary claims about two kinds of local organizations operating in Ojibwe conversation: preference organization and conversational sequencing.

5

'The Tail of the Lynx': Interactional Resources in Ojibwe Storytelling

Bush life is still an important part of their everyday world for most people in Pikogan, as it is in many northern Aboriginal communities. Some families still live in the bush year-round and use their houses in the community as their headquarters when they come back from their camps and hunting grounds to go shopping for essential goods and to make contact with the rest of the community. People seem to feel more at home at their bush camps. It was a place where you could relax and be yourself without the hassles and frustrations that so often go along with life on the reserve. After all, most of the elders spent more than half of their lives in traditional lifestyles: hunting, trapping, and fishing. The elders were always so patient and kind with me, inviting me to go with them for moose hunting, beaver trapping, and fishing. We would sit around the fire at night in summer or in a cozy cabin in winter and talk, drink tea, tell stories, and laugh together. One of the elders who had a great influence on my thinking and my life was Mr Albert Mowatt (also known as Okinawe). He and his wife Anna often invited our family to go with them to the bush. Those times were very special for me and I learned much about Native ways of thinking and living by listening and observing.

Okinawe loved going to the bush. It just seemed like a more natural environment for him than on the reserve. The two legends we explore below were told by Okinawe. One summer a non-Native friend from the United States came to visit me. He was an avid fisherman and asked if Okinawe would take us fishing. I asked Okinawe and he agreed. As soon as we arrived at his camp, we all got into his canoe to set his nets out on the lake. Back in the cabin we were sitting together having tea, and my friend asked me to ask Okinawe when we were going fishing.

By this time I had started to catch on to what was happening, but I asked anyway: 'My friend wants to know when we're going fishing.' Okinawe replied, 'We just did.' My friend was puzzled by this. He had brought his fishing rod with him, packed up in small carrying bag. He got it out, showed it to Okinawe and asked me to ask him where he could go fishing. Okinawe suggested that he could fish on the shore of the lake. So he did. I went down to the shore with him to watch. The shoreline was quite rocky and after a while my friend had lost the lures he had brought with him. He asked me to ask Okinawe if he had any lures or hooks in his cabin. By this time I realized that there was a deep cultural gap in this situation, but I went ahead and asked Okinawe if he had any fishing hooks. He said he did and he came down to the shore with a huge gaffing hook; it looked designed to catch a whale! The point is that Okinawe had no concept of sport fishing or sport hunting. As he said to my friend later that evening over tea, 'With a hook you can only catch one fish at a time. With a net you can catch lots of fish at one time.'

The Strength and Value of the Oral Tradition

This experience with Okinawe gave me a clue as to how fundamentally different his thinking and way of perceiving the world is from my own. There is no doubt there exists a tremendous conceptual difference between my tradition's sense of sport fishing and Okinawe's sense of why one fishes and what that tells us about Anishnaabe ways of thinking and doing things. With regard to the cultural place accorded telling and listening to stories, too, I believe there are great differences between Native people and non-Natives. In effect, I believe that the place and importance of storytelling in Aboriginal traditions is quite different from that of Euro-Canadian society. It doesn't take long, when hanging around Anishnaabe people, to discover that the purpose for telling and listening to stories appears to be much more conventionalized in Ojibwe culture than in non-Native society. As Beck, Walters, and Francisco write:

Traditionally among Native Americans the oral tradition of its tribe was its most important vehicle for teaching and passing on the sacred knowledge and practices of *The People* ... The human memory is a great storehouse ordinarily filled to only a fraction of its capacity. The elders knew this and tested and trained the memory along with the other senses, so that the history and traditions of *The People* could be preserved and passed on. (1993:57)

In talking with people from my own non-Native tradition, I sense that we tend to underestimate the strength and power of what is commonly referred to as the oral tradition. We make our evaluation of what we consider to be the oral tradition from the perspective of people steeped in a tradition of books, libraries, radio, and television. Since we consider our own memories to be so faulty we tend to think that the memories of all peoples are equally weak. Beck, Walters, and Francisco continue:

One of the most important of the oral traditions is storytelling and the preservation of the origin histories. In these [stories] we are told where we came from,
how the stars were created, where we discovered fire, how light became divided
from darkness, and how death originated. It is through these stories too that we
are given the basic tools and ways of knowledge with which to survive in the
world: healing ceremonies, prayers, dances, games, herbs, and models of behavior. (1993:57–8)

It is a common misconception that Aboriginal traditions in the Americas possessed no formalized ways of learning, that traditional Native
ways of teaching were primarily informal and ad hoc. But every Aboriginal tradition has culture-specific methods, techniques, and teaching/
learning philosophies which are relevant to their own particular needs,
and every Aboriginal tradition had (and many continue to have), formalized lodges and societies for teaching their young and developing a
common stock of knowledge and experience. Long before the first
Europeans arrived, First Nations had their own systems of education
that were practical, begun almost at birth, and continued throughout
life. Every culture has its own distinctive ways of ensuring that the next
generation carries on the culture's stock of knowledge and the practices
necessary for survival for individual and collective growth.

In the North American Aboriginal context, traditional teaching and
learning is viewed quite differently from what is commonly thought of
as education in a Euro-Canadian sense. From her own Anishnaabe tradition, Linda Akan writes: 'Education as the Elders understood it contains a spiritual message. It is about giving and taking the good, without
apology or expectation. Essentially it is about knowing the Creator's
will for us; this is a necessary part of living' (1992:194).

A key component of education shared by virtually all First Nations
people is that the unknown is made accessible by its connection to the
known. The principle here is that learning is enhanced not only when
one understands the relationship of new ideas to what is already known

and understood, but that there is a linkage of the known to the unknown (by non-western sources of knowledge). For example, the kind of knowledge required to make such decisions as where to move one's camp or where to hunt for moose was and is commonly received through dreams, visions, spirit visitors, ceremonies, and so on, rather than through books or theories as in the western tradition. What Linda Akans writes reminds me of what I heard from many Anishnaabe people of her generation:

As a 37-year-old Saulteaux woman, I have not lost the vision that the Elders had for us. I was inspired by the words of my grandparents before I left the reserve to come to the city to be educated, when they told me, 'Grandchild, don't ever forget who you are. Someday you are going to need it.' The old people know that the indigenous cultures have something of value that the western cultures needed to know. (1992:191)

It seems to me that the foundation for traditional teachings is the belief that true learning is flexible and open-ended, that change is a permanent part of life, and that absolute knowledge is not the goal of the quest. What can be learned is the capacity to pay attention to all the details which may influence the outcome of a particular course of action, a capacity learned as much by the way one lives as by what one hears. Even in the contemporary context of band-run schools and Aboriginal students in Canadian universities, these fundamental aspects of traditional Native education remain viable.

From the perspective of the elders in the communities of Pikogan and Winneway, teachers are those who can demonstrate the relationship between philosophy and practice. It is important to remember that one's way of life is a model for what one is trying to transmit. Who do people in a community seek out for advice, prayer, guidance, instruction, and so forth? Different people in a community have different powers and different ways of gaining knowledge, and therefore, have different responsibilities to those around them.

The elders at Pikogan taught me in subtle ways that everyone is at times a teacher and at times a learner, from children, strong dreamers, interpreters, visionaries, and skilled hunters to storytellers, orators, and ethnohistorians. Traditional education prepared Aboriginal children to become fully functioning members of their communities and nations. While some formal educational institutions existed through ceremonies, societies, specific apprenticeships and training, education was usually carried out in intimate community and family settings. There was no need for school buildings since the educational atmosphere included the entire community and its natural ecosystems. All members of the community participated in teaching and shared the responsibility for nurturing upcoming generations. This form of education is practical, lifelong and integrated into the fabric of community and society.

Aboriginal culture-specific ways of teaching and learning continue today in modified forms, sometimes used as the philosophy guiding the creation or modification of existing school systems. In many communities traditional ways of teaching and learning are still the primary methods used to transfer skills and values to youth in areas not covered by school curricula. In these communities, subjects such as hunting, trapping, or traditional medicines are still presented in the context of the land and indigenous knowledge of the environment and nature. The approach is holistic, bridging technological skills with scientific knowledge, social behaviours, history, legends, and the beliefs and teachings of traditional ceremonies.

Interactional Resources in Ojibwe Storytelling

In this chapter. I am proposing that legends, stories, and traditional teachings transmitted in Ojibwe are intricate and artful discourses; that is, the stories and teachings that are told are elaborately designed to do several things. They may display potentially related topical orientation, implicate the storyteller as a principal character in the story, direct the ones listening to attend to certain features of the story or teaching in subtle but specific ways, conceal some of the ways a story or teaching impacts on those listening, make a moral point or illustrate a maxim, and so forth. When Ojibwe people tell stories giving teachings they are capable of employing some complex and intricate interactional devices with the listeners in mind. In this chapter I want to concentrate on one such device found in the context of storytelling, that of *verb tense organization*. I do this by comparing a short story told in English with two Ojibwe legends.

Few would argue that storytelling is a commonplace conversational activity in any culture. In examining the sequential aspects of story forms, the late Harvey Sacks (1972, 1974, 1978) proposed that conversational storytelling is composed of three serially ordered and adjacently placed types of sequences: the preface, the telling, and the response. Jefferson (1978) demonstrates how a series of conversational utterances can be sequentially analysed as parts of a storytelling, with the talk being used to engage conversational co-participants as story recipients and to negotiate whether, and how, the story will be told, whether it is completed or in progress, and what it will have amounted to as a conversational event. She explicates two features of stories which are integrated with turn-by-turn talk: stories are locally occasioned in that they emerge from turn-by-turn talk; and upon completion stories re-engage turn-by-turn talk. Goffman (1974) suggested that talking often involves the reporting of an event, such as in storytelling, and that this reporting is commonly presented as something to re-experience. Ryave (1978) points out that the actual telling of a story, the recounting portion, is notable for its particular delineation of some event, usually requiring a number of utterances tied together by some developing course of action.[1]

The two legends we explore in this chapter were told by Okinawe and started me thinking about how he went about structuring his stories. He is a good storyteller and people would regularly ask him to tell them stories. I assumed that when he told stories he was not merely stringing together utterances in haphazard fashion, so I began to take an interest in the details of the stories and the language features embedded within them. I found that stories told by monolingual speakers are incredibly elaborate and complex, even though the storyteller may not be aware of that richness and complexity. I will begin, then, with some examples from non-Native English speakers telling stories and then make some comparisons with Ojibwe ways of telling and structuring stories.

VERB TENSE ORGANIZATION IN NON-NATIVE ENGLISH NARRATIVES

I want to begin by presenting an analysis of a story elicited years ago by Harvey Sacks (1971). In the story, Sacks begins to explicate a verb tense device which, among other things, does the work of providing for a point of decision in the storytelling. The business of the story involves the reporting of a date and the setting up of a decidedly focused characterization of the occurrence of physical intimacy on the date. The story is being told to a partial colleague, another unmarried teenager. Both the teller, Louise, and the story recipient, Ken, are seventeen years old. Sacks argues that the story is told in such a way so as to specifically locate what Louise did, why, and with whom.

Louise:	One night (1.0) I was with this guy	(1)
	that I liked a real lot. An' uh (3.0)	(2)

	we had come back from the show, we	(3)
	had gone to the (1.0) Ash Grove for	(4)
	awhile, 'n we were gonna park. An' I	(5)
	can't stand a car. 'n he has a small	(6)
	car.	(7)
Ken:	Mm hm.	(8)
Louise:	So we walked to the back, an' we just	(9)
	wen' into the back house an' we stayed	(10)
	there half the night. (1.0) We didn't	(11)
	go to bed – t' each other, but – it was	(12)
	so comfortable an' so nice.	(13)
Ken:	Mm hm.	(14)
Louise:	Y'know? There's everything perfect.	(15)

Sacks makes the initial claim that the storytelling (lines 1–7; 9–13) is intricately organized and that its organization is recipient-designed. One aspect of this organization is the teller's use of various verb tenses within the telling. Verb tense organization appears to be one of the devices available to tellers for putting a story together and focusing its business.

Sacks approaches the tense organization in this story by considering an alternative verb tense organization. Insofar as the whole story takes place in the past, the telling could have been organized by employing a simple past tense format, e.g., 'we did this, then we did that ...' and so on. Sacks suggests that the use of a past tense for stories is 'a perfectly natural, if not canonical, form to stories' (1971:4). In listening to and looking through numerous transcripts of storytellings, I found many stories in which the speaker employed such a sequential past tense format exclusively. The above story, however, does not adhere to that format. Sacks claims that the form of this story involves the arrangements of its tenses in such a fashion as to focus the story recipient's attention to the crucial point of decision in the story.

He first concentrates on the utterance ''n we were gonna park' (line 5), in that it occurs following lines 1–4 in which the past tense, 'I *was* with this guy,' and the past perfect tense, 'we *had come* back from the show,' 'we *had gone* to the Ash Grove,' are employed preceding the past participle in the utterance ''n we were gonna park.' At this point, Sacks suggests that 'we're in a present, looking forward to something' (1971:5), while keeping in mind that the something has already taken place. The interesting thing in relation to the verb tense organization is that the storyteller, Louise, switches back to a straightforward past tense format for much of the rest of the story in lines 9–13. The result is that the utterance ''n we were gonna park' is isolated, indicating that the past tense sequential narrative format before the past participle 'were gonna' is employed to bring the story recipient, Ken, into the present, and is presumably used to project the future.

Before proceeding further, however, we need to take into account the final outcome of the story, which is set up initially as a sexual encounter but does not actually come to completion. The story builds towards a different ending than it would have had if Louise had said something like: 'After we had come back from the show he dropped me off at my house and I went straight to bed.' It seems, then, that a real issue for her giving the story is the extent that what happened was planned. I propose that the tense organization employed by Louise is important in helping to resolve this issue.

I noted earlier that, along with verb tense variety, Louise appears to use an elaborate verb tense organization. Building upon Sacks's initial claim, it seems reasonable to suggest that there is an explicit form to her story. The first tenses she employs, the past and past perfect tenses, are already laying the groundwork for some later verb tenses, particularly the past participle in the utterance ''n we were gonna park.' A form is already emerging. Perhaps another way we might approach the issue is to suggest that, having established the earlier tenses, Louise then decides to change tense in order to get the temporal organization she finds she needs for her story, and it just so happens that this can be accomplished quite nicely with the use of a past participle.[2] This type of organization also tells us something about the organization of talk in more general ways. For example, some choices a speaker makes in the course of talk, such as the choice of a word or a verb tense, already works towards something the speaker has not formulated to say but will formulate a few seconds down the line. Somehow, then, it appears that Louise's story is getting organized before the actual telling takes place and that this feature is apparent in all sorts of talk. After all, we do have the feature of verb tense switching to consider in this story; that is, we'll examine when verb tenses occur and how they appear to work together. In order for the verb tenses to do the work which the speaker wants them to do, they must necessarily rely on the earlier verb tenses.

We are faced at this point in Sacks's argument with some rather slippery issues which we need to clarify in order to get a good grasp of how a verb tense organization device might be working in this story. First, when Sacks uses the term 'tense organization' he is actually referring to a type of temporal organization. That is, when Sacks talks about being in the present, he is not referring to the teller using a present tense, but rather to the work that is done by the employment of the past participle 'were gonna' to engineer the listener into a temporal present, a point of decision. It is quite common for a past participle to do that kind of temporal work. In this story, then, Louise narrated some rather common instances of what happened, using past and past perfect tenses. She then switched to a past participle in order to bring Ken to a point of decision in her story and to bring him to that point of decision as well. She tells, then, through the use of the past participle, what didn't happen.

Secondly, Sacks argues that one aspect of the design of the story is that Louise would be telling a completely different story if she had left out the utterance ''n we were gonna park.' What she is indicating by the temporal organization of her story is that there was a rejected alternative to what actually happened, and her use of a past participle does the work of bringing the listener into the middle of the story and focuses his attention on the point of decision. That is, Louise evidently felt compelled to include something that she did not do (i.e., park). Depending upon the story recipients, then, a teller may or may not choose to leave what didn't happen allusive. If, however, the teller decides to include what didn't happen in the telling, this can be accomplished via verb tense organization, as illustrated in this story.

Sacks's argument is that the verb tense organization is isolated by design in Louise's story in that she uses tense format to do certain kinds of work: in this case, to put Ken into the present, and to produce the desired effect. This temporal organization relates to the telling of what didn't happen as leading up to what did happen. So the story has an intricate organization in which a wide range of verb tenses is used in order to isolate a decision point in the story, although perhaps not in the precise way which Sacks specifies. The purpose of beginning with an analysis of Sacks's treatment of this particular story is to locate how a storyteller may employ a verb tense organization device in order to fashion a story and focus its business.

VERB TENSE ORGANIZATION IN OJIBWE STORYTELLING

Now we can explore two Ojibwe legends with an interest in discovering and describing how a storyteller organizes verb tenses in a legend can be of interactional value. After some initial explication of these two legends, we will be in a position to see how verb tense organization in Ojibwe narratives compares with similar machinery at work in English. I encourage you to read carefully the following Ojibwe legends before proceeding with the analysis.

'The Lynx and the Marten' (*Bizhiw ashij waabishtaan*)

1. *Bizhiw ashij waabishtaan babaa-anokiiwaagoban.*
   The lynx and the marten were hunting around.
2. *Amikwan babaa-anoojiihaawaagoban.*
   They were hunting for beavers.
3. *Babaa-eshkewaagoban.*
   They were fishing for them.
4. *Gegapiich nigodin e-eshkewaagobanen gii-bagidawaawaagoban.*
   After a while in fishing around they set some nets.
5. *Gegapiich ogii-inaan owiijiiwaaganan waabishtaan, 'Giin giga-babaa-minizhawaag amikwag.*
   After a while the lynx said to his friend the marten, 'You make the beavers run around.
6. *Gadaa-bidaahamoj.*
   They will be caught in the net.
7. *Niin niga-gaanawenimaa gidasabinaan.'*
   Me, I will watch our net.'
8. *Gegapiich bidaahanaadog waabishtaan amikwan.*
   After a while the marten catches a beaver.
9. *Ezhi-jaagizhegwaagonedaabiigwen odamikoman waabishtaan.*
   The marten must be hiding his beaver.
10. *Gaawin owiidamawaasiwan owiijiiwaaganan.*
    He doesn't tell his friend.
11. *Bizhiw megaa dash owiijiiwaan aha waabishtaan e-anokiiwaaj.*
    Of course the lynx always goes with the marten to hunt.
12. *Gegapiich gichi-bakadedog ahawe bizhiw.*
    After a while that lynx is getting really hungry.
13. *Gichi-wii-wiisini gegapiich.*
    He really wants to eat.
14. *Gegapiich ikidowidog bizhiw, 'Aaniga nidoowiisinaadog,' ikidowidog bizhiw.*
    After a while the lynx says, 'I must have lots of fat [to eat]' that lynx says.

15. *Gegapiich ezhi-bagojiindizogobanen bizhiw.*
    So then the lynx opened his own stomach.
16. *E-ndawaabadag owiis ezhi-giimoozaabimaaganiwij e-dinakamigizij bizhiw,*
    ezhi-giimoozaabimaajin owiijiiwaaganan.
    While looking inside for his own fat he is secretly being watched.
    His friend [the marten] is secretly watching him.
17. *Mii dash wiin waabishtaan ezhi-gichi-baapigwen e-gizhigaabamaajin*
    owiijiiwaaganan e-bagojiindizonjin.
    So then the marten really starts laughing at his friend when he sees
    him open up his stomach.
18. *Mii ezhi-gichi-goshkomaajin.*
    So that really startles (the lynx).
19. *Mii dash ezhi-bakibinaajin onagizhiin aha bizhiw e-gichi-goshkomaagani-*
    wij.
    So then he breaks off his intestines when he is startled.
20. *Mii dash gaa-oji-dakwaabikenagizhij bizhiw.*
    So then that was how the lynx got short intestines.
21. *Gichi-dakwaabikeziwan onagizhiin bizhiw.*
    They're really short his intestines

'The Lynx and the Fox' (*Bizhiw ashij waagoshan*)

1. *Bizhiw giiyaabaj.*
   Lynx again.
2. *Onagishkawaagoban waagoshan bizhiw.*
   The lynx met up with the fox.
3. *Ihi apiich ogwagwejimaan, 'Aadi e-doodaman gizoo gaa-oji-gichi-*
   minwaashig?'
   So he asks him, 'How did you get your tail to be so beautiful?'
4. *Waagosh ikido, 'Nidwaawahan, nibagonewaa mikwamii.*
   The fox says, 'I break a hole in the ice.
5. *Mii dash ezhi-bakobiihamaan ihimaa nizoo.*
   Then I put my tail in the hole.
6. *Mii dash apiich ezhi-mashkawadig ezhi-gichi-obigwaashkoniyaan.'*
   Then when it's frozen I really jump up.'
7. *Ikidowidog dash gewiin aha bizhiw.*
   That's what the lynx must have said [he'd try it] too.
8. *Gegapiich ogwagwejitoonaadog gewiin bizhiw, giji-dwaawahag, giji-*
   bagonewaajin mikwamiin.
   After a while that lynx tries it, too, to break a hole in the ice.

9. *Gegapiich mashkawadinni ozoo aha bizhiw.*
   After a while his tail freezes in the hole.
10. *Mii dash e-gichi-obigwaashkonigwen apiich e-ishkwaa-mashkawadinnig ozoo.*
    So then he jumps up really fast when his tail is frozen.
11. *Zaagiskwadinni ozoo.*
    So then his tail breaks off.
12. *Ezhi-giishkaanowesegobanen ahawe bizhiw e-gichi-obigwaashkonij.*
    His tail broke off when he jumped up.
13. *Mii dash ihi gaa-oji-dakwaanowej bizhiw.*
    So that was how the lynx got a short tail.

CHARTING THE VERB TENSE ORGANIZATION

The first thing we want to do is to chart the pattern of verb tense switching in these two legends. Following is the verb tense organization chart for the first story.

'The Lynx and the Marten'

tense	line(s)
past	1–7
present	8–14
past	15
present	16–19
past	20
present	21

   The first point I want to make is that the verb tense switching (from past to present to past) in this legend is doing some important interactional work for the storyteller. The narrator is able to focus on the immediacy of the situation being described and make the action more vivid through the use of switching from the past to the present tense – that is, to the historical present.
   'The Lynx and the Marten,' is interesting in a number of ways, the most important for our purposes being that, although the verb tense organization appears at first glance to be relatively simple, a closer investigation reveals it to be more elaborate. I want to first concentrate on lines

9 and 10. This sequence does some important interactional work in the story and provides us with some clues as to how a verb tense organization device may be employed.

We can begin to grasp what that interactional work is by noting that the storyteller is proceeding to tell about the temporal sequence of action: 'They were hunting for beavers' (line 2), 'They were fishing for them' (line 3), and 'After a while the marten catches a beaver' (line 8). The next three utterances, however, are not part of the action sequence but rather an aside inserted at this point for a specific purpose. Thus lines 9–11 are doing something other than continuing the narrative. Before we begin to explore what that is, I want to point out another kind of change in the storytelling which occurs in line 11, 'Of course the lynx always goes with the marten to hunt,' which puts the marten's action of hiding the beaver into context. This three-part utterance sequence is not a continuation of the narrative or a report of the next action that follows, 'After a while the marten catches a beaver.' What lines 9–11 are doing is some kind of explanatory work for the listeners.

Clearly this legend departs from the simple, canonical story model mentioned earlier in this chapter in a number of ways. For example, line 9, 'The marten must be hiding his beaver,' does the work of putting the listeners in a state that one of the story characters, the marten, had been in when the action was actually taking place.[3] Then the storyteller goes right back to the action sequence in line 12 with the utterance 'After a while that lynx is getting really hungry.' We have, then, a kind of embedded sequence in lines 9–11, interpolated between action sequences, which provides information which is important for the listeners to know in order to make sense of the story. We might characterize this section as follows: line 9, 'The marten must be hiding his beaver,' does the work of setting up the rest of the story properly, and the storyteller can then proceed to the punchline of the story, knowing that the listeners are aware of what is happening in the story and why the lynx acted as he did. Another interesting aspect of the story is that the narrative section in which the sequence is embedded also marks a shift in the storytelling from the past tense to the present tense in line 8. In the analysis which follows we will be interested in finding out what kind of work the switch in verb tenses is capable of doing for Ojibwe storytellers.

We have still not paid much attention to the actual working of the verb tense organization device in this story. The approach I want to take here is to divide the story into Time 1 and Time 2. Time 1 refers to the time at which the event(s) being recounted took place, while Time 2 corresponds to the time of the actual telling of the event(s). The linguist Jakobson

(1957) made this initial distinction between *proces de l'enonce* (Time 1) and *proces de l'enonciation* (Time 2). Any storyteller intent on telling a story that makes sense to the hearer must necessarily be oriented to both aspects. For example, the actual telling of the story itself is designed to simulate what the story characters were experiencing in the Time 1 part of the story and makes it clear to the listeners at Time 2 that what has happened at Time 1 has already taken place. In this story, then, the utterance 'The marten must be hiding the beaver' brings the listeners into Time 1; it is saying, 'You aren't necessarily aware of it yet, but when the marten caught a beaver he didn't share it with his friend, the lynx, but instead hid it from him.' Goffman (1974) suggests that in many instances what people telling stories in naturally occurring conversation attempt to do is not merely to provide information to a listener but to present a drama to an audience. In relation to Time 1 and Time 2, the point is that, when someone tells a story, she/he is not merely recounting past events (although that is one alternative), but as Goffman suggests, 'he is recounting ... And this is likely to mean that [the teller] must take his listeners back into the information state ... he had at the time of the episode but no longer has' (1974:508). Goffman is elaborating on the temporal aspects which we are calling Time 1 and Time 2. At the time of the telling (Time 2), the storyteller attempts to take the listeners back to the time of the action (Time 1).[4]

But what is the utterance 'The marten must be hiding his beaver,' doing *where* it is? That is, how does the work it is doing derive from where it is located in the storytelling? We have already laid some groundwork in reference to the positioning of this utterance: it helps to organize the narrative format; it shifts the focus to what the listeners need to know in order to make sense of the story action; and it allows the storyteller to control, to a large degree, the type of story it is and the purpose for telling the story. The important thing about this story at this particular point in the telling is that the marten hid his beaver from the lynx. As to what the utterance is actually doing, then, we are able to argue rather forcefully that the storyteller is able to instruct the listeners as to how the story is to be heard and what they should focus upon. This leads us to the notion that when people tell stories they are artful and competent in employing various interactional devices which do things for their stories.

THE HISTORICAL PRESENT IN OJIBWE STORYTELLING

Sacks has argued that the interesting thing about any kind of verb tense shift in a story can be determined by considering an obvious alternative to a storytelling with multiple tense switches. As an alternative, the whole story could take place in the past and be told employing a simple past tense format throughout. The form of this story, however, involves the arrangement of a simple past tense format in lines 1–7, followed by a switch to a present tense format in lines 8–14, a one-utterance switch back to the past tense in line 15, another present tense sequence in lines 16–19, and the story conclusion back in the past tense in line 20. So what is the verb tense organization in this story doing for the storyteller?

To answer this question I want to look a little closer at one particular use of the present tense in this story, the historical present. This is a feature in which the present tense is used to refer to past events (Wolfson, 1979; Valentine 1992, 1995). In order to try to explicate what kind of work the historical present is doing in this story, we turn to Goffman for a starting point:

A replaying [such as a story] is not merely any reporting of a past event. In the fullest sense, it is a statement couched from the personal perspective of an actual or potential participant who is located so that some temporal, dramatic development of the reported event proceeds from that starting point. A replaying will therefore be something that listeners can emphatically insert themselves into, vicariously reexperiencing what took place. A replaying, in brief, recounts a personal experience, not merely reports on an event. (1974:504)

It is apparent from the legend we are looking at that there are quite a few instances in which the present tense is used to refer to past events. I take it that the past tense format is a completely normal, even canonical, form for stories to have. In this story, and in many other stories which I have looked at and listened to over the years, whenever the present tense is employed to refer to past events it is never used exclusively but always involves a switching back and forth between tenses. We noted that in this story the teller begins by employing a past tense, switches to a present tense, returns to the past tense, then back to the present tense, and finally returns to a past tense at the end of the story.

In order to get at what the tense switching is doing in this story, I want to refer back to Time 1 and Time 2. The traditional explanation in the literature concerning the use of the historical present in storytelling is that its use causes the action being recounted to orient to the listeners (Time 2) as if it were happening at that very moment (Time 1). However, this does not account for the work that is done by the switching between past tense and present tense or tell us what exactly that work is. That is, if the historical present merely does the work of bringing the listeners closer to Time 1, then why doesn't the storyteller employ the present tense exclusively to refer to past events? After all, if the storyteller's purpose is to draw the listeners into the story, the historical present is seemingly best equipped to accomplish such a task. In this story, however, some parts of the legend are told in the past tense. Thus to say that the historical present tense is used only to bring the listeners into a Time 1 perspective does not altogether hold true. Rather, the important aspect regarding the historical present vis-à-vis other verb tenses is the switching that is employed by the storyteller. It is this switching that does much of the temporal/organizational work of the tense organization device. It would, after all, be quite a different kind of telling if the storyteller had used the past tense format throughout. Both the use of specific verb tenses and the organizational switching between them during the telling comprise the working of the verb tense device in this story. Also, it should be kept in mind that it is the storyteller who employs the device and chooses how to organize the story. And the crux of the matter is that this organization is necessarily recipient-designed.

COMPARISON OF VERB TENSE ORGANIZATIONS

Now let us look at the tense-switching in 'The Lynx and the Fox' in order to compare the verb tense organization with that of 'The Lynx and the Marten.' This is what the verb tense organization chart looks like.

'The Lynx and the Fox'

tense	line(s)
past	3
present	3–11
past	12–13

The verb tense organization for this story is not as complex as in 'The Lynx and the Marten.' Both stories are relatively short when compared with other Ojibwe legends. For our purposes it is better to use shorter legends in order to grasp some of the quite detailed and intricate resources available to Ojibwe speakers for structuring their stories. One way of approaching the tense organization in these stories is by considering an alternative verb tense organization. As we have seen in the previous stories explored in this chapter, both in English and Ojibwe, insofar as the whole story takes place in the mythic past, the telling could have been organized by employing a simple past tense format with no direct discourse or verb tense switching. Such a telling of this particular legend would amount to more of a reporting of the storyline than a storytelling performance.

Building upon our preliminary analysis of 'The Lynx and the Marten,' it is evident that there is an explicit form to this story; that is, from the point at which the storyteller begins his narration, he seems already to be setting the stage for some later verb tense organization. In particular, we can see the use of the historical present tense as we find in utterance 3, 'So he asks him ...' A form is emerging. Having begun the recounting of the legend in the past tense, the storyteller then decides to change tense in order to get the temporal organization he feels he's going to need in order to perform the legend rather than merely narrate the storyline, and one of the nifty ways of accomplishing this is by employing some tense switching.

When I talk about a storyteller making decisions and employing devices, I am referring to subconscious decisions and employments which may not even be apparent to the storyteller her/himself. I remember working with the language teachers in the Algonquin community of Winneway in the mid-1980s, all of whom were mother-tongue speakers of their Aboriginal language. They had recorded themselves talking together and telling stories. We transcribed their conversations and stories and then proceeded to analyse them together. When we began to discover emerging discourse patterns and the artfulness and complexity of their conversations and stories, they were amazed at how expert they were in using quite complex and unformulated discourse devices both in talk and storytelling. They initially figured that they were just telling stories before realizing that they were relying on their own competence as mother-tongue speakers to produce elaborate and intricate talk and stories using discourse devices available to them in their language. It was a startling discovery for most of them, usually followed by comments such as (and I'm paraphrasing here), 'I never realized what a good storyteller I am!' and 'Now I know things about how my language works which I never thought about before.' As a corollary to their discoveries, over the next few months they found they were better able to teach their language because they understand better how it worked.

Returning to the verb tense organization in this particular legend, it appears that Okinawe's story is getting organized before the actual telling takes place, a feature apparent in all sorts of naturally occurring talk. As we saw in our analysis of the stories presented earlier in this chapter, in order for the verb tenses to do the work the speaker wants them to do later on in the story, they must necessarily rely on the earlier verb tenses. This device is at work near the end as the storyteller delivers the punchline in line 11, 'So then his tail breaks off,' which is actually the end of the storyline, and then switches back to the past tense in his explanatory epilogue in lines 12–13, 'His tail broke off when he jumped up,' and 'So that was about how the lynx got a short tail.'

Conclusion

I have attempted to discover and describe a kind of machinery, an apparatus, which explains how it is that verb tenses in conversational storytelling in Ojibwe may be organized by the teller to 'do things' for the story, in particular, for making the storytelling a performance rather than a mere recounting. In the two legends recounted by Okinawe we found that stories told by monolingual speakers are incredibly elaborate and complex, even though the storyteller may not be aware of that richness and complexity. Also, in attempting to understand how such a device may be employed, we have touched on some general features of Ojibwe-specific reasoning in relation to storytelling and story listening. The type of apparatus proposed here is intended to be general in application while at the same time viewed as an adequate analysis of the stories which we have examined and the tense organization device we have explicated.

I would characterize the two Ojibwe legends we have investigated in this chapter as having some definite generalizable features: sequential depictions of past events, various teller perspectives, organized tellings leading to climactic endings, and so on. That the verb tenses may be organized to 'do things' for the storyteller in an interactional sense is one such technique involving one device that may be employed by a storyteller. Following is a summary of the verb tense organization device.

1. The verb tense organization in conversational storytelling in Ojibwe may take one of two forms: an exclusive past tense format; or a combination of verb tenses.
2. The storyteller may organize the verb tenses so as to make it a performance rather than a mere recitation of the storyline by being able to

organize the storytelling for the following purposes: (a) to focus attention on what the storyteller considers to be important or wants the listeners to focus on; (b) to partition important events in the story for the benefit of the listeners; (c) to tell the story from different perspectives; and (d) to set up and make recognizable the punchline/ conclusion of the story.

The verb tense organization device is used in the following way: follow all the capabilities of the apparatus and if the verb tense organization in a story can be heard in the way that the device provides for, then hear it that way. I have attempted to build an apparatus which explains how Ojibwe storytellers can organize the verb tenses in a story in such a way so as to be recognizable to the listeners. In the next chapter we explore how the principles of conversation analysis can be applied to humorous talk and teasing contexts.

6

'What's So Funny?': Humour, Laughter, and Teasing in Ojibwe Storytelling

In his article 'Striking the Pole: American Indian Humor' (1987), Joseph Bruchac tells about an Abenaki story he heard from a Native elder that epitomizes the nature of American Indian humour.

Many years ago there was a white trader who had a slippery reputation. He was known for having a bad temper and for cheating the Indians when they came to trade with him. When Indians would bring in their skins to trade, the white trader would use an old-fashioned balance scale and would pay them by the pound for their skins. Instead of using a counter-weight on his scales, however, he would just place his hand on the tray and say, 'My hand weighs exactly one pound.' One day the Indians who came to trade with him got tired of being cheated. They purchased a set of weights and came to the trader's store to confront him with his dishonesty. The trader, though, became angry at being accused of cheating, pulled a rifle out from underneath the counter and began shooting at the Indians. The Indians responded by firing back and the white trader was killed in the exchange of gunfire. Then, just out of curiosity, the Indians cut off his hand and weighed it on their own scales. They felt kind of bad to discover that his hand weighed exactly one pound!

Bruchac goes on to mention how some non-Natives to whom he's told this particular story don't see the humour of it. I think he puts his finger on the pulse of an important truth: if you can understand what makes a people laugh, you are closer to understanding and appreciating them.

This chapter builds upon and departs from the previous ones by showing how the methods of conversation analysis can be of tremendous value in understanding Ojibwe-specific ways of thinking and doing things. It does this by exploring stories told in naturally occurring conversation in Ojibwe with an interest in discovering and describing some of the methods that people engaged in ongoing conversation use to initiate, sustain, and terminate a series of topically related utterances in the context of humorous talk. In her discourse analysis of a Severn Ojibwe text, Valentine (1995:202–3) identifies such paralinguistic phenomena as laughter and coughs as performative features found within the text and suggests that laughter, in at least one instance, 'comes at a point in the narrative where the ... audience knows that the crux of the tension, the essence of the story, has been set up.' Rich Rhodes (1988), in his analysis of positive politeness strategies, includes the feature of laughter in presenting evidence that Ojibwe speakers form a single, cooperative in-group. This chapter will explore not only some ways in which laughter and humour are managed in Ojibwe conversation, but also some of the culturally defined humorous themes at stake in Ojibwe.

Funny Stories and Conversational Structures

What are some of the methods that people use in any culture to recount funny events so as to reproduce the funniness of those events for their listeners? While those methods may change from one culture to another, I take it that, when producing a story, all storytellers are obligated to build into their stories an account of why they are telling the story. That account usually proceeds through the use of a turn-taking system – that is, a system of rules which allows everyone to participate in the conversation while preventing overlapping talk (Sacks, Schegloff, and Jefferson, 1978). When one speaker tells a story, the normal turn-taking system is temporarily suspended to allow the teller a longer turn. The story itself should justify the temporary suspension.

There are several different methods which storytellers in any culture have available to them for telling stories. For example, a story could be told because it recounts an incident that was funny or unusual or frightening. When telling the story the teller ought to show that the story was so funny, unusual, or frightening that its telling is justified on those grounds. Often this will involve the storyteller in developing an elaborate structure for recounting the events so that listeners not only appreciate the humour, unusualness, or scariness of the events intellectually, but will also come to experience them in a manner similar to the way they were experienced by the teller or by the characters in the story. One way the teller can do this is by framing the events in a setting that highlights those features. That is, I take it for granted that people are capable of using such things as contrast devices and setting devices in order to orient listeners as to the point of what is being recounted. Such devices can, for example, be used to give listeners privileged access to the story-teller's or story characters' thoughts at the time the event being recounted took place. Because there is a need to produce and account for the telling of the story, there are good structural reasons for the artful construction of stories in naturally occurring conversation.

The storyteller ought to be concerned with two particular aspects in recounting the story (Gardner and Spielmann, 1980). One is sifting through experiences in order to find an event that members of a common culture will find interesting and relevant to the ongoing conversation; the second is employing telling devices that will allow the listeners to appreciate the relevance of what is being recounted. For example, a humorous story might go something like this: 'I saw a man walking down the street yesterday with his suit on backwards.' Here, the teller depends upon the fact that listeners would also find such an event funny given their knowledge about the proper way to wear suits.

Now consider how that story might be elaborated by building a contrast device into the telling: 'I was walking down the street yesterday feeling really together, y'know, for the first time in months, and then I see this guy walking down the street with his suit on backwards.' The humour still depends on the ability of his audience to see the strangeness of the man's apparel, but now the hearing is set up to focus on contrasting the mood the teller was in *before* seeing the man, with the imagined mood the teller would have been in *after* seeing him.

Now I want to move from non-Native English examples to Ojibwe-specific instances of humorous talk and laughing together in naturally occurring conversation.

Native-specific Humorous Themes

In Kenneth Lincoln's book *Indi'n Humor*, he suggests that, 'A joke is a play upon form ... where two sets of thoughts scratch against each other' (1993:64). My friend Gordon Polson, Anishnaabe scholar, educator, and hunter, showed me many times that laughter and humour are ways of dealing with oppression and tragedy, and that learning about a people also means learning something of their history. A number of humorous stories told to me over the years by Anishnaabe people are clearly responses to the long history of dispossession for First Nations people in Canada. As Lincoln also notes, humour in the Native community at large is commonly used as a way of deflecting hostility into a lesson. In my own experience, the elders in Pikogan would regularly tell me jokes and humorous stories which were clearly meant to teach me something or to inform me gently that I had made a cultural 'mistake.' As the Native scholar Vine Deloria Jr put it many years ago in his book *Custer Died for Your Sins*, humour and teasing were methods of social control:

Rather than embarrass members of the tribe publicly, people used to tease individuals they considered out of step with the consensus of tribal opinion. In this way egos were preserved and disputes within the tribe ... were held to a minimum. Gradually people learned to anticipate teasing and began to tease themselves as a means of showing humility and ... advocating a course of action they deeply believed in. [People] would depreciate their feats to show they were not trying to run roughshod over tribal desires. (1970:263)

Bruchac demonstrates also that teasing and humour have conventionalized rules in any Native context:

In some Native American cultures there are people you are not allowed to tease. Elders ... were not to be teased by the very young ... Among the Iroquois, the strike-pole dance afforded the opportunity for clansmen to tell jokes about each other. These jokes might satirize the person's hunting ability or exaggerate some physical characteristic.
...
One of the things which binds Indian people together ... is the complex phenomenon which might be called 'Indian humor.' Wherever you go in 'Indian Country' you will find laughter – a laughter which may be bawdy one minute, sacred the next. But whichever it is, you can be sure that it is a humor which makes its points clearly to Native Americans, and those points include the importance of humility and the affirmation that laughter leads to learning and survival. (1987:26–9)

The writings of Drew Hayden Taylor capture both the complexity and dynamics of Ojibwe-specific humour and humorous themes, and he seems to have a special knack for uncovering the underlying themes in which such humour is grounded. I want to provide you with just a few examples from Taylor's writings because I believe they illuminate shared humorous themes among Ojibwe people, particularly in relation to Native/non-Native perspectives. In his essay 'Pretty Like

a White Boy,' Taylor makes some keen observations on that relationship:

There's a lot to be said for both cultures. For example, on the one hand you have
the Native respect for Elders. They understand the concept of wisdom and
insight coming with age. On the White hand, there's Italian food. I mean, I really
love my mother and family, but seriously, does anything really beat good Veal
Scaloppini? Most of my Aboriginal friends share this fondness for this particular
type of food. And wasn't there a warrior at Oka named Lasagna?
...
Also, Native people have this wonderful respect and love for the land. [We]
believe we are part of it, a mere link in the cycle of existence ... On the White
hand, there's breast implants. Darn clever of them White people. That's something that Indians would never have invented ... We just take what the Creator
decides to give us. But no, not the White man. Just imagine it, some serious looking White doctor sitting around in his laboratory muttering to himself, 'Big tits.
Hmmm, how do I make big tits?' If it was an Indian, it would be, 'White women
sure got big tits,' and leave it at that. (1996:13)

I often use the writings of Drew Taylor to begin my classes; they are
usually thought-provoking and there is a kind of a biting humour to
them. Sometimes non-Native students approach me after class and tell
me that they are offended by a particular reading. I usually invite them
to try and take off their own cultural glasses and, at least for a moment,
put on Anishnaabe glasses and try to grasp a fleeting glimpse of the
world through the Anishnaabe perspective. It really is a totally different
world from a Native perspective, and I believe understanding the differences can go a long way to building bridges of mutual respect and
understanding between Native people and non-Natives in Canada, and
humour can help in this activity.[1]
But the humour in Taylor's writing is not exclusive to the Native/
non-Native relationship. He also makes fun of his own people, especially those who seem to have fallen into the trap of becoming living stereotypes. I noticed while living with Anishnaabe people that humorous
talk was often self-deprecating. According to Gordon Polson, making
fun of yourself and your own people's way of thinking and doing things
can also be part of an individual's and a people's healing. I never
laughed so hard as I did living at Pikogan. Sometimes the jokes, stories,
and teasing revolved around White people; but just as often it was
grounded in Aboriginal experience, laughing at themselves as much as

they did about people and perspectives from non-Native traditions. Taylor is not afraid to take aim at his own people. In his essay 'Pow-wows, They Are a' Changin'' he makes a humorous critique of the commercialization of the pow-wow circuit:

The spectre of commercialism has also reared its head at today's Pow-wow. At some of the larger gatherings, it's not uncommon to see tens of thousands of dollars or prize money up for grabs ... [and] the list of traditional 'Native Foods' being offered has grown to include pizza, candy floss, tacos, baloney on a scone, etc. My favourite were these two stands side-by-side, one selling Buffalo Burgers (made from real buffalo), and the other peddling something called an Indian Burger. (1996:103)

Finally, Drew Taylor includes in his book *Funny, You Don't Look Like One* what he considers to be philosophies of life on the reserve. As he suggests, 'you don't need a Ph.D. to understand them either':

- Never trap on another person's trap line.
- Enjoy the variety of life; that's why the Creator made
  four seasons.
- Family will be there when strangers won't.
- Beware of unusually coloured snow.
- Life is a circle, try not to get lost.
- Whenever you hunt an animal, make sure it's not hunting you.
- Be careful who you date, they could be your relation.
- Nobody can see tomorrow without first looking at yesterday.
- Check the authentic Indian totem pole for a 'made in Korea' label.

There are a number of humorous themes at play in all of Taylor's essays, and I believe his writings can help to clue non-Natives in as to what makes Anishnaabe people laugh, which brings us full circle back to the important maxim: if you can understand what makes a people laugh, you are closer to understanding and appreciating them.

Laughing Together in Ojibwe Conversation

I now want to look at some naturally occurring conversations containing humorous sequences in order to see how Ojibwe people introduce into their recounting of funny events devices that are designed to let listeners in on the humour of the original incidents. I hope to show, first, that people telling stories in naturally occurring talk normally want to make sure that their listeners understand why the story is being told, and secondly, that there are rules in conversation which constrain the telling of certain kinds of stories. As a result of these constraints, people often build into their stories a second element which is built with some of the same materials as a joke-like structure, and it is important to distinguish between the two. Insofar as the events in real-life stories are assumed to be true, then 'funny' stories are limited in the kinds of coincidences or set-ups which would enable people to produce a story which is tellable just because it is funny. As a result, tellers often build into their funny stories another structure which allows them to display the appropriateness of the telling on the grounds that the stories are either thematically relevant to the ongoing talk or that the humour of the story is sufficient to justify its telling. The proclivity for tellers to continue after the punchline has been delivered is attributed to their inclination to display the thematic relevance of the stories they tell.[2]

Gail Jefferson (1979) has demonstrated how, among non-Native English speakers, the onset of laughter by the current speaker in natural conversation can initiate a 'laughing-together' with all of the conversational participants becoming involved. The term indicates that all the participants in the conversation laugh simultaneously. In the Ojibwe examples below, we were able to locate a phenomenon similar to the laughing-together instances found by Jefferson in non-Native conversation. However, the structure here can have different interactional consequences, as the laughing-together evolves into a series of utterances which refer back to the original utterances which initiated the laughing-together. I hope to show how a laughing-together plays an important part in Ojibwe conversational interaction and helps to elucidate some of the culturally-defined humorous themes in Ojibwe culture.

The stereotype that Aboriginal people are humourless and rarely laugh is clearly false. In the examples below, the conversations taking place are fuelled by humour and laughter. These examples come from the Algonquin community of Winneway, where for many years I offered courses in language instruction for the Native teachers as they pursued their undergraduate degrees. These teachers, as well as others in the community, were deeply concerned that the young people were not hearing the language being spoken very much any more. The community radio station was going strong in those days and the language teachers decided to record themselves talking together. They wanted to build up a corpus of tape-recorded conversations in their Native language that could be played over the community radio. The conversations, excerpts of which are presented below, were not scripted beforehand; they just got together and talked. As we look at parts of those conversations, it should be noted that the analysis tends to get quite technical, and I encourage you to be patient as we explore the phenomenon of laughing-together and the natural use of humorous themes in these examples.*

In the following examples we can see that people listening to the ongoing talk laugh in response to the current speaker's laughter. When producing an utterance designed to initiate a laughing-together, speakers are obliged to position their utterances so as to show their relevance to the ongoing talk. Note how a laughing-together is initiated by speaker laughter in example 1:M1–M3 and example 2:L2–L4.

Example 1

H1:   *Aagim dash niin nigichi minwenimaa e-pimoseyaan giji-pabaa maagimeyaan.*
      I really like to use snowshoes when walking around on the snow.
L1:   *Mii geniin, nigichi minwendaan noopiming e-bimoseyaan.*
      Me, too, I really like walking in the bush.
H2:   Mm-hmm.
SH1: *Agwaa giga-bagishin.*
      Watch out, you'll fall.
L2:   *Nookaagonagaag sa wiinana ge izhi bagishiniyaan mikwamii dash wiin* gichi mashkaawizi!
      I'll fall for sure on the soft snow the ice is *really hard!*
      (simultaneous laughter – 3 seconds)
H3:   *Mikwamii wiin gichi-mashkaawizi.*
      The ice is really hard.

---

* A word of explanation is needed on some of the transcription devices used here. When the current speaker laughs or laughter occurs overlapping or following an utterance, the word 'laughter' is placed within parentheses with the time of the laughter immediately following. When conversational participants laugh at the same time, the term 'simultaneous laughter' is placed in parentheses with the time of the laughter and unassociated with any single speaker. When the current speaker laughs during the uttering of a word or phrase, I marked the beginning and ending of the laughter by putting the word or phrase into italics.

L3:   Mm-hmm.

M1:   *Niminwendaan geniin e-zhooshkwaadaheyaan aadidok sa giyaabaj ge-*
        oji-gashkitowaaban. Noongom mayaa nidaa-gichi-bagishin!
        Me too I like to skate, I don't know if I should still do it.
        Now I would really fall down !
        (simultaneous laughter – 2 seconds)

M2:   *Nidaa-gichi-kizhiiyaabonan noongom mayaa !*
        I would really glide fast right now !
        (simultaneous laughter – 2 seconds)

M3:   *Ihimaa nidaa-gotaadabonaaban!*
        There I would be gliding out of control!
        (extended simultaneous laughter – 7 seconds)

L4:   *Giin dash Susan, giin gizhooshkwaadahenaaban ako weshkaj?*
        You then Susan, did you used to skate a long time ago?
        (conversation continues)

Example 2

H1:   *Ehina dash ninoodawaabanig ako Amos ekidoj 'manaadizi.' Bakaan*
        ikido na?
        I heard them before at Amos saying 'manaadizi.' He says it dif-
        ferent, you know?

SH1:   *Ehe.*
        Yeah.

H2:   *Bakaan gewiin ikido 'manaadizi' ekidoj.*
        He says it different 'manaadizi' she says.

SH2:   *'Manaadizi' ikidonaniwan wedi, gaa na?*
        'Manaadizi' they say there, don't they?

H3:   *Gaawin, ninoodawaabanig ako, gichi kokom ako noodawaaban ekidoj*
        bakaan, ikidoban 'manaadizi' ekidoj.
        No, I heard them before, I heard an old woman saying it differ-
        ent, she said 'manaadizi' she says.

L1:   *Aandi dash e-ikidomagag?*
        So what does it mean?

H4:   *'Wawiiyaazinaagozi' ikido.*
        'Wawiiyaazinaagozi' she says.

L2:   *Ohhh, gaawin gadaa minosesinoban wa-izhi-aabajichigaadeg !*
        Ohhh, it wouldn't work to use that !
        (simultaneous laughter – 2 seconds)

L3:   *Gidaa-gizhimaa!*

You should make him mad!
(simultaneous laughter – 3 seconds)
M1:   *Mii ge-izhi*-nishkaadiziwaapan!
He would be *really angry*!
(simultaneous laughter – 3 seconds)
L4:   *Ohhhhh, gotaaji maane!*
Ohhhhh, lots of them [would be]!
(extended simultaneous laughter – 6 seconds)

In these examples, we find instances where those engaged in the ongoing conversation start to speak after the onset of laughter and, at times, before it subsides. In Example 1, M in lines M1–M3 seems to be building a series of utterances generally related to the topic of skating and, more specifically, to her self-perceived incapacity to participate successfully in the activity.

When I first heard this conversation it seemed that M was building an utterance series, the listeners' laughter binding the sequence together as a recognizable activity. We can see that M1–M3 has a three-part structure based on laughter timing. It starts with an initiating utterance (in M1), followed by an utterance which sustains the series (in M2), and concludes with an utterance which terminates the series (in M3). When M first speaks, following L3 and the two-second pause, she makes the topically relevant statement in M1, and laughs at two different places in the midst of her utterance. At this point in her turn at speaking her laughter does not generate a laughing-together.

Current-speaker laughter, such as we find in M1, can accomplish a number of purposes, the two of immediate importance to us being that it can inform those listening to the ongoing talk that something funny is coming up in the current or next utterance, and it can initiate a laughing-together. M's laughter in the middle of utterance M1 appears to be accomplishing the former, while speaker laughter at the end of M1 does the job of generating a laughing-together. The three-part structure of the series and the laughing-together can be seen as a concerted achievement between the one talking and those listening to that talk. However, as we shall see, there are times when co-conversationalists decline the invitation to laugh together, which has the potential to generate trouble for both speakers and listeners. The series of utterances in M1–M3 demonstrates one form of interactional cohesion: a topically relevant humorous sequence with laughing-together as the first salient feature and a distinct three-part structure as the second. Now, if we intend to make claims for organized conversational structures in Ojibwe, we need to look at other conversational sequences to see if this organization can be found in other conversational contexts.

With the above comments in mind, I want to compare the three-part utterance series in example 1 with a similar structure in example 2. First, note that the laughter timing in example 1, lines M1–M3, and example 2, lines L2–L4, indicates that the sequences are seen by the participants as complete. In example 1, after speaker M initiates a laughing-together in M1, the first laughing-together lasts for two seconds. The second utterance in the series is also followed by a laughing-together of two seconds and then the final utterance is followed by a laughing-together of seven seconds. In example 2, L's first utterance in her series (L2) is followed by a laughing-together of three seconds, her second utterance (L3) by a laughing-together of three seconds (as is M's paraphrase of L3 in utterance M1), and L's final utterance by a laughing-together of six seconds. In both examples 1 and 2 we can see a recognizable three-part series of utterances and structures of laughing-together, with a recognizable structure to the timing of the laughing-together in both examples. The longest laugh time comes after the third (and final) utterance in each series and marks the end of the series and of the laughing-together.

Further, the talk in these examples can be seen to be interactionally cohesive insofar as the three-part series of utterance structure (with laughing-together as one salient feature) may be specifically deployed to accomplish topic closure. Lisa Valentine (1995:202–3), in her analysis of a Severn Ojibwe narrative, shows that there is a kind of structure to current-speaker laughter within the structure of a story being told in naturally occurring talk. She claims that narrator laughter in Severn Ojibwe can be used to highlight informational aspects of the story being told that are important to the dramatic effect the narrator is trying to achieve. More closely related to our interests here, she shows how narrator laughter can be an accomplice to episode closure and segments the telling and recap portions of the narration.

Now let us take a look at examples 3 and 4 and compare the laughter positioning and timing with examples 1 and 2. These pieces of talk are also taken from the recordings made by the language teachers of Winneway.

Example 3

L1:   *Susan, giwii-gwagwejimin gaa-ijiseg giin giigikinoamaagebakesagaa-
       kaag gegoon baapishise goonigoj gii-majise.*
       Susan, I want to ask you what happened you in your school class-
       room, something funny or [something] that went wrong.
       (L laughs by herself – 1 second))
S1:   *Baapishise?*
       Something funny?
L2:   *Gaa-gizhebaawagag.*
       In the morning.
S2:   *Nigii-waabadahag abinoojiizhesag naa 'flash cards.'*
       I showed the small kids, y'know flash cards.
       *Bepezhig dash 'Grade One' dash wiin gaawin ogii giikendasinawaa naa
       baanimaa dash niiwaaadahag naa niin sa gooj nidizhitaa.*
       Each one of them in Grade One then they didn't know, y'know?
       So I had to show them, y'know, exactly what I'm doing.
       *Bezhig dash ahaa abinoojiizhesis niwaabamaa sa niin, Freda ogwizisan,
       ogwizisesan, Buck. 'Wegonan ohoo' nidinaa, 'Aandi ezhitaaj abinojiizh?'*
       So one of those small kids I see him, Freda's son, her small son,
       Buck. 'What's this?' I say to him, 'What's the child doing?'
       'Niimi' ikido, 'Ehe, anishinaabe niimi' (laughs – 1 second)
       'Aandi ezhitaaj, aashkwe saa waabadahishin.' Gichi-niimi !
       'He's dancing,' he says, 'Yeah, the Indian is dancing.'
       (laughs – 1 second)
       'What's he doing? Show me.' *He really dances!*
       (simultaneous laughter – 4 seconds)
S3:   *Wawiiyaazinaagozi.*
       He looks cute.
L3:   Mm-hmm.
S4:   *Gichi baapiwag abinojiizhesag.*
       The small kids are really laughing.
       (speaker laughs – 2 seconds)
       (7 second group pause, then a change of topic)

Example 4

M2:   *Aazha dash ahaawedi bezhig 'biidigen' odinan Brian ogichi baapizhi-
       taawan e-ikidonjin e-biidigenjin!*
       Now then that one there [child] 'come in' he tells him Brian really
       laughed when he said for *him to come in*!

(simultaneous laughter – 3 seconds)

M3: *Buckley maa inaaganiwii ahaawe mii 'kwe' e-ikidowaaj abinoojiizhesag*
biidigenaaniwanig 'Biidigen' ogaa-inaawan awiayagoon.
Buckley he is told that one then 'kwe' that the small kids say
when someone is coming in 'Come in' they will tell him.
(simultaneous laughter – 3 seconds)

M4: *Niintam ako ikidobanig e-ako-biidigenjin 'kwe, kwe' odinaawaabaniin,*
They used to say 'kwe, kwe' when someone walked in,
aazhaa maamaj megaa gaawin gii-gikinoamaagoziisiiwag ganabaj dash
gii wanikewag.
now they aren't taught that, [so] they forgot about it.
Meshkooj dash noongom ikidowag ako 'Biidigen,' mii ge-ikidowaaj.
(speaker laughs – 2 seconds)
It's changed then, now they'll usually say 'Biidigen' [Come in!],
that's what they'll say.
(3 second group pause, then a change of topic)

First, note that in example 3, lines S2–S4, and example 4, lines M1–M4, we find instances where the ones listening to the story do not laugh but respond with noticeable silence to someone recounting a humorous anecdote. Notice in particular S4 in example 3 as the speaker ends the telling sequence with a kind of recap utterance. In example 4, utterance M4, we find a similar structure where M has finished her anecdote with a kind of explanatory statement followed by speaker laughter.

In neither instance does current-speaker laughter generate a laughing-together. Instead the listeners are silent. This appears to run counter to the procedure in Ojibwe interaction whereby those listening to the ongoing talk are expected to display affiliation with a prior speaker, as we saw in example 1: M1–M3 and example 2: L2–L4. Certainly co-conversationalists can decline to join in with current-speaker laughter, as we see happening following S4 in example 3 and M4 in example 4, and it seems reasonable to suggest that current-speaker laughter can do the work of preparing co-conversationalists to look for something humorous in the next utterance. In Example 4, however, it appears that the laughing-together following utterances M2 and M3 is taken to be sufficient by her co-conversationalists. But why is this?

It seems that M4 offers no new information or humorous content for her audience and is thus sequentially deleted by those listening. This claim can be substantiated by noting that utterance M4 receives no responses or appreciation tokens and by noticing how, in examples 1

and 2, the three-part same-speaker utterance series contains new information and/or humorous content. I claimed earlier that same-speaker
laughter and laughing-together can be a valuable resource in conversational interaction. A laughing-together appears to be the product of a
methodical and concerted activity on the part of speakers and hearers in
Ojibwe interaction. In these conversations, it seems to be achieved
through audience laughter in reference to a prior speaker's laughter, as
we noted in example 1: M1–M3 and example 2: L2–L4.

Two orderings of laughter in the environment of requested stories can
now be identified. In the first ordering, co-participants can be recognized as declining to join in laughing-together as in examples 3 and 4. In
an analysis of request deliveries and response types in Ojibwe, Bertha
Chief and I (Spielmann and Chief, 1986) noted instances in Ojibwe conversation when the response to a request for a favour provided for the
possibility of a conversational trouble, where responses to questions fall
outside the category of preferred responses. It may well be, then, that
silence may be a preferred response among Ojibwe people in a variety of
conversational contexts. Indeed, this appears to be quite widespread in
Native American interaction patterns (Basso, 1979; Wild, Nalonechny,
and St-Jacques, 1978; Darnell and Foster, 1988; Darnell, 1993). What
might be some of the reasons for this?

PREFERRED AND DISPREFERRED ACTIONS

For a variety of first actions, such as attempting to initiate a laughing-
together, it seems that dispreferred second actions, such as declining to
laugh or delaying a response, are routinely avoided, whereas preferred
actions, such as responding to an invitation to do laughing-together, are
usually performed with little or no delay. In conversational interaction
people are expected to display continuously that they are talking to each
other about the same things. It would seem that declining to participate
with current-speaker laughter could constitute a conversational trouble
for the speaker. In example 3: S2–S4 and example 4: M1–M4, however,
we can begin to see how declining to laugh in tandem with the current
speaker is not a dispreferred response. This claim is based on the positioning of the laughing-together earlier on in the sequences, and the
position of current-speaker laughter in the structure of the story
sequence.

Note, first, that the positioning of the laughing-together occurs at the
end of the sequence as opposed to the completion of the telling sequence

itself, which is extended by an evaluation of the anecdote by the teller. Looking again at example 3 we find that S does initiate a laughing-together following the punchline of the anecdote in S2, *'Gichi-niimi!'* ('He's really dancing!'). Then in S3, S comments *'Wawiiyaazinaagozi'* ('He looks cute'), which is responded to only by L's token acknowledgment consisting of *'Mm-hmmm.'* In S4, S offers a further evaluative comment on the story: *Gichi baapiwag abinojiizhesag.* ('The little kids are really laughing').

Similarly, in example 4: M1–M4, M initiates a laughing-together following the end of the story in M2, then in her story elaboration and evaluation in M3–M4 she is the only one who laughs following each utterance. The point here is that it appears that, while a laughing-together is a preferred response at story end, it is not necessarily a preferred feature at sequence completion. So an environment exists in which declining to laugh following the laughter of the current speaker may not be considered a dispreferred response, which is contrary to what we find among English-speaking non-Natives (Jefferson, 1979).

Such an environment can be clearly seen in examples 3 and 4 where, following each anecdote, the listeners indicate that they have paid attention to what has been recounted and that they have understood the punchline. Nevertheless, both speakers in examples 3 and 4 produce utterances following their anecdotes which elaborate or comment on them. The anecdotes do not necessarily need elaboration. However, in example 3: S3–S4, S's two utterances following her anecdote are not produced to explain the punchline of the story in S2, but to show how recognition for the rule that tellers ought to pay attention to in the culture: that stories be accountable in relation to the ongoing talk and that topical relevance is one possible account. Thus S does not merely rely on the funniness of her story in S2 to account for its production, she demonstrates that her story is tied sequentially to a request for a story in L1 by producing utterances (S3 and S4) which lead back to the original request to recount something funny that happened that morning in L's classroom.

These comments about the sequential structure of an utterance series bring us back to the placement considerations of topic closure. One feature of topic closure in these Ojibwe conversational sequences is the relationship between what Sacks and Schegloff (1974) call pre-closings and laughter/pause positioning. We have already noted one pre-closing device in an utterance series: the three-part structure of laughter timing where the laughing-together begins with a short burst (at least twice as long as the two previous instances of laughing-together within the sequence). Another feature of the pre-closing operation is that the laughing-together at sequence end indicated to the participants that the floor is open to any speaker to introduce a new topic without violating topical cohesion in the ongoing talk.

Teasing and Its Response in Ojibwe Conversation

I want to shift gears in this section and focus on a particular conversational activity occurring in examples 5 and 6 (below). In his article 'Pro-faced Receipts of Teases,' Paul Drew explores teasing practices and responses to teasing in non-Native English-speaking interaction. He found that, even where it seems that people recognize that a tease was meant to be humorous, the ones being teased display a tendency to 'correct' the tease, and in only a small number of instances in Drew's materials do they play along with the teasing. The most common response to teasing is to take it seriously. He writes:

Humorous remarks in conversation are not always treated humorously ... And for one kind of humorous remark ... teases ... I have been finding that recipients of teases rarely respond by going along with the humor of the tease. It is this phenomenon of responding to teases seriously to which I am referring as *pro-faced receipts* of teases. (1987:220)

Drew makes the case that, in non-Native English-speaking interaction, teasing and whether or not people feel comfortable teasing each other tells us something about their relationship. He draws a comparison between teasing and what Gail Jefferson (1984) discovered with the use of obscenities in naturally occurring conversation: that the introduction of obscenities into talk can act as an index of intimacy. Drew writes: 'As a means of displaying and assessing informality, intimacy, close acquaintance, and so on, teasing can be an index' (1987:220). Why, then, are teases so often responded to in a serious vein by the one being teased? My own sense is that teasing tends to catch people by surprise and often requires some 'recovery.' You can monitor your own response to teasing, regardless of your tradition, by thinking back on instances where you have been teased and how you responded. While teases are most often spontaneous, their production creates a climate for a potential interactional trouble. That is, teasing someone can be risky. It could be misconstrued, taken as serious, or cause the one being teased to feel hurt. Even when teasing is recognized as such by the one being teased, Drew found that 'the overwhelming pattern is that recipients treat something about the tease, despite its humor, as requiring a serious response: even when they plainly exhibit their understanding that the teasing remark is not meant to be taken seriously ... recipients still *almost always put the record straight'* (1987:230).

Drew includes a number of examples drawn from transcripts of natu-rally occurring conversation, but for our purposes just one will give us a better sense of what he means when he refers to 'pro-faced receipts' of teases. This example comes from an excerpt of a recording of a tele-phone conversation between Del and Paul.

Del: What are you doing at home?
Paul: Sitting down watching the tube.
Del: Watching daytime stories, huh?
Paul: No, I was watching this, you know, one of those game shows.

Drew's analysis of this conversation suggests that Del's utterance, 'Watching daytime stories, huh?' is a tease. After all, sitting around watching television when one should be doing something else can cre-ate a climate for teasing. Paul then overtly rejects Del's teasing (by answering no), and then corrects the tease by setting the record straight by saying, 'I was watching ... one of those game shows.'

But the question remains. Why is it that, despite the fact that teases are usually recognized for what they are (that they are not meant to be taken seriously as real versions of anything), people nevertheless tend to treat them as requiring serious responses? In order to suggest an answer to that question, I want to return to something I noted at the beginning of this chapter.

In many cultures, teasing has a social control function which occurs in the context of face-to-face interaction. In my own interactions, with both Native people and non-Natives, I have noticed a difference in how people respond to teasing. With my non-Native friends, people gener-ally tend to respond to teasing by trying to set the record straight. When teasing is done in Native-to-Native interaction, the tendency is for peo-ple to not only laugh along with the teasing but to participate in it by teasing themselves. Recall that Vine Deloria (1970) claims that Native people tend to use teasing with individuals they considered out of step with the consensus of tribal opinion (as a mechanism for social control), and that people being teased (for whatever reason) are most likely to

anticipate the teasing and go along with the teasing as a means of showing humility and solidarity with others. In other words, where conversation analysis research has shown that non-Natives will generally rely
upon pro-faced receipts when being teased, Native people most often
respond to teasing with self-deprecating humour and participate in the
teasing themselves.

With these comments in mind, let us consider the following conversational exchanges in the tapes made by the community language teachers
in Winneway.

Example 5

A1: *Gakinaa gii-maashkaawadan ziibii, gigii-waabadan naa zhebaa?*
   Did you see that the river was all frozen this morning?
B1: *Ehe.*
   Yeah.
A2: *Naaniizaaniwag ako abinoojiizhag, gaa naa?*
   It's pretty dangerous for the kids, y'know?
D1: Uh-huh.
A3: *Apiich gibwaadig ziibii.*
   When it's starting to freeze.
B2: *Zhooshgwaadenaaniwan nogom ziibiikaag?*
   Is there skating on the river yet?
C1: *Zhooshgwaadenaaniwan naa?*
   Skating?
B3: *Ehe.*
   Yeah.
A4: *Gaa mashii minoziisii.*
   It's not strong enough yet.
D2: *Nogom mochi ozhichigaade, gaa naa?*
   It's just getting made, isn't it?
A5: *Ehe, ozhichigaade noogom ge- zhooshgwaadenaaniwag.*
   Yeah, it's getting ready for skating.
B4: [to A] *Gizhooshgwaadane naa?*
   Do you skate?
   (simultaneous laughter – 6 seconds)
C2: *Ehe, gaawenasabii!*
   Yeah, she watches the (hockey) net!
   (simultaneous laughter – 4 seconds)
D3: *Gotaazinaagozii ahaa gookom!*

She's scary that old lady!
(simultaneous laughter – 3 seconds)

B5:   *Gaawin wiikad miinawaaj nidaanimwesii!*
      I'm not talking anymore!
      (simultaneous laughter – 3 seconds)

C3:   [to A] *Giga-oji-bookoogaadeshin!*
      You'll break your leg!
      (simultaneous laughter – 4 seconds)
      (conversation continues)

Example 6

B1:   *Aadii-e-dashieg ntaawigieg noopimig?*
      How many of you guys were born in the bush?

A1:   *Niin.*
      Me.

C1:   *Geniin.*
      Me, too.

B2:   *Mii eta?*
      That's all?

E1:   *Noopimig gaa-izhi-ntaawigiaan.*
      I was born in the bush.

B3:   [to D] *Giin dash, aadi gaa-izhi-ntaawigian?*
      You then, where were you born?

D1:   *Aadidoog.*
      I don't know.
      (simultaneous laughter – 4 seconds)

A2:   *Gaa naa Rock Lake gigii-dazhiikesii weshkaj?*
      Didn't you live at Rock Lake a long time ago?

D2:   *Rock Lake? Ohh, ehe, niinwiin okoonimakaag e-paamibitowaan.*
      Rock Lake? Ohh, yeah, I used to run across the power dam.

When I first listened to this tape I noticed two instances of teasing. Structurally, the first instance is characterized by a question which is followed by an utterance that could not be interpreted as an answer (example 5). In the second instance the answer to a question is followed by laughter (example 6). In the case of the former, instead of an answer, the question was followed by laughter. Further, the questioner, A, seems to treat the laughter as something produced in response to the question, although not as an answer to it. Normally in Ojibwe conversation, questions provide a slot which enables the next speaker to produce an utterance which is to be heard as an answer. In this instance, we can see that the laughter did not stand as a substitute for the answer, but seemed merely to delay it. Certainly the utterances in example 5 are sequentially connected, although perhaps not in the strong way that, for example, adjacency pairs are connected. Instead, the utterances are tied together because the production of a 'funny' question (in B4) had caused a disruption in the conversation which the participants respond to in the laughter and talk which follows.

It should be noted, too, that all of the participants were in approximately the same visual range and share a common culture-specific sense for recognizing what is funny. The laughter is responsive to the question because it acts as a comment on the question. In example 5, B is faced with two interactional problems: first, she has not received an answer to her question, which may constitute a problem for B's continued participation in the flow of conversation; and secondly, she has been temporarily disaligned from the other participants and seeks some way of fitting back into the flow of conversation. The problematic sequence is handled by B with a self-deprecating comment (B5) relating to the inappropriateness of the question. Her comment in B5, 'Gaawin wiikad miinawaaj nidaanimwesii!' ('I'm not talking anymore!'), does the work of indicating that B has heard the laughter in response to her question in B4 and is treating it as some kind of conversational move. Utterance B5 also elicits laughter, which allows B to regain her status as a participant. How so? By producing a self-deprecating utterance, B indicates that she considers the laughter to be part of the conversation she is having with the others and not part of some private conversation that her funny or inappropriate question may have generated.

What exactly made B4 such a funny question that it provided the other participants with an opportunity to engage in teasing? I think B's question was treated as humorously inappropriate and thus open to a tease because the other participants heard the question as expressing ignorance about the social organization of skating in the community, who does and does not skate, something B should know about. As I kept listening to this piece of interaction on tape, I was puzzled by the laughter that followed B4. I went and asked A why everyone had laughed at the question. She told me, 'An old woman like me doesn't skate.' She was thirty-eight years old at the time.

Certainly people engaged in conversation can be expected to bring with them a certain amount of shared knowledge, particular motives, and culture-specific attitudes and beliefs. Interaction generally proceeds smoothly in any culture because these assumptions are continually reaffirmed by the relative ease in which participants produce meaningful utterances. For instance, in example 6 it struck me that D's response of *'Aadiidoog'* ('I don't know') in D1 displays a lack of what would surely be considered common knowledge. After all, one is surely expected to know where one is born, unless there are extenuating circumstances. Behind every utterance people attribute a whole culture of knowledge, attitudes, and motives. In example 6, then, rather than hearing B3 as an inappropriate question, it appears that D1 is treated by the other participants as an inappropriate answer. D's stock of common knowledge is temporarily brought into question. We can support this claim by noting that, in the conversation prior to B's question to D, three other participants have already successfully responded to and treated the question as natural (in lines A1, C1, and E1). D's response in D1 displays that she does not possess this same piece of proper cultural knowledge that is assumed by others.

In Drew's response types to teases in non-Native English-speaking interaction, he claims that simultaneous laughter by other participants can, in itself, constitute a tease (1987:225). The most common response to laughter-as-teasing in Drew's materials is for the one being teased to initially join in with the laughter, as we see D doing in example 6, followed by a serious rejection of the tease (a pro-faced receipt). In this Ojibwe sequence we are able to observe a different pattern. While teasing does occur in the form of simultaneous laughter in response to D's utterance in D1, D herself does not respond with any kind of utterance, pro-faced or otherwise. The show of solidarity among the conversationalists occurs when A attempts to help D remember where she was born. Another component of D's response to the teasing – her participation in the laughter which is generated as a result of D1 – demonstrates that, while D realizes that the other participants took her response to display an ignorance of what is considered to be common social knowledge, she also finds her own ignorance as funny and worthy of being teased about. Rather than teasing being met by pro-faced resistance by the ones being teased (as Drew describes for non-Native English-speakers), the conversation shows a preference among Anishnaabe people for self-deprecating humour and laughing-together, with no sign of attempting to correct the tease by employing a pro-faced receipt. Our look at how Anishnaabe people respond to teasing in naturally occurring conversational interaction again helps us to understand how the techniques of conversation analysis can be of tremendous value in exploring culture-specific ways of thinking and doing things, and informs us of yet another different way of thinking and doing things between Native people and non-Natives.

Conclusion

In this chapter we have looked at a number of examples of laughter positioning in naturally occurring Ojibwe conversation in order to show how laughter can be used as an interactional resource in ongoing conversation. Further, we saw how laughter and teasing can be used to accomplish a variety of activities in Ojibwe interaction, such as topic closure, expressing recipient appreciation, initiating a laughing-together and, in collaboration with other structural features of Ojibwe conversation, initiating, sustaining, and terminating an utterance series. In any culture, laughter, humour and teasing can help to generate and sustain communication, friendship, and a sense of cultural solidarity. In Ojibwe interaction we can see how culture-specific humorous themes and laughter positioning throw light on what are considered to be important cultural values: group solidarity, interpersonal harmony, patience and tolerance. Finally, this chapter describes a conversational environment in which declining to laugh following the laughter of the current speaker can also be used to facilitate topic closure and topic change. We also discovered a teasing-response pattern which appears to work much differently from non-Native English-speaking interaction, again demonstrating how different and culture-specific the ways of thinking and doing things are between Native people and non-Natives.

7

'Almost Burned': Conversation Analysis and Culture-Specific Ways of Accomplishing Interactional Tasks

We left our cabin in the bush and walked for about a mile until we reached the river. I had gone to the bush with one of my friends from the reserve. We were about the same age, still considered to be in the category of *gaa oshkii bimaadiziwaaj* (young people) from the elders' perspective, and we were scouting out places to set beaver traps. It was early spring and the ice on the river was getting a bit treacherous. We thought it would be worth crossing the river to check out some areas on the other side. My friend walked to the edge of the river, took a few steps, then beckoned me to come with him. After a few more timid steps, he took his ever-present .22 rifle and shot a hole in the ice. He got down on one knee to examine the hole. Then, satisfied that the ice was thick enough to hold us as we crossed, he said to me in his language, 'Oh, yes, the ice is strong enough. You go first.' I took a few confident steps and then plunged through the ice. Fortunately we were still close enough to the bank that I was able to gain some footing and, with my friend's help, scramble back onto the ice and then off the river completely. We had a good laugh as we hurried back to his cabin (although I think he was laughing harder than I was). But I learned something from that experience. Part of the humour of the story that my friend told and retold when we got back to the reserve was how fortunate that he had sent me first! But the important thing in my mind, and which relates to what we will explore here, is that he had used a method for testing the ice that made the elders who heard the story shake their heads.

I can't remember exactly when I started keeping a list of 'complainable states of affairs' that I heard the elders talk about in everyday conversation, but over the years I began to pay attention to what people in Pikogan complained about and how they complained. I regularly heard the elders complain about the young people and their actions and behaviours. In fact, one of the things that I heard quite often was how the *gaa oshkii bimaadiziwaaj* no longer knew how to act appropriately in the bush and how dangerous it was becoming for them to go to the bush without the supervision of elders. In the eleven years that we lived in the community there were a number of accidental deaths and close calls of young people alone in the bush. So this was a real concern and the elders talked regularly about how important it was for the young people to learn proper bush skills.

In exploring this phenomenon, I came to realize that there are differences between complaint structures and complaint deliveries in Ojibwe culture as compared to my own non-Native culture. The 'complainables' most often voiced over the years are the following: not listening to the elders any more; not speaking the language; not knowing about bush skills; too much drinking and *maji maashkikii* (bad medicine – drugs); too much playing (referring to the great number of hockey and softball tournaments); not praying or going to church; lack of understanding about Anishnaabe ways of doing things; and not knowing the traditional legends and stories.[1] At one point I was inspired by reading Scollon and Scollon (1981) to keep a list of what I refer to as preferred and dispreferred behavioural characteristics that I heard the elders talk about over the years, and began to notice that the dispreferred characteristics were often the same as the things the elders would complain about. Before we get into an analysis of complaint structures and deliveries in naturally occurring talk, I invite you to peruse the list of preferred and dispreferred behavioural characteristics that I compiled.

Preferred characteristics	Dispreferred characteristics
Participates in community life; listens to the elders	Keeps to oneself; a 'loner,' doesn't listen to the elders
Speaks the Native language; or at least tries to learn and appreciate it	Makes no effort to learn or speak the Native language
Shares freely with others: money, moose-meat, possessions, etc.	Hoards goods and possessions, moose-meat, and money
Doesn't drink or use drugs	Drinks too much/uses drugs
Accords others freedom of choice, doesn't offer advice unless asked	Tells others what to do and how to do it; is considered pushy

Makes information known but lets people make their own decisions	Forces people into making verbal commitments
Always ready to help others, looks for ways to help and be hospitable	Doesn't readily offer to help others, looks for excuses not to help
People more important than things, activities, or following the rules	Things/activities and following the rules of primary importance
Prays often. Visits people and is ready to pray with them when asked	Rarely prays and rarely takes the time to visit other people
Expresses a deep trust in and reliance on the Creator and helping spirits	Trusts exclusively in self and the value of looking out for number one
Dreams and pays attention to dreams as messages from the Creator	Doesn't pay much attention to dreams or the Creator
In short, acts like an Anishnaabe	In short, acts like a *Zhaagnaash*

Complainable States of Affairs

When I speak about a complaint I am referring to a conversational event; that is, to some formulation of a trouble or perceived problem which one cultural member delivers to another. I use the term complainable to refer to a state of affairs which a complaint formulates. With these terms we have a way of indicating when we are referring to the conversational event being analysed or to the states of affairs which occasion these events.

In listening to elders talking about heart-felt complainables over the years it seems that complaints are normally generated to accomplish one or both of the following: to seek remedy of a perceived problem in the social reality of the one making the complaint; and to seek some form of sympathy or solidarity. Upon the completion of a complaint, those hearing the complaint will, more often than not, produce a next utterance which acknowledges the complaint or an utterance which shows some appreciation for the complainable state of affairs. Whether the sought response is remedy or sympathy (or both), the timing of the complaint with the occurrence complained of seems to be crucial. Clearly, for example, someone contacting the Amerindian police to complain about a stolen item ought to make their complaint as soon as possible upon discovering the item was stolen.

In listening to the elders sitting around talking together over the years, I noticed that the sought response when someone generated a complaint more often than not seemed to be sympathy and solidarity rather than seeking remedy. That is not to say that people in the community do not generate complaints in order to remedy some complainable state of affairs. They most certainly do. It also appears that occasions for complaints in Ojibwe provide legitimate grounds for transmitting and reinforcing cultural values.

When I was teaching a course in the Ethnography of Communication in Winneway a few years ago, we spent some time talking about how people voice their complaints in the community: how people complain, what they say, what people complain about, and so on. In my notes on our discussions I noted that one of the students, a teacher in the community, said, 'When I hear someone complaining about another person and uses her name, I usually agree with them even if I don't really agree. Or I try not to say anything.' Richard Rhodes (1988) offers support for this attitude. Speakers and hearers both assume and display that they are cooperators, and that the cooperation principle seems to be quite strong even in contexts where people are formulating complaints. Another person told me: 'If I have to complain about a person and I know that that person is related to the person I'm talking to, I won't mention his name.' And another said, 'I don't like using a person's name when I'm complaining about something she did. If they find out, they might try to get back at me.'

In order to establish recognizable grounds for complaining, some kind of documentation becomes an essential component of the complaint. Surely the absence of a recognizable reason for a complaint in everyday interaction could occasion questions as to its appropriateness. In the story that we are looking at here, for example, the complainable can be characterized as follows: it is a state of affairs whose troublesome nature has become evident and the complainable is captured in the recounting of a specific event. Read through the following story excerpts before proceeding on with the analysis.

'After the Tournament'

1. *Mii dash e-gii-maaji-odaminonaaniwag, gaa-niiogaazhikwagag e-onaa-goshig.*
   So then there was the start of playing last Thursday evening.

2. *Gaa-bi-nda-odaminowaaj Anishnaabeg.*
   Indians came to play.

3. *Gii-maaji-odaminonaaniwan e-onaagoshig, naano-dibahiganiyaag biinishi dash zhaagidachin.*
   The playing started at five o'clock in the evening until nine.

4. *Gii-doohewag mikwamiikaag wedi arena-kaag.*
   They played on the ice there at the arena.

5. *Miinawaj idash e-waabag ihiwedii, aazha miinawaj gii-maaji-odaminon-aaniwan gaa-ishkwaa-aabita-giizhigag e-doohaaniwag wedi mikwamii-kaag, zhooshkwaadahewag ashij 'broomball' ikwesesag.*
   Again in the morning now again they started playing in the after-noon there was playing there on the ice they skated and the girls [played] broomball.

6. *Gabena gii-odaminowag biinishi ishkwaa-aabita-dibikag, aadidog apiich mayaa gaa-ishkwaataawaaj.*
   They always played until after midnight, I really don't know when they finished.

7. *Miinawaj e-gizhebaawagag gaa-Maanigiizhigag niizhwaachin e-gizhe-baawagag gaa-maaji-odaminonaaniwag.*
   Again at seven o'clock in the morning they started playing again.

8. *Gabe-giizhig wedi gii-odaminowag gichi-miigiwaamikaag arena-kaag.*
   They played there all day at the big house at the arena.

9. *Zhooshkwaadahewag ashij ikwesesag odaminowag ayahii 'broomball.'*
   They skate and the girls play broomball.

10. *Maane gii-dewag wedi Anishnaabeg.*
    There were a lot of Indians there.

11. *Ashij ohomaa gaa-dewaaj Anishnaabeg gegaad gabena wedi gii-dewag e-gizhigaabamaawaajin awiyan e-odaminonjin.*
    And the Indians from here were almost always there to watch other Indians play.

12. *Gii-gichi-maanenaaniwan wedi arena-kaag.*
    There were really a lot of people there in the arena.

13. *Mayaa goj debwe gii-gichi-maanenaaniwan ashij gii-gichi-giiwashkwebii-wag awiyagoog, bizhishig naandam, mii ezhitaawaaj eta e-minikwewaaj.*
    Truly there were a lot of people there and some of them were always drunk, they were there only to drink.

14. *Gakinaa goj ihiimaa dazhi gegoon giiwashkwenaagwan wedi.*
    Everything there is really a mess.

[Later.]

50. *Gii-minose sa bekish gaa-odaminonaniwag.*
    Just the same it went well when there was playing [hockey].
51. *Gaawin awiyag oji-nibosii, gakina awiiyag gii-bimaadizi, wewenda ogii-ganawenimigowaan Gizhe-Manidoon megwaaj e-odaminowaaj.*
    No one died, everyone was doing well, the Creator kept [everyone] safe while they were playing.
52. *Aanish dash bezhig gegoon.*
    But one thing.
53. *Gaa-maajitaaniwag e-odaminonaaniwag e-onaagoshig, gaa-Niiogaazhik-wagag.*
    The playing started on Thursday evening.
54. *Gii-ashamigoonaaniwan ohomaa dazhi Anishnaabewakiig, daso-giizis gaa-ashamaaganiwiwaaj Anishnaabeg.*
    Rations were given out [welfare cheques] here at the reserve, each month the people are given rations.
55. *Gii-dagwan ihiwe gaa-Niiogaazhikwagag.*
    It was there on Thursday.
56. *Nawaj idash giiyabaj maane awiyag gii-minikwe e-dibikag.*
    Then there were lots of people who were drinking at night.
57. *Naandam gii-gichi-giiwashkwebiidogwenag ohomaa Anishnaabeg e-dibikag.*
    Some were really drunk here at the reserve.
58. *Ashij idash ohomaa dazhi wiibaj e-gizhebaawagag gaa-Jiibayaatigo-giizhi-gag e-gizhebaawagag.*
    And then early here at this place [Pikogan] it was Friday morning.
59. *Nizhoomisim wii-miikimo gewiin, odaa-bimibidetoon odaabaanni.*
    My husband wants to work also, he should/would drive his car.
60. *Wiibaj idash gii-wanishkaa.*
    He woke up very early.
61. *Aazha dash nigii-wiidamaag gii-bii-biidige nizhoomisim, 'Bezhig ishk-waade miigiwaam!'*
    Then he told me when my husband came inside, 'A house is on fire!'
62. *Geniin nigii-wanishkaabatoo.*
    Me, too, I woke up quickly.
63. *Aazha niwaabadaan gichi-baashkine.*
    Now I see a lot of smoke.
64. *Debwe gii-ishkwaade bezhig miigiwaam.*
    It's true that a house was burning.
65. *Gegaad mayaa gii-jaagaakide, aabita mayaa gii-ishkwaade.*
    It was almost burned up; half of it had burned up.

66. *Gegaad naandam gii-izhkwaazowag ihimaa dazhi.*
    Some people were almost burned there.

67. *Naandam anooj gaa-ojiiwaaj, Lac Simon gii-ojiiwag ihimaa
    nibaawaagoban ihimaa.*
    Some were from another place, some from Lac Simon were sleeping
    there.

68. *Ashij idash igiwe ihimaa gaa-dazhiikewaaj omiigiwaamiwaakaag.*
    And there were also the ones who lived in the house.

69. *Gegaad mayaa gii-ishkwaazowag niizhin.*
    Two of them were almost burned.

70. *Gii-gichi-zanagiziwag giji-zaagijihaaganiwiwaaj, ozaam megaa bezhig
    ahawe baazhigobii, bezhig idash ahawedi gichi-nibaa.*
    It was really difficult to get them out, because of course one is quite
    drunk and the other one is fast asleep.

71. *Mii dash wiinawa gakina ogii-gashkihaawaan giji-zaagijihaaganiwiwaaj,
    gaawin awiyag gii-ishkwaazosii.*
    So then they were all saved when they were taken out, no one was
    burned.

72. *Mii eta miigiwaam, gii-ishkwaabadan miigiwaam.*
    Only the house, the house burned down.

73. *Mii eta ihimaa maawaji-gegoon gaa-izhi-gichi-goshkwendagwag, gaa-izhi-
    webag gaa-wii-maaji-odaminonaaniwag.*
    So the biggest thing was that it was really a shock what happened
    when the playing began.

74. *Ozaam maane minikwewin ashij.*
    There's way too much drinking, too.

75. *Ashij idash gaawin dibise naanigodin gegoon ginaagajitoosiin, naanigodin
    giwaniike gegoon, naanigodin giwii-nibaa, mii eta gaa-oji-gii-izhiseg gaa-
    ishkwaadeg miigiwaam.*
    And then sometimes you are not too careful, sometimes you forget
    something, sometimes you want to sleep, so it will happen for a
    house to burn down.

76. *Debwe misawaaj naniizaanad ishkode gaa-izhinikaadeg.*
    For sure, fire, as it is called, is dangerous.

77. *Moozhag igoj wewenda giji-naagajitoowan ishkode aagwaa giji-inendaman
    wii-nibaayan, ashij e-gizhebaawagag gii-boodaweyan, moozhag aagwaa
    giga-inendaan ishkode gaa-izhinikaadeg.*
    You always have to be very careful with fire, to think about it when
    you want to sleep, and when you light a fire in the morning you
    have to be careful to think about the fire, as it is called.

78. *Mii eta ge-ikidowaan noogom gaa-biboog.*
That's all I will say [about] this year's [tournament].

FORMULATING COMPLAINTS IN OJIBWE CONVERSATION

In formulating a complaint in face-to-face interaction the complainable state of affairs is not necessarily ascertained apart from who is seen to be responsible. In this story, the one being complained about is formulated as a general category rather than as a specific identity. The complaint is highlighted with line 52, *Aanish dash bezhik gegoon* (But one thing). Thus far the story is concerned with talk about the recent Indian hockey tournament: that it was a fun time, that there were a lot of people there, and so on. Earlier on in the conversation, when the speaker was telling about who was at the tournament, we find the first use of a general identification in line 13, *gii-gichi-giiwashkwebiiwag* (A lot of them were drunk), and *bizhishig naandam, mii ezhitaawaaj eta e-minikwewaaj* (Some are always there only to drink). In this story, then, those complained against are both involved and characterized in ways intended to render intelligible the cause of the complainable state of affairs. While we can gloss what they were doing as, say, 'drinking,' what that amounts to is perhaps not so easily arrived at without line 14, *Gakinaa goj ihimaa dazhi gegoon giiwashk-wenaagwan wedi* (Everything there is really a mess). Surely people who are drinking have plenty of ways of disrupting social events, but line 14 provides a possible way of seeing *what* is happening precisely by seeing *who* is doing it. The fact of their status as 'people who are drinking' is used as a resource for formulating the ones who are being complained against as such persons who would do just what they are, in fact, doing.[2]

In the examples of complaining under analysis here, the complainable is so conceived that some category of persons is seen to be responsible for the state of affairs at issue. Further, the complaints report on complainable states of affairs which do not contain specific identities of persons – at least, they are not mentioned by name. Nevertheless, categories of persons responsible for the complainable states of affairs are identified. My first thought was that it may be the preferred way in Ojibwe culture to preserve anonymity when possible. Such a preference would appear to be in contrast to North American English-speaking culture; if possible, non-Native English speakers prefer to use actual names (Turner, 1974; Sharrock and Turner, 1978).

A preference for categorial identities over naming names in Ojibwe complaint deliveries would be understandable in light of other typically

Native features of interpersonal relations, such as cultural deference as seen in requests for favours, for example. In everyday interaction in the community where we lived, too, I noticed that complainable states of affairs regularly centred on categories of people – young people, drinkers, fast drivers, and so on – and that complaints were expressed in terms relative to these categories. This is not to say that names are not used when complaints are formulated. They sometimes are and there are interactional benefits accrued by using names on certain occasions. But categorial formulations are more common and different kinds of interactional benefits arise from their use.

The articulation of a complaint can have side effects. One may generate a complaint about how a certain category of the community's population – young people, for example – don't pray any more or don't respect the elders or drink too much or play too much, and so on, without reference to a specific complainable state of affairs. Such general complaints are common in elders' talk and provide the opportunity for cultural members to exhibit solidarity with and sympathy for one another. Another kind of side effect can be seen where those of a certain category – for example, those who drink – are related to a community disaster, such as a house burning down, which can have long-lasting negative effects on the community. No names are mentioned, although generally everyone in such a small community knows who was involved. See, for example, the lines 66–7, *Gegaad mayaa gii-ishkwaazowag niizhin* (Two people were almost burned), and who started the fire. Certainly telling about something that happened can be transformed by the narrators, with the result that talk about one thing can undergo a shift so as to become talk about something else. Talk which contains complaints, too, can undergo such a shift so as to yield talk now focused on the one complained against.[3]

It is reasonable to assume that complaining is relatively commonplace in any culture. And certainly complaints can be and are used to get things done, such as gaining revenge or making an individual look bad in the eyes of others, for a variety of reasons. More often than not, naming names is useful in these circumstances. But in other contexts we find a conversational environment for evasiveness where one of the tasks of the people delivering complaints seems to be to avert suspicion that the complaint is designed to gain revenge or carries some other motive toward the person or persons to whom the complaint is being addressed. This consideration takes us back to the preference for using categorial formulations rather than specific identities. It explains my friend's comment about agreeing with someone who is using a name in making a complaint even if she disagrees with the complaint assessment. We understand also why others are hesitant to use a person's name in a complaint for fear of some kind of retribution. One person with whom I recently spoke said this: 'The only time I would use a name if I was complaining about someone, it would have to be someone very close to me, like my husband. I'm pretty sure my husband wouldn't go tell that person, "This is what my wife said about you." Even if it was my best friend, I still wouldn't use a person's name.'

MEMBERSHIP CATEGORIES

Thus far we have looked at the structure of a mundane conversational activity (complaining) in Ojibwe with an interest in coming to a better understanding of Ojibwe-specific ways of thinking and doing things. I want to return briefly to the work of Harvey Sacks (1970) and see how his development of the notion of membership categories can take us to an even deeper understanding of the thoughts of a mother-tongue Ojibwe speaker as she formulates a complaint in the midst of telling a story about what happened after the hockey tournament. We can use a simple linguistic example to show how important it is that people engaged in talking together share certain background assumptions with each other. Sacks used the following example to illustrate this point. It comes from his exploration of children's stories, one of the stories containing the two-part sequence: 'The baby cried. The mommy picked it up.' I use this illustration in the classroom by writing it on the blackboard and asking students to interpret what is going on in this simple sequence. Invariably, all agree that the 'mommy' is the mother of the 'baby.' Then I ask how they know that. After all, there are no semantic or syntactic features in the sentences which tell us that. The point I try to get across to my students is that the connection between mommy and baby is not marked linguistically, but is actually taking place in our minds. Sacks claims that what we are really relying on, and what people of all cultures inevitably are required to rely upon in order to make sense of what other people say, are membership categories. He claims that in conversational interaction we regularly rely upon this device in order to interpret correctly the meaning of words such as mommy and baby. But that connection is made in our minds and we can only come to a shared understanding of that connection with others when we all share the same membership categories; that is, a shared sense of what goes together naturally. Thus we understand that the mommy in the sequence is the mother of the baby. But why would this be so?

At the risk of getting too technical, allow me to reiterate that we all use membership categories every day as we listen to and engage in conversation; we just don't necessarily realize that we're using them! After all, the baby in this example certainly could be categorized in a variety of ways, as can the mommy. But then it would be quite a different sequence if other categories were used. For example, we could refer to the same two people using different membership categories by saying, 'The Indian cried. The lawyer picked it up,' the baby being of Native ancestry, say, and the mommy being a lawyer by profession. But then it is not so easy to make the connection between membership categories and thus make sense of what is being said. The point here is that we use and understand membership categories naturally, and know that certain things go together. One of Sacks's assumptions in exploring membership categories is that the world around us is ordered in such a way that there are certain categories of relationships that are expressed through language, and to interpret accurately a word, utterance, or sequence of utterances one must have some shared knowledge in order for conversation to proceed smoothly (which, if you think about it, is most often the case). This knowledge, of course, is socially acquired and may differ from culture to culture.

MEMBERSHIP CATEGORIES AND PRACTICAL REASONING

The interesting thing about Sacks's approach to analysing everyday conversation is that he considered it imperative to pay careful attention to the semantic and theoretical strategies which people in any culture use to identify themselves or react to others. He initially made the connection between 'what goes on in the mind' and membership category devices by taking a detailed look at how people use something as common as nouns and verbs in their everyday conversational interactions, such as mother, baby, hairstylist, and activities such as crying, joking, having problems, and so on. The bottom line here is that the world around us, our reality, is something that people must constantly keep creating and sustaining for themselves. In this view, language and verbal interaction play extremely significant roles in creating and sustaining culture. What Sacks was really trying to get at, however, was how we use practical reasoning in our everyday lives, regardless of our cultural background. Practical reasoning refers to the way in which we make use of our shared stock of knowledge, our commonsense knowledge. What we are exploring here is how we employ that knowledge in our everyday lives, what we assume, what we accept as true, and how we make the various bits and pieces of our shared stock of knowledge fit together in social encounters so as to maintain normal appearances.

It is important to keep in mind, too, that practical reasoning is not the same as what we commonly refer to as scientific thinking. In going about their everyday lives, people do not normally think through the problems and complexities of life the same way that trained scientists go about solving a problem or understanding a phenomenon. One of the best articles that helps us to grasp this concept is one written years ago but still, I think, relevant here. The article, 'Notes on the Art of Walking,' was written by Alan Ryave and James Schenkein in 1974. They write:

The substantive focus of this discussion is the phenomenon of 'doing walking'. We use the verb 'doing' to underscore a conception of walking as the concerted accomplishment of people as a matter of course in its production and recognition ... [People] rely on an elaborated collection of methodic practices in the conduct of doing walking, and we want to try to ... gain access to the details of these methodic practices. (1974:265)

One might ask why we should talk about *walking* when we're supposed to be discussing *talking*? I think Ryave and Schenkein's article provides us with some clues to doing something which most of us engage in every day, yet without thinking about it. In that way, manoeuvring one's physical body around is similar to engaging in talking; both are done in taken-for-granted, unformulated ways. The fact is, though, we do have strategies for going about our everyday lives, doing such seemingly simple things as walking and talking. Most of us are competent cultural members in the sense that we can accomplish these kinds of activities with relative ease and with little or no forethought.

That being the case, think about the following. Say you're going to do some Christmas shopping on Christmas Eve (this is perhaps a good example for men). You know the mall is going to be crowded. Do you have a strategy for manoeuvring your body through the crowd? Of course not – at least, not consciously. You might come up with some plan of action, such as: 'When I get to the mall I'll go to the grocery store first because it's closest to where I plan to park, then I'll make my way around the mall and end up back at the grocery store,' or whatever. But do you have a strategy for transporting your body through the crowd?

What if you are with someone else or a group of people? Do you have a strategy for walking together in the crowded mall? Again, the answer to these questions is, of course not. Nevertheless, we do employ navigational strategies and we rely on them constantly as we move from store to store.

The point is that we are most often successful in navigating our bodies through crowds, and we accomplish this activity with little planning or thinking about navigational strategies. When you think about it, we all have a complex repertoire of strategies, of ways of doing things, that enable us to do something as simple (and yet as complex) as getting around in crowds at a mall, or walking with a friend down a crowded city street, or whatever. And if you *really* think about it, you can even begin to explicate, examine and describe what those strategies are.

In the past few paragraphs I have been trying to orient you to what we will be discussing in the next section. Keep in mind that we are using one conversational activity, that of formulating complaints in Ojibwe, in order to gain a deeper understanding of the methods that Ojibwe people (and people from any culture) rely upon when they're doing things via talk. And while people in any culture do similar things – greetings, leave-taking, complaining, joking, telling stories, and so on – it is important to remember that many of these things are done differently from culture to culture, and done in culture-specific ways. In the next section, then, we will look at how Ojibwe people rely upon membership categories as they engage in everyday interaction.

MEMBERSHIP CATEGORIES IN THE 'AFTER THE TOURNAMENT' STORY

We are now in a better position to see how membership categories are relied upon in Ojibwe verbal interaction, in this case for in-group solidarity or sympathy in the context of complainable states of affairs. One feature which is shared in all three excerpts from the story is that the complainable state of affairs involves the categorial identity of 'those who drink.' The deeper issue related to these complaints is that an activity such as drinking can serve as a basis on which people take stands, display commitments to health or other ideologies, and thus possibly lay claims to be more sensible, upright, or considerate than others. If this assumption is correct, then one natural outcome of a complaint using categorial identifications is to take the opportunity to make a stand against that activity as a basis for warning others against participating in the complained of activity. In all three texts grounds are provided for the speaker to warn the hearers about the dangerous consequences of drinking. Note in particular line 75, where there is a noticeable shift to the second person: *Ashij idash gaawin dibise naanigodin gegoon ginaagaji-toosiin* (And then sometimes you aren't too careful), *naanigodin giwaniike gegoon, naanigodin giwii-nibaa* (Sometimes you forget, sometimes you want to sleep).

Keep in mind, too, that in identifying where the storyteller in the 'After the Tournament' story is formulating a complaint, we are unable to locate any obvious syntactic or semantic properties that might be seen as linguistic features of a complaint. I take, further, that the one recounting this particular story may have begun the complaint, or set up the possibility of formulating it, in an earlier part of the story by referring to the membership category of those who drink. There is no *a priori* reason that an activity (such as complaining) should be expected to require certain words or utterances. We should have no difficulty in agreeing that the basis of the storyteller's complaint is a critique of those who drink. Let us assume for a moment that a critique of a certain membership category can be made by anyone. For the person affected by the perceived negative behaviour of those members of a certain category, it can provide the resources necessary for understanding what happened in a particular situation. More important, it can provide a person, as it most certainly does in this story, with the opportunity to get across a particular point or teaching which he/she deems important to transmit. What we have in this instance, then, is a characterization of an occasion structured in such a way that the story itself becomes a resource for constructing a complaint. Then the complaint is used as a resource for doing some practical teaching or exhorting, such as we find in lines 74–5. In effect, what we are dealing with is this person's concern to ensure the appropriateness of the complaint that is directed towards those implicated in a particular membership category, and how it can be accomplished in the midst of seemingly mundane talk about what happened after the tournament.

Recall that the choice of a membership categorization device, while accomplished subconsciously, is a product of practical reasoning. Whatever cultural tradition we belong to, we are competent members of that culture, as evidenced by our natural ability to engage in everyday verbal interaction.[4] Conversation analysis can show us how Ojibwe people achieve common purposes by doing and saying certain things in culture-specific ways. Ojibwe people, as people in any culture, naturally follow certain rules of cooperation, trust, turn-taking, and so on, and it is rare to confront others openly doubt them, insist that they be logical, or refuse to do their own part in creating and sustaining reality.

Conclusion

I have made two somewhat tentative claims from the story we have been looking at in this chapter: that members of Ojibwe culture are oriented to a preference for categorial identifications over name recognition in the context of complaint deliveries; and that complaints provide a culturally relevant slot for reinforcing cultural values and traditional ideologies. I have also explored how membership categories are commonly and naturally used by people engaged in verbal interaction to make sense of what is said in the context of that interaction. Another important thing we can glean from this analysis is that though the path from linguistic structures to interactional ones is not a straight line, not much may lie at the end of the path. That is to say, an utterance or a sequence of utterances can be categorized as a complaint only in reference to its interactional location. Certainly there are differences between complaint structures and complaint deliveries in Ojibwe culture as compared to non-Native English-speaking culture, and one task in trying to understand how Ojibwe people think is to analyse how people do things, how they accomplish activities in and through talk.

PART THREE
INTRODUCTION TO LINGUISTIC DISCOURSE ANALYSIS

8

'What Happens in Life': An Introduction to Linguistic Discourse Analysis

Not long ago I was asked by a close friend of mine, Karen Pheasant, what I was writing about. Karen is an Ojibwe woman and an internationally acclaimed jingle dress dancer. When I told her that the book was designed to be an introduction to discourse analysis in Ojibwe, she responded by saying, 'I should help you write your book. I know lots of good disco moves!' Perhaps Karen and I will collaborate on a book about disco analysis in the future, but the topic you are being introduced to in this chapter has more to do with talking than with dancing. The critical questions in doing discourse analysis, beyond translation and textual reconstruction, are ones of interpretation. In this context, what are we to make of the story or teaching or text before us? What can we actually find out about a people by taking close, interested looks at their legends, stories, teachings, and everyday interactions?

This chapter is designed to give you an introduction to linguistic discourse analysis (LDA) and presents a preliminary analysis of one traditional teaching from a monolingual elder in the Algonquin community of Pikogan. I then present an analysis of another traditional teaching from a bilingual speaker from the same community and compare the two analyses. One of my ongoing research projects has involved collecting stories, legends, and traditional teachings in Algonquin and Ojibwe. These stories, legends, and teachings contain a wealth of information on the complexity of the language and culture in a place where Native people are still considered to be not merely speakers of their language but masters of it. What we find behind the words, stories, and teaching is information on matters of culture. The elder in the first instance, Okinawe, is recognized in the community as one who understands his dreams, visions, and teachings to be an avenue of communication between humans and the spirit world for the protection and betterment of his people. The teaching we will be exploring was initiated by Okinawe in order to put on tape some of the things that he considered important for the next generation of Anishnaabe people to know. He recorded the teaching in private, had copies made of the tape, and then distributed the tape to his children, grandchildren, and to me. Okinawe firmly believes that his culture has something of value that the young people need. I would take that a step further by saying that I believe his teaching has tremendous value for non-Aboriginal people as well.

What I would like to do, then, is introduce you to the basic methodology used in LDA and then point out a few salient features in Okinawe's teaching, with the aim of discovering and describing some of the complex discourse features available to Ojibwe speakers for transmitting matters of culture, knowledge, and wisdom. The frustrating part for me is that we will not be able to spend much time on his teaching. I leave it to you to read it through on your own, my hope being that you will come to appreciate the richness and complexity of it. It has much to teach us about life through the eyes of one who speaks his Aboriginal language exclusively, and has spent more than half his life in a traditional lifestyle before being forced to live on a reserve in the mid-1950s.

An Introduction to Linguistic Discourse Analysis

When I teach discourse analysis in my university classes, I am often confronted with the question, 'What good is this?' and 'Why are we doing this?' Some students even go so far as to say, 'We shouldn't tamper with these legends and stories, they're sacred. We shouldn't be tearing them apart bit by bit and looking at them in such detailed ways.' What I try to get across in my classes is that we are not tearing them apart or analysing them just for the sake of being analytical. By taking a detailed look at how legends, stories, and teachings are told, we have the opportunity to get inside the heads of the elders and to discover and describe how they see the world and how they can teach us, both Native and non-Native, to see the world through indigenous eyes, with a Native sensibility and intuition. In other words, we can see how elders perceive the world and how that perception is accessible to us (and to everyone) by how they talk about it.

Perhaps the best place to begin to answer these questions is with a definition of what LDA really is. In general terms it is the discovery and description of language-in-use in a variety of contexts and forms: conversation, storytelling, joking, advising, telling how to do things, and so on (Burman and Parker, 1993; Norrick, 1994; Valentine, 1995; Kinkade and Mattina, 1996). Features of LDA include: the need to distinguish between linguistic forms of utterances and the actions they perform in actual talk, such as the historical present tense (what does it *do*?); sequencing: how some features of a story relate to other features in some kind of order, for example, tense switching; and understanding discourse types, which we'll be discussing in detail in the next section.

The traditional concerns of linguistic analysis have been with the construction of the sentence (Coulthard, 1977; Freedle, 1979; Renkema, 1993; Todorov, 1990; Wardhaugh, 1993). In recent years descriptive linguistics has begun to pay attention to how sentences work in sequence to produce coherent stretches of language, an interest building upon the interdisciplinary perspective on language from anthropology, sociology, psychology and education (Atkinson and Heritage, 1984; Button and Lee, 1987; Gumperz, 1982; Moerman, 1988; Tedlock and Mannheim, 1995; Lee, 1992; Tannen, 1988, 1989). Interpretive anthropology, for example, views speakers as located within a social world and the shared worlds that emerge out of talk and conversation are continuously being created and recreated. Such interdisciplinary approaches are not merely combining the methods of, say, anthropology with linguistics, but extending the methodological boundaries to see how the issues can be transformed in theoretically interesting ways.

As for methodology, LDA aims to discover and describe as nearly as possible a complete roster of the features that contribute to the purpose of a particular discourse or stretch of talk. The basic methodology in engaging in discourse analysis includes: the isolation of language features which help the speaker to fulfil her/his communicative purpose; discovering and describing the patterns of the particular discourse type being explored; and making the connection between linguistic features and performance ones. All three aspects of this methodology will be explored further when we take a close look at Okinawe's teaching. All that concerns me at this point is that you begin to develop a sense of what is meant when I talk about LDA.[1]

Within phonology and grammar, the traditional concerns of descriptive linguistics, the labels and structure of the units are well established. At the level of discourse analysis, however, there is very little agreement between the major traditions. There are no agreed labels and few agreed structures. Most discourse linguists agree that there are four main areas of discourse study.

1. *Morphology and context*: where morphological information ties in with the structure of a discourse type – that is, particles, dubitatives, and so on;
2. *reference*: story characters, reference to others, for example, how characters are introduced in a story, in what order and how marked;
3. *structure*: differences between discourse types, for example, request structures; and
4. *linkage*: paragraph boundaries, going from one topic to another.

The way I visualize LDA, then, is as an attempt to extend the procedures and analytical categories used in descriptive linguistics beyond the unit of the sentence. The essential procedures used are: the isolation of a set of basic syntactic categories or units of discourse for analysis; the stating of a set of rules which differentiate coherent discourses from ill-formed or incoherent discourses; and taking a text and giving an analysis of all the structural features of the discourse. These basic procedures are used by the text grammarians, under which I classify Longacre and his students, as opposed to those who base their work on speech act theory. The work of the former has been mainly neglected by those approaching discourse from a multi-disciplinary perspective, while the work of the latter has been severely criticized as being fundamentally misconceived (Turner, 1976; Gardner, 1982; Levinson, 1983; van Dijk, 1997).

ASSUMPTIONS ABOUT LANGUAGE IN LINGUISTIC DISCOURSE ANALYSIS

According to most discourse linguists, we can say most about language by filtering out two different things: the decisions a speaker can make regarding what and what not to say; and the structures that are available to the speaker for implementing the results of those decisions in a way that communicates with another person (Grimes, 1975, 1978; Gavin, 1980). Grimes (1975) refers to these decisions which the speaker makes, and the relations between them, as the underlying formational structure or the semantic structure. The relation between this underlying structure and the speech forms that are uttered is called the transformation.

One assumption shared by discourse linguists is that, in everyday life, we all use different types of speech in different circumstances. A public school teacher, for example, will adopt a different kind of speech when being interviewed for a job from the one when relaxing with friends over a beer. We express most of what we say in strings of sentences, but not just random strings. There are features of language which may constrain later utterances in relation to earlier ones, and large-scale structure within which individual utterances play their parts (Grimes, 1975, 1978; Longacre, 1983). Not only do we use different types of speech in different circumstances, but we may have marked reactions when a discourse type is used inappropriately. The relevant factors in such situations are the relationships between the speaker and the one(s) being spoken to, and the nature of the message. Linguists involved in discourse studies are interested in explicating and describing discourse types; for example, if a speaker is exhorting a hearer to do something, certain discourse types or forms will be appropriate. If one is arguing, instructing, or passing on information, other types will be more fitting.

DISCOURSE TYPES

What are some examples of discourse types? Most discourse linguists agree that there are six major discourse types: narrative, procedural, hortatory, expository, argumentative, and conversation. *Narrative* discourse recounts a series of events usually ordered chronologically and in the past tense. *Procedural* discourse is designed to give instructions for accomplishing some task or achieving an objective. *Hortatory* discourse attempts to influence conduct, while *expository* discourse seeks to provide information required in particular circumstances, and often does so by providing detailed descriptions. In addition, it is designed to inform others about how and why things are the way they appear. *Argumentative* discourse tries to prove something to a hearer and tends to exhibit frequent contrast between two opposing ideas. *Conversational* discourse takes place between two or more people. Oddly, although discourse linguists express interest in this last type, most analyses are limited to the other five and rely mainly on edited texts, although most agree that attention to naturally occurring talk is lacking in the linguistic discourse analysis literature and should be pursued more fervently (Longacre, 1983, 1990; Jones, 1983; Poole, 1990).

A linguist brings his/her own distinctive mode of reasoning and perspective to bear on language. Generally speaking, the discourse linguist sees distinctiveness and contextual influence, constituency and matching of complex relations, and tries to generalize about them. Longacre (1983, 1990) insists that it is impossible to achieve a comprehensive understanding of a language without accounting for its discourse level features. He maintains that discourse analysis used to be regarded as an option for the linguist in supplementing the description of lower levels (word, phrase, clause). He contends that it is now understood by most linguists that all work on the lower levels is lacking in perspective and considered inadequate when the higher level of discourse has not been analysed. He asks, 'How can one describe the verb morphology of a language when one cannot predict where one uses a given verb form?' and 'How can one describe a transitive clause in terms of what is obligatory and what is optional when the conditions for optionality are not specified?' (1983:67). Longacre contends that the answers to these questions require a discourse perspective.[2]

In relation to the discourse analysis of narratives, for example, the linguist seeks to discover and describe how speakers sign on and sign off to their audiences, how speakers make side comments in their stories, where and how characters are introduced, how major and minor characters are differentiated, where background information most often occurs, how story action is introduced, how the end of the action is signalled, and how conclusions are accomplished. Thus we can see that the discourse linguist is seeking to explicate and describe a formula for a complete narrative, the difference between written and spoken forms, and possible options available to speakers when telling a story.

THE INTERACTIONAL NATURE OF DISCOURSE

The LDA view of context usually refers to the immediate surrounding discourse. There is, however, some redefining taking place. More emphasis is being placed on the interactional context, sometimes referred to as the ethnographic perspective (Mandelbaum, 1991). Discourse linguists are realizing that, as in the definition of context in conversation analysis, comprehensive understandings and interpretations of language-in-use are only possible when one has access to context in terms of past events, local epistemologies, and what constitutes appropriate verbal interaction in an endless variety of conversational settings and backgrounds. In that sense, a great many discourse units are now being explored. What is being explored is not so much linguistic patterns (although these are important as well for understanding language-in-use), but patterns of talk. In this sense, many kinds of discourse units have been studied in naturally occurring talk: telling about one's experiences (Jefferson, 1978; Gardner and Spielmann, 1980; Gardner, 1982; Basso, 1983; Sacks, 1992; Valentine, 1995), how people deal with ambiguity (Schegloff, 1987; Hopper, 1989), how people respond to compliments (Pomerantz, 1978), how people tease (Drew, 1987), how people offer and refuse invitations and requests (Drew, 1984; Spielmann and Chief, 1986), to name but a few.

The movement in LDA, then, is increasingly towards describing both linguistic structures and interactional contexts. It is based on the premise that language is organized interactively and is designed to be listener-sensitive. Moerman goes so far as to say:

No model of natural speech events that does not take account of the properties of ... interaction can be correct. Utterances, social actions, and the expressing of cultural themes are simultaneous and mutually constitutive ... Because conversation is a process of social interaction, the content and boundaries of its units are sometimes essentially unclear: not because of faulty analysis, but because participants are themselves centrally engaged in negotiating, interpreting, and disputing them. (1988:11)

Moerman appears to be addressing what he considers to be a deficiency in LDA by suggesting that our understanding of language must be grounded in naturally occuring talk rather than what we might think about language. His definition of context, then, is anchored by the question: Given some occurrence of talk, what do we need to know about the situation in which that talk is embedded in order to understand it? Moerman is not making an elitist claim here. Many discourse linguists recognize this deficiency quite explicitly. In *The Grammar of Discourse*, for example, Robert Longacre ends the chapter on repartee with the comment: 'All that we have written here needs eventually to be supplemented by and compared with the current research into the nature of live conversation' (1983:75).

Larry Jones, too, writes about the need for a broader linguistic vision which encompasses the social sciences: 'One of the new frontiers of linguistics, discourse analysis, is in fact a part of a larger frontier, the study of how people think and how they express their thoughts ... In exploring this new territory, the discourse linguist ... who chooses to remain close to his own linguistic ... border will be, I believe, infinitely the poorer' (1983:137).

Another linguist, Wilbur Pickering, brings the issue of interdisciplinary integration in linguistic discourse analysis to the forefront of current linguistic concern: 'While I insist that situation and culture are part of the prior context upon which given information [in discourse] may based, I freely confess that I do not know how to handle it' (1979:170).

Other discourse linguists have more recently echoed the same concern (Burman and Parker, 1993; Lee, 1993; Renkema, 1993; Fleming, 1995). '*You're So Fat!*' is intended to be one step towards what Moerman refers to as the study of 'talk-in-interaction' (1991:176) and may, in part, be seen as a response to an invitation emanating from the linguistic community.

Some Discourse Features of Okinawe's Teaching

With the above considerations in mind, I invite you to take a look at Okinawe's teaching and what he considers to be important in relation to 'What Happens in Life.' I hope that it will give us a glimpse of the eloquence, complexity, and richness of the thinking of one of the last generation of monolingual speakers in Canada.

Bimaadiziwin Ezhiseg ('*What Happens in Life*')

1. *Bimaadiziwin Ezhiseg.*
   This is what happens in life.
2. *Maawaji niitam ge-doodaman.*
   Here's the most important thing to do.
3. *Giga-manaajihaag giniiigihigoog giishpin ginwezh wii-bimaadiziyan.*
   You will respect your parents if you want to live a long life.
4. *Gaawin wiikaad giga-ashidamaasiiwag gegoon wiidamawikwaa.*
   You will never turn away from what they tell you.
5. *Misawaaj gikenimadwaa banahaagewaaj mii bezhigwan wewenda giga-doodawaag.*
   Even if you think they're off the path, still you will carefully do what you are told.
6. *Miinawaaj godag gegoon.*
   So then another thing.
7. *Gaawin wiikaad giga-majenimaasii awiyag.*
   You will never treat someone badly.
8. *Giga-gichi-inenimaa moozhag.*
   You will always think highly of her/him.
9. *Giishpin majenimaj awiyag, gwagwe-waniiken gaa-majenimaj.*
   If someone treats you badly, try and forget it.
10. *Giishpin egaa waniiken awiyag e-majenimaj, mii ihimaa wejiseg nisidiwin.*
    If you don't forget it when someone treats you badly, that's where murder comes from.

11. *Gaawin dash ginwezh giga-bimaadizisii, gii-nisaj awiyag goonigoj giin giga-nisigoo.*
    You won't live long, you'll kill someone or someone will kill you.
12. *Miinawaaj godag gegoon.*
    So then another thing.
13. *Gaawin wiikaad ozaamikaaken gaa-izhi-odaminonaaniwag.*
    Don't spend all your time where there's playing.
14. *Ozaam gichi-zanagan naanigodin awiyag naanigodin.*
    Because sometimes it's hard for someone to get away from something.
15. *Naanigodin opitahogoon.*
    Sometimes someone will get hurt.
16. *Mii ge-ani-izhi-aakozij.*
    So she/he will get sick.
17. *Gegapich gadaa-nibo e-gii-ozhigoshig.*
    After a while she/he will die.
18. *Miinawaaj godag gegoon.*
    So then another thing.
19. *Gaawin izhaaken gaa-izhi-minikwaaniwag ozaam mii gegiin ke-izhi-minikweyan.*
    Don't go where there's drinking because you, too, will drink.
20. *Gegapiich giga-giiwashkwebii gegiin.*
    After a while you, too, will be drunk.
21. *Gegapiich gaawin giga-gikendasiin aadi enakamigiziyan.*
    After a while you won't know what you're doing.
22. *Ashij gaawin giga-gikendasiin wegonen gaa-minikweyan, goonigoj anooj gegoon giga-minikwe.*
    And you won't know what you're drinking or you'll drink something else.
23. *Mii dash ge-izhi-bichibowan goonigoj giga-nisigoo.*
    So then you'll poison yourself or you will be killed.
24. *Gaawin megaa awiiyag ogikendasiin enakamigizij e-giiwashkwebiij.*
    Because, of course, a person doesn't know what she/he is doing when she/he is drunk.
25. *Miinawaaj godag gegoon.*
    So then another thing.
26. *Gaawin babaamibizowan gidoodaabaan e-gichi-majigiizhigag, egaa minwaashig miikana ozaam giga-oji-bekakanawehe.*
    Don't drive around in your car when it's a bad day because you will drive off the road.

27. *Mii dash ge-izhi-ozhigoshiniyan goonigoj giga-abajishin.*
So then you will get hurt or you will have an accident.
28. *Giga-nibonan dash.*
So then you will die.
29. *Miinawaaj godag gegoon.*
So then another thing.
30. *Gaa-mazinaateseg noodaagwachigan gaawin apichi minwaashisinoon abinoojiizh giji-gizhigaabadag anooj gegoon, gaa-inaagwag gaa-babashkiz-idowaaj ashij gimoodiwinniig.*
It's not very good for a child to be watching just anything on TV that appears [like] violence and thieves.
31. *Gii-waabag abinoojiizh mii mayaa gewiin gaa-gwagwe-inakamigizij.*
That child will try to act like the one she/he sees.
32. *Gegapiich gadaa-maajitaa giji-gwagwe-gimoodij.*
After a while she/he will try to steal.
33. *Gegapiich oga-nisaan awiyan.*
After a while she/he will kill someone.
34. *Miinawaaj godag gegoon.*
So then another thing.
35. *Gaawin gabaashimoken giiwashkwebiiyan.*
Never swim when you're drunk.
36. *Apiich bakobiiyan giiwashkwebiiyan mii ge-izhi-opinigowan.*
When swimming while drunk you will get cramps.
37. *Apiich dakaabaaweyan mii ge-izhi-nisaabaaweyan, mii giji-ishkwaa-bimaadiziyan.*
When you go under you will drown, then your life will be over.
38. *Miinawaaj godag gegoon.*
So then another thing.
39. *Gaawin wiikaad wiibaj giga-bimaadagaakosii e-dagwaagig.*
Never walk on the ice in the fall [too quickly].
40. *Baanimaa gechinaaj minosej mikwamii.*
You must be sure that the ice is strong.
41. *Mii bezhigwan e-ziigwag maanaadizi nanigodin mikwamii.*
Same thing in the spring, sometimes the ice is bad.
42. *Moozhag mitig giga-dakonaan bimaadagaakowan.*
Always poke the ice first with a stick.
43. *Mii dash ihi ge-maajihigowan oji-dwaashiniyan.*
So then you won't fall through the ice.
44. *Miinawaaj godag gegoon.*
So then another thing.

45. *Gaawin wiikaad mosawendaken giji-gichi-ozhooniyaamiyan.*
Never be too greedy to have lots of money.

46. *Giishpin gichi-ozhooniyaamiyan, gakina gegoon giga-inakamigiz, goonigoj gegoon giga-wanaajihigon.*
If you have a lot of money you'll want to do everything or something will destroy [ruin] you.

47. *Goonigoj giga-nisigoo goonigoj giga-nisigon ishkodewaaboo.*
Or you will be killed or you'll be killed by fire-water.

48. *Miinawaaj godag gegoon.*
So then another thing.

49. *Ndawimineyan gaawin aabajitooken e-makadewekag biizikawaagan.*
Never wear a black coat when you're picking berries.

50. *Naniizaanizi makwa giji-mikanik.*
It's dangerous, a bear may find you.

51. *Nawaj minose e-mikwaag goonigoj e-waabag.*
It's better to wear a red or white coat.

52. *Ashij gaawin zagime giga-bamenimigosii.*
Also, the mosquitos won't bother you.

53. *Miinawaaj godag gegoon.*
So then another thing.

54. *Wanishiniyan gaawin zegiziken.*
Don't get scared when you're lost [in the bush].

55. *Giishpin zegiziyan, gaawin giga-gikendasiin aadi ge-inakamigiziyan, giji-gii-mikaman aadi ge-izhi-giiweyan.*
If you're scared you won't know what you're doing in order to find your way home.

56. *Gegapiich bizhishig giga-bimibatoo.*
After a while you'll just be running around.

57. *Newad giga-bookogaadeshin bagishiniyan.*
Maybe you'll fall and break your leg.

58. *Newad giga-bookonikeshin goonigoj gishkiizhig giga-wanaajitoon.*
Maybe you'll break your arm or you'll lose your eyes.

59. *Miinawaaj godag gegoon.*
So then another thing.

60. *Gaawin miijiken awesiiz obimidem agwaajiig e-dakaayaag.*
Don't eat animal grease when you're outside where it's cold.

61. *Giishpin miijiyan awesiiz obimidem mii ge-izhi-mashkawadig gigondashk-waakaag.*
If you eat animal grease it will freeze in your throat.

62. *Mii dash ge-izhi-egaa-gashkitoowan giji-neseyan.*

So then you won't be able to breathe.
63. *Miinawaaj godag gegoon.*
So then another thing.
64. *Gaawin wiikaad giga-maanenimaasii awesiiz anishaa giji-nanekaajihaj.*
Never treat an animal badly just for the fun of it to get it angry.
65. *Ogikendaan megaa maanenimaj awesiiz.*
Because of course the animal knows what you're doing.
66. *Naanigodin giga-mamidawinishahog goonigoj giga-nisik.*
Sometimes you'll be injured or she/he will kill you.
67. *Gekwaan mooz, makwa goonigoj.*
A moose or maybe a bear.
68. *Mii dash ishkwaayaag gegoon.*
So then the final thing.
69. *Aabadan ayamihewin ikidonaaniwan.*
It is said that prayer is useful/appropriate.
70. *Maamidonendaman baanimaa gwayak e-bimaadiziyan ohomaa akiikaag.*
Remember that you should live a straight life on this earth.
71. *Mii baanimaa ge-waabamaj Gizhe-Manidoo.*
So then you will see the Creator.

First, I want to point out some basic discourse features of this teaching. As I mentioned earlier, LDA is concerned with language-in-use in a variety of contexts and forms. It aims to discover and describe as nearly as possible a complete roster of the features that contribute to the purpose of a particular discourse or talk. One of the more noticeable discourse features that Okinawe uses is a technique for dividing his teaching into manageable chunks for the listener. The most common device for this purpose is his use of the phrase *Miinawaaj godag gegoon* (So then another thing). If we had the time to examine hundreds of stories, legends, and traditional teachings, we could compare the discourse features in a variety of different discourse genres and among different speakers. In this way, we could begin to see the techniques available to and used by monolingual speakers of the Algonquin dialect of Ojibwe for guiding their listeners through their respective stories and teachings. That, unfortunately, is beyond the scope of this chapter, although we will be comparing some of the features of Okinawe's teaching with those of another speaker in the next section.

Two elements of Okinawe's teaching deal with content and the interaction of discourse features and what, specifically, is being taught. At first glance, this teaching seems quite disjointed. The introductory part of the teaching in lines 1–11 and the concluding lines 68–71 seem to be of a qualitatively different nature from the middle portion. Over the years, as I had the opportunity to listen to dozens of different traditional teachings by a variety of elders, I began to see a pattern emerge which suggested that the most important parts of a particular teaching occur at the beginning and end. The middle portions are meant to be heard as grounded in the beginning and end of the discourse. This kind of structure, used with hortatory discourse such as traditional teachings, while used subconsciously by Ojibwe speakers, attests to the richness and complexity of both the Ojibwe language and traditional ways of thinking embodied in the minds of monolingual-speaking elders.

Being a non-cultural member, one of the techniques I use to understand Aboriginal stories, legends, and teachings is to explore those things that strike me as different from my own tradition. One of the things that really jumped out at me in Okinawe's teaching were the linkages between his specific teachings and what will happen if his teachings are not followed. Initially his links seem a bit morbid, usually ending with something like 'If you don't follow this teaching, you will die,' or 'You will be killed or you will kill someone.' We can see instances of this linkage of teaching and the consequences of not paying attention to the teaching in lines 10–11, 17, 23, 28, 33, 37, 47, and 66. Of the twelve components of Okinawe's teaching that are bounded by the opening and closing sections, all twelve end with the same conclusion that one faces imminent death or serious injury if one fails to attend to what is being said.

Taking a deeper look, however, and keeping in mind the word that Okinawe uses a few times in his teaching, *bimaadiziwin*, we can understand what he is trying to do from a distinctly Ojibwe point of view. *Bimaadiziwin* is virtually impossible to translate accurately into English. Each time I asked bilingual Anishnaabe people for a translation, they seemed to agonize over the problem, and every translation was a bit different. There are, however, some common themes that come through in the translation, revolving around such things as, 'a worthwhile life,' 'a long, fulfilling life,' 'our walk in life,' 'walking the straight path in this life,' and so on. While no single translation was ever agreed upon, and while most of the people I asked were not happy with their own translation, the picture that emerges of *bimaadiziwin* is one which is reflected in Okinawe's use of the term. And that, perhaps, is the best way to try to understand the concept, by how it is so naturally used by a monolingual speaker of the language.

From that perspective, then, Okinawe's links between teaching and *bimaadiziwin* are not morbid at all. They are designed to impress on the listener the great importance of *bimaadiziwin* – living a long, fruitful life in communion with family, community, other-than-human persons, the environment, the Creator and the spirit world – and the responsibility of using the gifts that we are given in the best way that we can. It would not be too strong a statement to say that the central goal of life for Algonquin people is expressed by the term *bimaadiziwin* – life in the fullest sense, including longevity, health, and freedom from misfortune. Achieving *bimaadiziwin* involves not only the help of the Creator and other people, but also the help of other-than-human persons as well as one's own efforts.

The subject matter of Okinawe's teaching is also interesting. In the first two sections (lines 1–11), he speaks in relatively broad terms about respecting your parents and other people. Then in section three (lines 12–17) he begins to get specific by talking about the category-bound activity of playing (in this context a reference to sports tournaments). In section four it appears that he reverts back to speaking in quite general terms about the dangers of drinking, but this, too, is usually talked about as a category-bound activity and when juxtaposed with the previous section seems to be a natural fit with the unfolding discourse. Then in sections five through thirteen (lines 25–67) he continues on with teaching grounded in the concept of *bimaadiziwin*. Most of this portion takes us back to one of the common complainable states of affairs that we explored earlier: that the younger generation is lacking in bush survival skills (lines 34–9; 48–67), something which is still considered to be extremely important in the minds of the elders. We thus have a clearly defined discourse structure of generic-specific-generic in this teaching. Okinawe begins the teaching with relatively universal maxims about respecting one's parents and respecting other people, then moves into quite specific and context-bound teachings in lines 12–67, and back to a general teaching about the importance of prayer and trusting the Creator in lines 68–71. Our task in the next section, then, will be to compare this teaching with at least one other in order to gain a sense of what may be conventionalized features of hortatory and expository discourse in the Algonquin dialect of Ojibwe.[3]

Comparison of Hortatory and Expository Discourses

Ideally, anyone engaging in discourse analysis should have access to a variety of tapes and texts which capture the essence of naturally occur-

Linguistic Discourse Analysis   161

ring talk. For our purposes in this section, recall that expository discourse provides answers or explanations to real or imagined questions and represents a speaker's way of presenting facts, explaining what something means, how something works, or why it is important. Hortatory discourse, such as Okinawe's teaching on 'What Happens in Life,' is designed to tell young people how to live properly. Before we take a comparative look at hortatory and expository discourse in Ojibwe, read through the following teaching on prayer. The speaker in this instance, Alice Mowatt-Kistabish from the community of Pikogan, made this recording in the fall of 1983.

Ayamihewin E-mikoojigaadeg (*'Talking about Prayer'*)

1. *Wegonen ge-mikoodaamaan noogom ayamihewin, wegonen weji ayami-heyaan niin.*
   What I will talk about now is prayer, why I pray.
2. *Nidayamihe ako apiich gegoon wii-nadotamaayaan ashij majendamaan*
   I usually pray when I want to hear something and when I am sad
3. *nigad-ayamihe ashij miigwech giji-inag sa gaa-Dibenimiyag*
   I will pray and to say thank you to the Creator
4. *gegoonni e-gii-miinizhij goonigoj miigwech giji-inenimag*
   for something that He gave me or thank you that He thinks about
5. *e-gii-wiisiniyaan, anooj igoj.*
   what I should eat, or whatever.
6. *Ashij ayamihewin baanimaa gii-ganawendamaan e-bimaadiziyaan.*
   And it's important to keep praying while I am alive.
7. *Mii ihiwe ge-waabadahigoowaan giji-bimaadiziyaan sa, niigaan giji-bimaadiziyaan.*
   So that I will be shown how to live in order that I may live right.
8. *Nigii-gikendaan egii-boonitaawaan sa egaa babisiskendamaan ayami-hewin.*
   I knew when I stopped that I shouldn't ignore prayer.
9. *Nidinendaanaaban sa gaawin maamakaaj ga-gichi-ayamihesii debinaak bimaadiziwin, nidinendaanaabaan.*
   I thought that it wasn't necessary to pray in order to live, I thought.
10. *Gii-majise gaa-ako-miinawaaj-bi-giiweyaan eshkam ani-minose gegoon.*
    Things went wrong since I came back home, now things are getting better.
11. *Ganabaj dash nidinendaan, 'Dibahigeyan awiyag e-gizhigaabamik,*
    Maybe then, I think, 'Someone is watching over me

12. *giga-minose giji-bimoseyan sa niigaan,' nidinendaan.*
it will go well for you in order to live right,' I think.

13. *Naanigodin dash gigad-ayamihe, giga-nda-nadotimaa gegoon.*
Sometimes then you will pray, you will ask for something.

14. *Nidikidonaaban dash apiich ako ayamiheyaan ako*
I was saying then when you pray habitually

15. *naanigodin gaawin gi-nadotaagosii.*
sometimes you are not heard.

16. *Nidinendaan dash ako naanigodin mayaa sa goj niwebinigoo,*
I often think that sometimes I am truly rejected,

17. *nidinendaan sa ako.*
that's what I usually think.

18. *Goonigoj nimajendaan sa ezhiseg egaa awiyag e-ndotawizhij enenda-maan.*
Or I am really unhappy when somebody doesn't listen to what I think.

19. *Gaawin dash misawaaj nidaanawenjigesii miinawaaj giji-ayamiheyaan.*
But then when I pray I am no longer discouraged.

20. *Naanigodin ako e-doodamaan giji-wiijihigoowaan sa gegoon giji-ayami-heyaan.*
Sometimes it happens that it really helps me when I pray.

21. *Mii sa ako enendamaan.*
So that's what I usually think.

22. *Newad niin eta gaa-inendamaan goonigoj mii sa ezhi-waabadamaan*
Maybe I only think about it or that's what I see

23. *niin giji-wiidookaagoowaan nidayamihewin.*
in order that I may be helped by my faith.

24. *Misawaaj igoj gaawin ninadotaagosii nidinendaan sa.*
Even when I think that I'm not being heard.

25. *Gaawin sa misawaaj giga-aanawenjigesii giji-ayamiheyan.*
Even when you are too discouraged to pray.

26. *Ashij dash nidinendaan abinoojiizhag giga-gichi-wiijihigoog.*
And then I think how children will really help you.

27. *Wiinawaa mii mayaa bezhigwan aajeniig.*
They are just like angels.

28. *Apiich zegiziyaan goonigoj gotaajiyaan, nidinendaan ako dewag abinooji-izhag*
When I am scared or afraid I usually think of my kids

29. *giji-wiidookawizhiwaaj, egaa giji-gotaajiyaan, egaa giji-zegiziyaan.*
how they help me not to be afraid, not to be scared.

30. *Moozhag nigii-dazhiike niin eta, mii dash ako enendamaan abinoojiizhag ako niwiidookaagoog nidinendaan.*
   Often I stay [am] alone, so that's when I usually think, that my children help me.

I want to begin by comparing some of the surface structure features of this teaching with those we found earlier in Okinawe's teaching. I want to focus on discourse features rather than communicative purpose for two reasons: in listening to elders tell stories and give teachings, I found that such discourse could represent more than one communicative purpose; and I want to develop a detailed understanding of some of the salient features of hortatory and expository discourse in order to understand better how they work. In expository discourse, a speaker's intention may be multi-faceted; it may be to explain and to prove. In hortatory discourse, a speaker's purpose is to influence or change ideas or behaviour. Certainly Okinawe's teaching represents this kind of communicative purpose. Okinawe's teaching is actually a mitigated, or softened, kind of exhortation designed to influence the thinking and behaviour of the younger generation (his primary audience). And when the speaker's intention is mainly to exhort and persuade, one can begin to see some of the persuasive strategies available to Ojibwe speakers for doing just that. In the case of 'What Happens in Life,' one such device is the linkage Okinawe creates between what one *ought* to do and the consequences of not doing it.

The tone of the teaching about prayer seems to be substantively different than Okinawe's teaching. Here there is little or no exhortation, no sense of trying to persuade the listener to change her/his thinking or behaviour. In that sense, Alice Mowatt-Kistabish's intention appears to be more to explain rather than to persuade, whereas Okinawe attempts both, with heavy emphasis on the latter. This teaching is more of a self-contained unit focusing on one ongoing topic, the importance of prayer in the speaker's life. Okinawe's teaching ranges over a broad spectrum of topics with a number of well-defined units and clear boundaries. Further, Okinawe's teaching employs discourse features designed to orient the listener to the hortatory (persuasive) nature of his teaching. As we saw earlier, he uses the second person (you) frequently, imploring the listener to think carefully about what is being taught with the hope that the listener will take the teaching to heart and put it into practice in everyday life.

There are, however, some structural similarities between these two discourse types. Both teachings begin with a conventionalized sign-on designed to orient the listeners to what is going to be talked about. In 'What Happens in Life,' Okinawe begins his teaching with the utterance *Bimaadiziwin Ezhiseg* ([This is] what happens in life), and Alice orients her listeners with a similar utterance, *Wegonen ge-mikoodaamaan noogom ayamihewin, wegonen weji ayamiheyaan niin* (What I will talk about now is prayer [and] why I pray). While Okinawe uses the second person regularly, Alice's discourse uses the first person most often, with the exception of lines 13–15 and 25. We noted earlier that Okinawe's teaching is replete with a topic-boundary utterance, *Miinawaaj dash godag gegoon* (So then another thing). Alice's teaching doesn't have such clearly defined discourse boundaries. In fact, she doesn't use that phrase or any of its variations at all. While one might argue that the teaching on prayer is not designed to teach listeners what happens in life, there are some parallel discourse boundary utterances which point to the main difference in communicative purpose between the two teachings. One device that she does employ is embodied in the utterances *nidinendaan sa ako* (that's what I usually think) and *Mii sa ako enendamaan* (So that's what I usually think). These phrases play a similar role to Okinawe's *Miinawaaj dash godag gegoon* in that they orient listeners to the flow of the teaching and the movement from point to point. It may be that Okinawe's teaching is necessarily more structured because of the complexity of the teaching and the nature of the discourse type itself, while Alice's exposition focuses almost exclusively on one topic, prayer, until the very end (lines 26–30) when she makes an interesting link between prayer and children.

Let us explore that linkage for a moment. We noticed earlier that Okinawe makes some clear linkages with what he is teaching in relation to the concept of *bimaadiziwin*. In Alice's discourse she, too, makes some interesting links, particularly with *abinoojiizhag* (children). In fact, she ends her teaching with that very explicit link (lines 26–30).

What, exactly, is the nature of the link that she is making between prayer and children? I'm not sure. But I did talk to a number of elders about this particular linkage and the consensus seems to be as follows. The topic focuses on prayer and implies a certain kind of relationship between human beings and the Creator. In a very real sense, parents are implicated in a similar relationship with their children. The Creator is our parent, one who watches over us and interacts with us in our everyday lives. Parents, too, fulfil a similar role with their children, at least ideally. The teaching thus acts as a kind of living parable. It tells us something about how much the Creator cares for us and loves us and assures us we can gain a practical sense of this caring by monitoring our own love and concern for our children. Note, too, that there is a reciprocity to the relationship. Children are portrayed in this teaching as being helpers at times in line 26, *Ashij dash nidinendaan abinoojiizhag giga-gichi-wiijihigoog* (And then I think how children will really help you). As a corollary to that, Alice uses an analogy with angels in line 27, *Wiinawaa mii mayaa bezhigwan aajeniig* (They are just like angels). What such teaching tells us, according to the elders I spoke with, goes beyond human relationships to the very nature of our relationship with the Creator. Again we see how Ojibwe people create and sustain their social world by talking about it, and how that talk opens up a window on the psyche and thinking of a people.

Conclusion

Much more could be said about the richness and complexity of the two teachings we explored in this chapter. This is merely an introduction to linguistic discourse analysis, and my main purpose is to nudge you in the direction of looking for discourse patterns and observe how the structure of discourse can teach us much about Ojibwe-specific ways of thinking, doing things, relationships, and perceiving the world.

The analysis of naturally occurring stories, legends, and teachings, the analysis of discourse, can open up a world of appreciation of and learning from the elders. By exploring some of the salient discourse features of Okinawe's teaching on 'What Happens in Life' and Alice's teaching on prayer, we realize that these are no mere pie-in-the-sky teachings but down-to-earth expressions of how Anishnaabe elders view the human condition and what our responsibilities and privileges are as we walk this earth, regardless of an individual's specific tradition. This kind of knowledge is meant to be earned, it is not something that can be learned from a book or even from reading this book. While living in the community of Pikogan the elders in their kind and patient way would teach by example that it takes hard work, perseverance, a firm belief in *bimaadizi-win* and a faith in the Creator who gives us the gift of life. By giving their teachings to others, others are able to keep it alive.

9

'The Bear Facts': Using Discourse Analysis to Understand Ojibwe Cosmology

While living in Pikogan I often wondered at the different realities engulfing me. My own world seemed so at odds with the world of Anishnaabe people with whom I was becoming intricately connected. The whole area of dreams and visions, for example, created a stark contrast with my own thinking developed in the incubator of western rationalism. It was not merely in the area of competing cosmologies, though, that I felt this stark contrast. It also revolved around everyday life and the integration of one reality (and its expectations) with another.

Not long after moving to Pikogan I was invited to go moose hunting with a man my age and his girlfriend. He told me that we would canoe down the river and stay in a nice cabin located on his father's hunting grounds. After a few hours of paddling, I asked, 'Are we almost there?' (I used to scold my own kids for asking that question when we were travelling). He kept telling me, 'It won't be long.' Seven hours later, when I was just about to request that I be thrown overboard and put out of my misery, we arrived at the 'nice' cabin on the riverbank. Cabin is not the word that I would have used to describe the structure where we would be staying. It was about the size of an outhouse and had barely enough room for one small single bed. Needless to say, my friend and his girlfriend took the bed, and I unfurled my sleeping bag under the bed. 'Hmmm, this could be interesting,' I remember thinking as we turned in for the night. For whatever reason, I had packed a battery-operated electronic baseball game in my knapsack and so I pulled it out and asked my friend if he wanted to give it a try. I'll never forget that night. Here I was crammed under the bed in total darkness, my body wracked by the pain of paddling the canoe most of the day, trying to communicate with my less-than-proficient competency in the Native language and wondering what the hell I had gotten myself into! My thoughts were disrupted by the electronic pings emanating from the baseball game my friend was now playing in the dark. The strangeness of that cross-cultural scene (from my non-Native perspective at the time) stays with me to this day and helps to set the tone for the dream stories we will be examining below.

This chapter explores teachings about bear dreams and lucky dreams with an interest in discovering and describing some of the performative features of Ojibwe narrative and expository discourse.[1] Careful attention to the features of spoken discourse sheds light on what at first appears to be common knowledge but in the final analysis reveals something previously unexplored about the nature of Ojibwe ethnography of speaking (Spielmann and Chief, 1986; Spielmann, 1987).[2] When these features are explored in the context of teachings about bear dreams and lucky dreams and then compared with teachings about warning animals and dream visitors in a related dialect (Odawa), these teachings enable us to understand better the relationships between performative features of Algonquian discourse, culture-specific techniques of transmitting cultural knowledge, and Ojibwe cosmology.

Spirituality and Ojibwe Reality

It may sound strange, but in the eleven years I spent in Pikogan, and in the years since, I have rarely met a Native person who does not believe in the Creator. And not just a belief in the existence of the Creator, but a belief that the Creator interacts with people in their everyday lives through dreams and visions, spirit visitors, circumstances, and the teachings of the elders. That is not to say that all Native people believe in God or the spirit world – I imagine one might encounter those who do not – but I have yet to meet very many of them. Compare that to non-Native culture, where a common question is, 'Do you believe in God?'

Spirituality underlies every aspect of Native ethics and behaviour, so it is essential to understand that fact as one seeks to demystify the Native perspective on life. Prayer and the exercise of spiritual power is still an important aspect of Ojibwe life and society. Healings, dreams, and visions are of vital importance in the Native community. Dreams and visions are seen as signs of spiritual power and the presence of the Creator. In fact, one of the ways people in the community talk about a foolish person or one who is seen as wasting his life is 'One who doesn't pray,' or 'One who doesn't follow the path of the Creator.'

I agree wholeheartedly with James Dumont when he suggests that perhaps the most fundamental shortcoming of the Euro-Canadian perspective on Aboriginal peoples and traditions is in failing to appreciate the centrality and the all-encompassing nature of spirituality. He writes:

Where the European-based view of the metaphysical remains grounded in a specifically-defined *rationalism* and supported by the *scientific method*, Aboriginal views share the feature of being enmeshed in mythological and spiritual beliefs. Aboriginal world views throughout the Americas generally share the theme that life is circular and governed by spiritual beginnings, spirit-centred reality and spiritual vision and destiny. None of the activities of most Aboriginal people today are carried out without the acknowledged primary place of the spiritual aspect of "self" and the spiritualization of reality. No actions are carried out independently of spirit-influence, nor are they separate from a collective whole. For most Aboriginal people today, as in the past, the *spirit* is the motivator of the individual and of the collective, and is central to the understanding of the culture and history of the people. (1993:9)

In his article 'Journey to Daylight Land' (1992), Dumont talks about the Native way of seeing the world as a primal vision that is unique to Native people, their cultures, and their ways of perceiving the world around us. He attempts to elucidate the nature of this vision and to show how Native people see the world in a special way. Dumont describes this way of seeing as a holistic vision, one that is all-encompassing in nature. Because of this way of seeing, Native people must be understood within their own cultural context and on the basis of their own unique world view. He continues:

Aboriginal traditions in the Americas share the belief that human beings are motivated by spirit; he/she is a 'spirit-walking-through-this-world.' As Aboriginal people we regard ourselves as being grounded in a strong sense of being spiritually connected with the Creator and the spirit world, and we recognize our cultures as being spiritually-based. Native Studies scholars have tried to define such concepts as *manido, orenda,* and *wakan* in the Anishnaabe, Iroquoian and Siouan traditions, respectively. (1992:9–10)

In portraying Aboriginal peoples and traditions as being spiritually based. I do not intend to imply that European-based (and other) traditions around the world are merely secular or pay no attention to the metaphysical. Every tradition has its own myths, legends, and stories which relate to the spiritual or metaphysical. My point is this: in the context of the Americas, I believe that indigenous traditions do offer a cultural critique of western rationalism. Is there perhaps something that can be learned from Aboriginal traditions? I invite you to keep an open mind as we explore these issues and themes which I see as fundamental to people indigenous to the Americas.

DREAMS AND VISIONS

Everybody dreams, no matter what culture they belong to or what they believe, but how people interpret their dreams depends greatly on what they believe. At Pikogan, for example, there is a strong belief that the Creator uses dreams to communicate with people, to warn them about possible misfortune, to help people make important decisions, to know where to go to find game when hunting, and so on (Albert Mowatt, personal communication). People would tell us their dreams regularly and matter of factly, as if to say, 'Of course it's the Creator communicating with us. What's so strange about that?' One very strong tradition at Pikogan is dreaming about a bear. Many of the elders believe that the bear is sent as a dream visitor to warn people about possible misfortune.[3] The elders at Pikogan would teach us about the importance of dreaming about a bear by regularly calling to tell us they had had such a dream the night before. Sometimes we would be warned not to drive on the highway for the next three days because the elder had dreamt about a bear on the side of the road. One time an elder told us about a dream where a mother bear was playing with her cubs and the mother bear fell down and was hurt. The elder said, 'Watch. Within three days something bad is going to happen.' The next day her daughter, who is a teacher at the community school, was out at recess with her Grade 4 students when she slipped and broke her ankle. When we saw the elder the next day she said, '*Ginisidotan naa?*' ('Do you understand?'). My daughter, the teacher, is like a mother bear to her students, who are like cubs.' It made sense and eventually we began to believe that these elders were tuned into something that escaped us.[4]

From the perspective of the elders, there exists a very fuzzy boundary between the natural and the supernatural (Spielmann, 1993b). In the minds of most people I know at Pikogan, everything that happens, including dreams, visions, dream visitors, and warnings, are all part of the natural. Animals who are sent to visit people in dreams or visions are not seen as somehow beneath human beings but are considered to be other-than-human persons and messengers from the Creator. Most people at Pikogan seem to experience something profound in their contact with animals, either in the bush or in dreams and visions. For them, the prime means of access to personal knowledge and spiritual awareness seems to be through dreams and visions. Most, if not all, people at Pikogan are motivated and directed by their dreams as a part of their everyday experience. That is just the way it is and the way it has been for thousands of years.

Dreaming about a Bear in Ojibwe Cosmology

What we are dealing with in these instances, however, are not specifically dream recountings, but a story and two separate but related aphorisms about bear-dream accounts and lucky dreams. In the community of Pikogan, a commonplace conversational activity is telling stories and listening to them. Here we have a series comprising a story and related teachings told contiguously. The storyteller, Mrs Anna Mowatt, is recognized as an elder in the community and is one who understands her dreams to be an avenue of communication between humans and the spirit world. Her stories are presented immediately below and the reader is encouraged to examine them carefully before proceeding to the analysis.

'Dreaming about a Bear Long Ago'

1. *Makwa e-aadisookanaaganiwij.*
   The story is told of the bear.
2. *Gichi-weshkaj-gookom gii-wiidamaage egaa e-minwaashig makwa bawaanaj.*
   A really old woman told about how it's not good to dream of a bear.
3. *Noopimig dazhiikewaagoban weshkaj-gookom ashij idash naabe ashij owii-digemaaganan ahawe naabe.*
   A long time ago an old woman and her man were staying in the bush.
4. *Gegapiich nigodin e-gizhebaawagag ikido ahawe naabe, 'oo, nigichi-min-wendan e-gizhebaawagag.*
   After a while one morning the man said, 'Oh, I'm really happy this morning.
5. *Makwa nibawaanaa,' ikido ahawe naabe.*
   I dreamed about a bear.'

6. *'Oo,' ikido dash gookom.*
   'Oh,' says the old woman.
7. *'Giga-wii-wiisin ihi gaa-inaabadaman. Gaawin minwaashisinoon gaa-bawaanaaj makwa,' ikido ahawe gichi-gookom.*
   'You will be hungry because of that dream. It's not good to dream about a bear,' that old woman says.
8. *'Aan dash wiin ihi?' ikido dash ahawe naabe.*
   'Why's that?' the man then says.
9. *Miinawaj idash ikido ahawe gichi-gookom, 'Gigikendaan naa?*
   Again then that woman says, 'Don't you know?
10. *Makwa gaawin wiisinisii gabe-biboon.*
    The Bear doesn't eat all winter.
11. *Mii eta nibaa.*
    She/he only sleeps.
12. *Mii dash ihi gaa-oji-egaa-minwaashig makwa bawaanaaj.'*
    So then that's why it's not good to dream about a bear.'
13. *Naabe dash wiin ahawe ikido, 'E-bawaanag makwa, nigichi-babeweyaa-badaan, nidinendaanaaban,' ikido ahawe naabe.*
    So then that man says, 'I thought when I dreamed about a bear that it was a lucky dream,' that man says.
14. *Gookom dash gii-wiidamaage, 'Gaawin minwaashisinoon e-bawaanaagani-wij makwa.*
    So the old woman tells him, 'It's not good to dream about a bear.
15. *Gimasagwaabadaan ihi gaa-inaabadaman.*
    It was an unlucky dream when you dreamed it.
16. *Giga-bakade naage, giga-gichi-wii-wiisin naage,' gii-ikido ahawe gookom.*
    You will be starving later. You will really be hungry later.' That's what that old woman said.

'Dreaming about a Bear Today'

1. *Ogaazhigag idash.*
   So then today.
2. *Mii giiyaabaj ezhiseg bawaanaaj makwa.*
   This is what happens when someone dreams about a bear.
3. *Giishpin makwa inaabadaman gigichi-masagwaabadaan ihi gaa-inaabada-man.*
   If you dream about a bear it will really be unlucky that you dreamed it.
4. *Gegoon giga-izhi-majise.*
   Something bad will happen to you.

5. *Goonimaa ogaazhigag, goonimaa waabag, goonimaa bezhigo dawateyaan.*
   Maybe today, maybe tomorrow, maybe in one week.
6. *Giga-gichi-majise gaa-inaabadaman makwa bawaanaj.*
   Something will go wrong for you if you dream about a bear.
7. *Mii giiyaabaj noogom ezhi-miikimoomagag ihi inaabadaman.*
   That's the way it still works [today] when you dream about her/
   him.
8. *Gigichi-masagwaabadaan makwa bawaanaj.*
   It's really unlucky when you dream about her/him.
9. *Goonimaa gaawin giga-mikasiin miikimowin.*
   Maybe you won't be able to find a job.
10. *Goonimaa giga-wanitoon ihiwe gimiikimowin.*
    Maybe it will go bad for you on the road in your car.
11. *Goonimaa giga-aakozinan.*
    Maybe you will get sick.
12. *Goonimaa miikanakaag gadaa-majise odaabaan bimibizowan.*
    Maybe something bad will happen to you on the road when you're
    driving around.
13. *Gegoon sa igoj giga-majise giishpin bawaanaj makwa.*
    Something bad will happen to you if you dream about a bear.
14. *Goonimaa gaawin gadaa-dagwasinoon debwe ge-miijiyan, anooj igoj
    gegoon gadaa-izhi-majise bawaanaj makwa.*
    Maybe you won't have anything to eat, something will go wrong
    when you dream about a bear.
15. *Mii giiyaabaj noogom ezhi-miikimoomagag ihiwedi makwa bawaanaj.*
    That's how it still works when you dream about a bear.
16. *Debwe igoj gekwaan gaawin anishaa ikidonaaniwasinoon gaa-inweyaan,
    mayaa igoj debwe igoj ihi ikidonaaniwan ihi inaaniwag.*
    It's true, I'm not just saying this for fun, this has been said [known]
    for a long time.
17. *Giishpin naagajitoowan ihiwedi giga-waabadaan, giga-debwetaan dash
    naage apiich gikendaman wegonen ihi weji-inaabadaman.*
    If you look carefully you will see it, you will believe it and then later
    you will know why you dreamed it.

'Lucky Dreams'

1. *Ohowedi dash, miinawaj godag, giishpin inaabadaman e-nibaayaan.*
   This one then is another, if I dream while I am sleeping.
2. *Nimikaan gegoon, gichi-weshaj gegoon, gonimaa igoj azhishkiikaag nimi-*

kaan gegoon, inaabadamaan, ni-gichi-minwaabadaan ihi gaa-inaabad-
amaan.
I find something, something old, maybe in the dirt I find it while I'm
dreaming, that's a really good dream.

3. *Mii bezhigwan, gichi-weshkaj miigiwaam nimikaan noopimig gaa-dazhii-*
   kaaniwag inaabadamaan, gichi-minwaashin ihi gaa-inaabadamaan.
   The same way, I found a really old house to stay in the bush once
   when I was dreaming, that was a really good dream.

4. *Mii bezhigwan nimikaan gichi-weshkaj onaaganan goonimaa gichi-weshkaj*
   akikwag nimikawaag inaabadaman, gichi-minwaashin ihi gaa-inaabada-
   man.
   Then I found some really old dishes or old buckets I found, it was
   good that I dreamed it.

5. *Giga-minose naage, goonimaa giga-mikaan miikimowin, goonimaa gigad-*
   ayaawaa zhooniyaa, gadaa-minose gegoon gimiigiwaamikaag giishpin ihi
   inaabadaman.
   It will be good for later, maybe you will find work, maybe you will
   have money, it will be something good for your house[hold] if you
   dream it.

6. *Naanigodin gidinaabadaan weshkaj gaa-dazhiikeyan ihi e-abinoojiizhi-*
   wiyan.
   Sometimes you dream of where you used to live as a child.

7. *Gakina giwaabadaan ihi, gakina gegoon gimikan ihimaa gaa-dazhiikeya-*
   ban, noogom dash aazha gaawin dagwasinoon ihi gegoon ihimaa.
   Everything you see, everything you will find it in that place you
   were living, though now those things are not there.

8. *Giiyaabaj idash giwaabadaan e-bawaadaman e-nibaayan.*
   Again you will see [those things] when you are dreaming.

9. *Ihiwe dash inaabadaman, gichi-minwaashin ihi gaa-inaabadaman.*
   That kind of dream is really good when you dream it.

10. *Gigad-ayaan gegoon naage, goonimaa gigad-ayaawaa zhooniyaa naage,*
    goonimaa miijim maane gigad-ayaan.
    You will have something for later, maybe you will have money later,
    maybe you will have lots of food.

11. *Mii ezhiseg giishpin weshkaj gegoon bawaadaman.*
    That's what happens when you dream of something from long ago.

12. *Mayaa goj debwemagan ihi gaa-inweyaan.*
    It is really true what I'm saying.

13. *Gaawin anishaa nidikidosii ihi gaa-inweyaan.*
    I'm not just saying these things for fun.

These teachings are examples of how traditional teachings and modes of learning have remained intact and still reflect the underlying philosophies and sacred ways of acquiring knowledge and power among Ojibwe people. A world where even inanimate objects possess a spirit indicates the severe clash with the viewpoint of the western tradition. Beck, Walters, and Francisco demonstrate this point: 'Aboriginally, basic education among Native Americans did not separate the search for knowledge from sacred learning or "religious" training. Native American sacred ways insisted on learning, on education, as an essential foundation for personal awareness' (1993:48).

To ensure the survival and perpetuation of Ojibwe culture, communication with the spirit world is essential and is the responsibility of all members of the First Nation. Although variations exist in the transmission of the sacred ways, in the Algonquin tradition the bear is a highly respected spirit and upon encountering or after killing the animal many of the elders will still address a speech to the bear's spirit, commending it for giving its life for the people. The ritual simultaneously signifies respect for the slain animal and to its spirit. This philosophy is still very strong among many Ojibwe and Algonquin people. The cultural significance of the bear is so strong that the elders rely on the Great Spirit to warn them of possible future calamity by sending the bear as a dream visitor.

In this first story the elder is identifying and portraying the living interaction with other-than-human persons, in this case the bear. All cultures change, yet traditional education, even in a modified form, is still maintained in Aboriginal societies today. These are not just old stories but are told by a living voice; they recognize and support the very real strength of the interaction between humans and other-than-human persons in Algonquin society, even though these teachings more often than not take place at the subconscious level in today's generation of Ojibwe learners. These beliefs are not merely relics of the past; they are integral to today's education in the Anishnaabe tradition. These are things Native people are taught and are expected to know as part of their identity as Anishnaabe.

While the first story is one which is being told and transmitted from what Mrs Mowatt learned as a child through her parents, the second story is her internalization of this teaching for her and those of her generation. This elder is not only maintaining the traditional teachings among those of her generation, but is now in the process of adapting and transmitting these teachings to the next generation and beyond.

Some Discourse Features of Ojibwe Narratives

Telling stories remains an important part of everyday life and relationships among most Aboriginal people today. Regna Darnell provides us with some first-hand insight into the importance of telling stories among Ojibwe people in the contemporary context when she writes: 'Perhaps the most pervasive feature of First Nations discourse ... is the emphasis speakers place on telling their personal stories as a necessary prelude to and authority for any further discourse' (1993:89).

One of the basic premises of *'You're So Fat!'* is grounded in the storytelling tradition and the importance of personal experience. Recall that an integral aspect of my approach to discourse analysis in this book includes taking personal experiences to be as important as the socio-cultural scaffolding of naturally occurring talk in which these experiences are grounded. In my own experience at Pikogan, it was common for the elders, in teaching me about what they considered important in order for me to become acculturated, to couch their teachings in story form. Only one elder at Pikogan ever told me and my wife explicitly what to do or instructed us in didactic fashion, and that was an elder whom we considered to be our surrogate mother. But I can recall countless experiences when the finer points of appropriate thinking and behaviour were embedded in the stories they told me. It may be a simple thing or a complex teaching, but telling a story was most often the medium.

In the storytelling portion of this series, Mrs Mowatt recounts the significance of dreaming about a bear *Gichi-weshkaj* (long ago). She uses the narrative format as a heuristic device to teach the listener about the importance of bear dreams and some of the reasoning behind their significance. It should be noted, as well, that the relations between the story and the two teachings are not capricious, but the products of Mrs Mowatt's attention and careful management. Her narrative which opens the series, which we have called 'Dreaming about a Bear Long Ago,' is structured in such a fashion that the underlying theme of the story (that it is not good to dream about a bear) is made clear in the following lines:

2. *Gichi-weshkaj-gookom gii-wiidamaage egaa e-minwaashig makwa bawaanaj.*
   A really old woman told about how it's not good to dream of a bear.
7. *'Giga-wii-wiisin ihi gaa-inaabadaman. Gaawin minwaashisinoon gaa-bawaanaj makwa,' ikido ahawe gichi-gookom.*

'You will be hungry because of that dream. It's not good to dream about a bear,' that old woman says.
12. *'Mii dash ihi gaa-oji-egaa-minwaashig makwa bawaanaj.'*
So then that's why it's not good to dream about a bear.'
14. *Gookom dash gii-wiidamaage, 'Gaawin minwaashisinoon e-bawaanaagani-wij makwa'.*
So the old woman tells him, 'It's not good to dream about a bear.'

Here is not a random cluster of utterances thrown into the story in haphazard fashion, but a sequence which is progressively organized and situated so as to highlight the important theme of the story. The technique of bringing the hearer's attention back to the important theme of the story via repetition is found throughout this text and, according to Lisa Valentine, appears to be typical of Algonquian discourse in general. She writes: 'Narrative texts from many Algonquian languages display a pervasive use of doublet constructions, which are repetitions of phrases or lines, occurring at crucial points in the narratives' (1995:202). Valentine claims that this feature is considered old-fashioned by some younger speakers, one of whom complained that 'the old people repeat themselves all the time.' Linda Akan writes that, in her Saulteaux tradition, 'Repetition [in stories and teachings] is made for refocusing in (an)other context(s). There is an implication of maturity or stage-development changes, as repetition checks the learner's understanding of these. A "good talk" has lots of repetition to help us draw verbal circles of existence' (1992:192).

In my analysis, it seems clear that this rhetorical device is important for storytellers in general and one which Mrs Mowatt uses in this story to great advantage as a means of adding force to the teaching she is giving through the repetition. Redundancy appears to be an extremely important means of highlighting the theme of the discourse and lightening the information load for the hearers.

There is another type of parallelism at work in this opening story in the series which other stories told in Ojibwe seem to exhibit. While telling this particular story, Mrs Mowatt not only takes on the task of structuring her narration, but she also gives the listeners some subtle and not-so-subtle clues as to what the story is about. In storytelling situations at Pikogan, the significance of individual stories is frequently impressed on the listeners within the context of the story itself. In the opening story in this series, for example, both aspects of story organization and their functions are represented. There is a recounting of a particular *aadisokaan* or legend which is prefaced by an introductory statement which informs the listener about what the story is about (line 2). This statement, which precedes the actual telling of the story, provides the listener with the appropriateness and relevance of the story which follows.

The story about the 'long time ago woman' and the 'old man' serves as a source of evidence which supports the two related teachings which follow ('Dreaming about a Bear Today' and 'Lucky Dreams'). The two teachings are, in a sense, informed by the opening story, and this reflexive relationship operating between the story and the teachings testifies to the competency of the speaker and provides the observer with a window into the speaker's mind. Mrs Mowatt was not merely stringing together a story and some teachings; rather, the teachings are occasioned by the opening story which gives the listeners a context for understanding the teachings. That is to say, Mrs Mowatt's opening story can be viewed as providing a source of testimony occasioning the significance and coherence of the teachings which follow. The means by which she introduces what she is going to teach seems to follow a pattern that is quite common in Ojibwe ways of transmitting tradition and culture.

Some Features of Ojibwe Expository Discourse

In the first teaching following the narrative, Mrs Mowatt uses a standard format found in most Algonquian expository teachings (Valentine, 1992). As we saw earlier when looking at Okinawe's and Alice's teachings, expository discourse in Ojibwe invariably begins with the speaker telling the hearers what is going to be told. Note the following from two stories above:

'Dreaming about a Bear Today'

1. *Ogaazhigag idash.*
   So then today.
2. *Mii giiyaabaj ezhiseg bawaanaj makwa.*
   This is what happens when someone dreams about a bear.

'Lucky Dreams'

1. *Ohowedi dash, miinawaj godag, giishpin inaabadaman e-nibaayaan.*
   This one then is another, if I dream while I am sleeping.

Another feature frequently found in Algonquian expository discourse is a generic-specific structure at the beginning of a discourse and a similar one at the end. Generic-specific refers to a contextual use of deductive reasoning (from general to specific) in transmitting cultural knowledge; specific-generic refers to inductive reasoning (from specific to general). The same features can also be found in another Algonquian language, Atikamekw (Boo Stime, linguist working among the Atikamekw, personal communication, 1984). One can see these features in operation in the two expository discourses following the opening story. First, the generic-specific feature in the first half of 'Dreaming about a Bear Long Ago' and the beginning of 'Dreaming about a Bear Today':

'Dreaming about a Bear Today'

7. *Mii giiyaabaj noogom ezhi-miikimoomagag ihi inaabadamaan.*
   That's the way it still works [today] when you dream about her/him.
8. *Gigichi-masagwaabadaan makwa bawaanaj.*
   It's really unlucky when you dream about her/him.
9. *Goonimaa gaawin giga-mikasiin miikimowin.*
   Maybe you won't be able to find a job.

'Lucky Dreams'

1. *Ohowedi dash, miinawaj godag, giishpin inaabadamaan e-nibaayaan.*
   This one then is another, if I dream while I am sleeping.
2. *Nimikaan gegoon, gichi-weshaj gegoon, goonimaa igoj azhishkiikaag nimikaan gegoon, inaabadamaan, ni-gichi-minwaabadaan ihi gaa-inaabadamaan.*
   I find something, something old, maybe in the dirt I find it while I'm dreaming, that's a really good dream.
3. *Mii bezhigwan, gichi-weshkaj miigiwaam nimikaan noopimig gaa-dazhii-kaaniwag inaabadaman, gichi-minwaashin ihi gaa-inaabadaman.*
   The same way, I found a really old house to stay in the bush once when I was dreaming, that was a really good dream.

We can see the movement from generic to specific in both of these instances. In 'Dreaming about a Bear Today,' the speaker moves from the generic *ihi inaabadamaan* (dreaming) in line 7 to *Goonimaa gaawin giga-mikasiin miikimowin* (Maybe you won't find a job) in line 9. In 'Lucky Dreams,' she moves from the generic *giishpin inaabadamaan e-*

nibaayaan (if I dream while I'm sleeping) in line 1 to *Nimikaan gegoon* (I find something) in line 2 and *gichi-weshkaj miigiwaam nimikaan noopimig gaa-dazhiikaaniwag inaabadamaan* (I found a really old house in the bush once when I was dreaming) in line 3.

Now let us look at the specific-generic structure near the end of the discourse.

'Dreaming about a Bear Today'

14. *Goonimaa gaawin gadaa-dagwasinoon debwe ge-miijiyan, anooj igoj gegoon gadaa-izhi-majise bawaanaj makwa.*
   Maybe you won't have anything to eat, something will go wrong when you dream about a bear.
15. *Mii giiyaabaj noogom ezhi-miikimoomagag ihiwedi makwa bawaanaj.*
   That's how it still works when you dream about a bear.

'Lucky Dreams'

10. *Gigad-ayaan gegoon naage, goonimaa gigad-ayaawaa zhooniyaa naage, goonimaa miijim maane gigad-ayaan.*
   You will have something for later, maybe you will have money later, maybe you will have lots of food.
11. *Mii ezhiseg giishpin weshkaj gegoon bawaadaman.*
   That's what happens when you dream of something from long ago.

At the end of each discourse we can see the speaker generating a specific-generic structure in 'Dreaming about a Bear Today' by moving from line 14 to line 15. In 'Lucky Dreams' we can see the specific-generic movement beginning in line 10 with the mention of specific benefits and leading back to the generic in line 11.

Another feature of expository discourse in Ojibwe is the appeal to personal experience and/or the defusing of contrary opinions with an appeal to authority, as in the following:

'Dreaming about a Bear Today'

16. *Debwe igoj gekwaan gaawin anishaa ikidonaaniwasinoon gaa-inweyaan, mayaa goj debwe igoj ihi ikidonaaniwan ihi inaaniwag.*
   It's true, I'm not just saying this for fun, this has been said [known] for a long time.

'Lucky Dreams'

12. *Mayaa goj debwemagan ihi gaa-inweyaan.*
    It is really true what I'm saying.
13. *Gaawin anishaa nidikidosii ihi gaa-inweyaan.*
    I'm not just saying these things for fun.

Expository discourse frequently includes a final challenge or advice along with the appeal to authority, as we see occurring in line 16 of 'Dreaming about a Bear Today' and line 13 of 'Lucky Dreams.' I have listened to many expository discourses over the years and virtually every one ends with some kind of appeal to authority such as we see in these instances. In other words, the speaker is saying something like: 'This isn't just me that believes this and I didn't just make it up. I'm passing down something that has been taught among our people for generations.'

The strength of the challenge at the end of these expository discourses is directly proportional to the relative positions of the speaker and hearer (i.e., mother-daughter, old person-young person), and the consideration of the importance in what is being said. In 'Dreaming about a Bear Today,' for example, the speaker uses the second person construction almost exclusively throughout the discourse, indicating the importance of what is being said, particularly highlighted in the final exhortation:

17. *Giishpin naagajitoowan ihiwedi giga-waabadaan, giga-debwetaan dash*
    naage apiich gikendaman wegonen ihi weji-inaabadaman.
    If you look carefully you will see it, you will believe it and then later you will know why you dreamed it.

By examining some of the salient features of Ojibwe discourse we can see that there are certain interactional benefits to transmitting traditional knowledge and teachings in the structural positioning of the stories and teachings themselves. That is to say, the meaning and relevance of a particular teaching, as exhibited in the story/exposition series we have been examining, is not something that can be determined merely by inspecting the details of the story and following teachings. What one can see happening in this instance is a social occasion, a traditional teaching which emerges in the context of the particulars of a culture-specific situation. The analysis thus far is best perceived as relating to how traditional teachings from one Algonquian tradition are structured and transmitted in a contemporary setting.

I have claimed that Algonquin narrative discourse is characterized by a form-content parallelism which turns on two different aspects of the accounts themselves; the *structure* of the accounts and their *significance*, the latter embedded within the former. When these features are explored in the context of teachings about 'animals who warn people of possible misfortune' and are compared with findings in a related dialect (Odawa), these observations enable us to understand better the relationships between performative features of Algonquian discourse and culture-specific ways of retaining and transmitting cultural knowledge.

Warnings and Dream Visitors in the Odawa Tradition

In comparing the bear-dream accounts found in the Algonquin dialect of Ojibwe with a related Ojibwe dialect, Odawa, I discovered that, while our Algonquin data suggest that the significance of bear dreams and bear visitors seem to be Algonquin-specific, there are some thematic similarities when examined in the context of 'animals who warn people of

between two related traditions, I asked my colleague Mary Ann Corbiere to interview some Odawa elders from her community of Wikwemikong, to find out what similar themes are at play involving dream visitors and animals who bring warnings in both conscious and dream states to Anishnaabe people. While we were, unfortunately, unable to elicit tape-recorded responses, we were able to ask four elders, all in their seventies, for their responses to the bear-dream tradition among the Algonquins and for their thoughts on animal warnings in their own tradition. Another colleague, Barry Ace, interviewed one elder in the same tradition from the community of Sagamok.

The strongest tradition of a warning animal for these elders involves the fox. All the elders agreed that the fox is one who warns of imminent misfortune, usually related to death. More specifically, it is the sound of the fox barking that gives the warning. One of the elders stated that the bark of the fox is, in her words, 'our relatives screaming' as a warning to prepare for the death of a relative or family member. In talking to some of the younger community members, there seems to be a strong sense of the reliability of the fox's warning. As one respondent in her early thirties noted, 'When I was growing up, the thing I heard most about was the fox and if you heard a fox bark at you or hang around your house that was a warning or a sign that something bad was going to happen.' Responding to this comment, one of the elders acknowledged, 'Yes, the fox is generally the big one, the one commonly associated with a bad sign.' As to the fox as a dream visitor, as in the Algonquin bear-dream teaching, one younger respondent answered, 'I've never heard of anyone dreaming about a fox. Hearing it [in a conscious state] is the important thing.'

During our visits with the elders at Wikwemikong, we related the Algonquin tradition of dreaming about a bear. All the elders were unanimous that they did not have those kind of stories. Interestingly, the elder we talked to from Sagamok, upon hearing of the Algonquin bear-dream tradition, agreed that 'It's a bad sign to dream about a bear.' When questioned further, she noted that the bad sign had more to do with the colour black than with the bear figure. This exchange did trigger a response from this particular elder, however, about dreaming about a horse. She told us that dreaming about a horse is a warning that someone (usually a relative) is going to become very sick.

Another animal who warns people of future misfortune is the woodpecker. Particularly strong in the mind of the elder from Sagamok, a woodpecker pounding on one's house is another warning of the imminent death of a relative. One elder recounted a story of how a man's dog began howling for three successive nights prior to the accidental death of its master. In fact, almost every response by these five elders was accompanied by real-life stories relating the particular warning animal with recent and not-so-recent experiences as evidence of the power and efficacy of the animal's warning.

In both traditions there does seem to be a sense that dream visitors, both human and other-than-human, are still active. We heard one story about a dream visitor where one family member who had recently died came to visit a relative in her dream.[6] One of his cousins was particularly shocked by his death and, according to the recounting, one night soon after his death she heard someone come around the house and go into the back. Then she remembers hearing the person come up the stairs and into her room. It was her cousin who had recently died. He said to her, 'I know you're really depressed about me dying, but don't feel bad. I'm very happy where I am, other family members are here, so put your mind at ease and don't be so sad about me anymore.' This kind of recounting seems to be common in the Algonquin tradition as well, with stories of the recently deceased visiting people in dreams in order to set the minds of family members at ease and encourage them to stop mourning and to go on with their lives.

Conclusion

Our exploration of bear-dream accounts and the teachings related to that tradition, while preliminary, give a number of insights into the discourse structures and interactional techniques available to Ojibwe speakers for retaining and transmitting cultural knowledge and traditional teachings. The field of discourse analysis among Algonquian languages is still relatively young and much remains to be done before one can begin to make rigorous connections between linguistic traditions. I have made the claim that Ojibwe narrative discourse is characterized by a distinct form-content parallelism which turns on two different aspects of the accounts themselves: the structure of the accounts and their significance. Ojibwe expository discourse is characterized by a generic-specific structure at the beginning of the discourse, a related specific-generic structure at the end, an appeal to personal experience and/or the defusing of contrary opinions with an appeal to authority in the middle, and the inclusion of a final challenge or related piece of advice along with the appeal to authority. I then explored the content of these teachings from one Algonquian tradition and compared them in a related dialect, using the theme of 'animals who warn people of possible misfortune.' I described some of the similarities and differences between traditions as a way of highlighting culture-specific teachings and structural and interactional transmission techniques. In this way we can reach a better understanding of the relationships between performative features of Algonquian discourse, culture-specific techniques of transmitting cultural knowledge, and Ojibwe cosmology.

10

'Leave It to Beaver': Discourse Analysis of a Traditional Anishnaabe Legend

One of the keys to understanding storytelling in its proper context is knowing that it comes with an often complex set of rules (Johnston, 1991; Steckley, 1994a). These rules can stipulate when stories should be told (e.g., winter rather than summer for some peoples), who has the right to tell the story (e.g., someone from the appropriate lineage or clan), and restrictions as to how much interpretation the teller can add. The most important key, however, is the strength of the oral tradition in most First Nations' traditions and the influence the myths, legends, and stories continue to exert on behaviour and ways of thinking among Aboriginal people. The legend we will explore in this chapter is designed to illustrate the strong link between Native languages and the oral tradition, for the recounting of these stories in the original languages is extremely important if the cultural and historical roots of the people are to be maintained.

Legends and myths in most, if not all, Aboriginal traditions create a unique reality not necessarily subject to factual or observable data. That is, legends and myths should not be construed as literal truth that can be proven and substantiated according to western scientific methods. For example, when we explored the story of how the lynx ended up with short intestines in an earlier chapter, the important consideration was not its actual truth, but what the legend teaches about ways of thinking and living. That is, legends and myths are viewed by Anishnaabe people as culture-based understandings which provide important lessons for living and give life purpose, value and meaning.

Passed down since time immemorial, these legends and myths, along with ritual, dance, and song, contain stories of the creation and establish an order of reality that is culturally distinct for a people. Legends and myths also create a unique understanding of the world which further

strengthens the social and cultural cohesiveness of a people. Understanding these legends and myths, according to the elders, is understanding yourself, understanding the world, understanding where you
came from, and understanding where you are going.[1]

In earlier chapters we have seen how the link between Aboriginal languages and culture-specific ways of thinking and doing things is an intimate one. I agree with the insight of John Steckley when he suggests that
a connection most certainly exists between the linguistic structure of an
Aboriginal language and a people's world view or philosophy. Julie
Cruikshank (1990) provides us with some important clues on the close
connection between place names, personal names, songs, and the life
stories of elders. This intimate link is demonstrated in the scholarly
world as well, another social context for language, albeit by its absence.
Steckley gets to the heart of the matter:

As many Aboriginal peoples have pointed out, academics study Native cultures
by trying to infuse life into bits of material culture through archaeology and into
isolated words and phrases, and translated passages of Aboriginal languages
recorded by outsiders such as missionaries, explorers and military men. The
study of the oral tradition, including myths, legends and traditional stories and
their place in the Aboriginal world view, has historically been undertaken by
people who do not share a sense of what it means to be from an oral tradition.
When this is attempted without any knowledge of the Aboriginal language
involved, true understanding is not achieved, the studies are as lifeless as
museum exhibits of mounted animals. More often than not we end up with a
confused and untrue picture of the richness and complexity of the oral tradition.
Particularly disturbing to Aboriginal peoples in this regard are collections published in English of traditional stories ripped out of context from First Nations
across the country like skulls and artifacts taken from sacred burial grounds.
Out of their natural context, these stories become subjects of curiosity, not tools
for understanding. (1994a:43)

As Steckley claims, in order for Native peoples to be able to recapture
the significance of the oral tradition and the myths and legends, Aboriginal languages and an accurate understanding of the oral tradition and
the place of myth and legend in people's lives must be restored. As
much traditional knowledge and wisdom that exists in the Aboriginal
languages is lost in translation, many Aboriginal peoples feel it is crucial
to revitalize the oral tradition in the original languages (Corbiere, 1997;
Christensen, 1993).

Discourse Analysis of a Traditional Algonquin Legend

Recent studies in linguistic discourse analysis have yielded insights into the structure of Amerindian oral narratives. The legend we are exploring here was taped by Rand Valentine during an evening of visiting and storytelling in Pikogan in the fall of 1982. Our interest in this type of analysis is to discover and describe some of the essential structural features of Algonquin narrative discourse, and to show the richness and complexity of the philosophy of the elders as they use these features. In the legend I look at seven basic features of Algonquin narrative structure: direct discourse, tense switching, doublet constructions, character focus, particles and other discourse markers, word internal constructions, and finally, general narrative structure.

I should reiterate a point which is likely to resurface as we begin taking a detailed look at this legend. Sometimes my students, both Native and non-Native, are concerned that we are tampering with these legends and stories by taking detailed looks at them and at how elders structure their tellings. But as we take a detailed look at this legend, our interest is not in tearing them apart or analysing them just for the purpose of being analytical. Rather, by taking a detailed look at how legends, stories, and myths are told, we have the opportunity to get inside the heads of the elders and to discover how they see the world and how they can teach us, both Native and non-Native, to see the world through indigenous eyes, with a Native sensibility and Native intuition.

BACKGROUND TO 'AMIK ANISHNAABEWIGOBAN'

Traditionally, the use of legend and myth narratives in Algonquian languages had two purposes: instruction in proper cultural behaviour and values, and entertainment. The storytellers were those considered to be elders in the community. The narrator of this legend, Albert Mowatt, or Okinawe, certainly meets those qualifications. The story 'Amik Anish-naabewigoban' was just one in a series of stories told by Okinawe. Others include the two narratives used in chapters 5 and 11; 'Bizhiw ashij Waa-goosh' ('The Lynx and the Fox') and 'Bizhiw ashij Waabishtaan' ('The Lynx and the Marten'). Okinawe has put stories and teachings on tape many times, thus the presence of a tape recorder seemed to have a minimal effect on the actual storytelling itself.

In Algonquian languages such as Ojibwe, Cree, and Algonquin, speakers of these languages differentiate between two genres of discourse; *aadisokaan*, or traditional legends and tales, and *tibaajimowin*, personal accounts and narratives about 'what happened.' As Rand Valentine (1996) notes, these two kinds of discourse have several distinctive features. The use of the historical present tense, for example, is a common characteristic of *aadisokaanan* (the plural of *aadisokaan*) and a high degree of what linguists refer to as the preterite dubitative mode verb forms.[2] The historical present refers to the use of the present tense when recounting a past event, and its use is common in narratives and stories by non-Native English speakers as well. In telling stories in English, people often use the historical present as a way of bringing the hearers into the immediacy of the event being recounted. For example, when telling a story about 'what happened last week on my trip to Toronto,' the historical present might be used like this:

Last week I was travelling to Toronto and I pulled into a gas station to fill up. As I was getting out of my car this guy was getting out of his car at the same time and he smashed his car door into mine. So I get out of my car and yell at him. He gives *me* a bad time for scratching *his* door and then hops back into his car and drives away. I was really mad that he blamed me for scratching his car when it was obviously his fault, but I didn't let it wreck my day.

Note that the story begins in the past tense and then moves into the present. The use of the historical present is used here as a highlighting device to bring listeners into the present as the story is being recounted and thus contributes to the immediacy of the event being recounted.

We explored verb tense shifts in Ojibwe narratives in chapter 5 and showed how it creates a sense of immediacy for the listeners, putting them into the thick of what is being recounted. In her analysis of the story '*Mii Tahsh Wenci-oshaawisic Pahpashki*' ('Why the Partridge Is Brown'), Lisa Valentine suggests that there are two orders of tense shifting taking place, similar to the tense shifting we saw at play in 'The Lynx and the Marten' and 'The Lynx and the Fox': from an expected past tense into the historical present tense. A second order of shifting identified by Valentine is from an expected past tense into what she refers to as a 'future, more vivid' tense. She claims that 'The historical present in Ojibwe, as in English, is typically found in particularly compelling parts of a story' (1995:201).

According to Nichols, the high frequency of the preterite dubitative mode verb forms informs us that it is 'most commonly used in the beginning and end [of stories] to establish the traditional nature of the events.' He goes on to suggest that 'Dubitative verbs mark the inability or unwillingness of the speaker to vouch for the certainty of the occurrence of the event ... This may be due to lack of personal observation, supposition or inference, forgetfulness or the traditional nature of the speaker's knowledge' (1980:124).

The story recounted here by Okinawe sheds light on the relationship between humans and other-than-humans, in this case between humans and beavers. The legend is presented below and I encourage you to read it carefully before moving on to the analysis.

'Amik Anishnaabewigoban'

1. *Mii oowe aadisokaan amik weshkadj.*
   This is the story of the beaver long ago.
2. *Amik Anishnaabewigoban.*
   The beaver was once in human form.
3. *Gegapiich babaamosegoban noopimig.*
   At one time he was walking around in the bush.
4. *Gegapiich weji-waabamaagwenin ikwewan anooj e-dazhiikenjin.*
   After a while he saw a woman where she was living.
5. *Mii dash e-ayamihaagobanen.*
   So then he spoke to her.
6. *Gegapiich odinaagoban,*
   After a while he said to her,
7. *'Giga-wiiji-dazhiikemin,' odinaan.*
   'Let's live together,' he says to her.
8. *Mii dash ekidoj ahawe ikwe,*
   So then the woman says,
9. *'Niga-gichi-minwendaan wiiji-dazhiikemizhiyan,'*
   'I'd really enjoy it living with you,'
10. *ikidogoban aha ikwe.*
    the woman said.
11. *Mii dash aazha onashowedogenag ke inakamigiziwaaj giji bimaajiowaaj.*
    So then now they're discussing what they're going to do in order to make a living.
12. *Ikidogoban ahawe amik,*
    The beaver said,
13. *'Gaawin mayaa ohomaa giga-dazhiikesiimin.*
    'We're not going to live here.
14. *Bagii bakaan giga-dazhiikemin.*
    We'll live in a different manner.

15. *Giga-maawajitoonaan nibii.'*
    We'll dam up the water.'
16. *Gegapiich maajaadog.*
    After a while he's leaving.
17. *'Niin niga-niigaanii apiich maajaayag.*
    'I will go first when we leave.
18. *Odaakanaag giga-bimose giin.*
    You will walk behind me.
19. *Inigik dash ziibii e-ani-bi-madaabiiyag, gakina nigad-aazhoganike.*
    And then any river we come to each one I'll build a bridge.
20. *Inigik igoj weyaabadamag zhiibiizhiishii, gakina nigad-aazhoganike.'*
    And then any old river that we see, at each one I'll build a bridge.'
21. *Mii dash gegapiich ezhi-waniikegwen bezhig giji-aazhoganikej ziibiini.*
    But then it seems that he forgot to build a bridge at one river.
22. *Gegapiich inendamodog ezhi-gwiinawi-biihaajin odikweman odaakanaag e-bimosenjin.*
    So then he's thinking that he forgot to wait for his woman as she walks along behind.
23. *Gaawin nanaazh odadiminewigosiin ezhi-gooki-giiwegwen.*
    Then he doesn't encounter her as he heads back [to look for her].
24. *'Aanigada nigii-waniike giji-aazhoganikeyaan gaa-bi-bimoseyaan ziibii,' inendamodog.*
    'Oh, I forgot to build a bridge at some river that I came upon,' he's thinking.
25. *Gegapiich odooditaanaadog gaa-izhi-waniikej ziibiini giji-aazhoganikej.*
    So then he finally reaches it where he forgot to build a bridge at a river.
26. *Ezhi-waabadag apan e-bakobiikanawenjin odikweman.*
    And there he sees the place where his woman has gone into the river.
27. *Gegapiich onanaadawaabamaadogwenin ezhi-bakobiigwen gewiin gega-piich.*
    After a while he goes looking for her and there he, too, goes into the water.
28. *Gegapiich omikawaan.*
    After a while he finds her.
29. *Nibiikag odji mikawaan odikweman.*
    There in the water he finds his woman.
30. *Gegapiich odayamihaadogwenan miinawaaj.*
    After a while he speaks to her again.

31. *Odinaadogwenan,*
    He says to her,

32. *'Nibiikaag ndawaaj giga-dazhiikemin, ge-bimaadiziyag.*
    'Well, we might as well stay in the water to live.

33. *Giga-ozhitoonaanaan ge-dazhiikeyag.*
    We'll make the place where we're going to live.

34. *Giga-ojitoonaanaan okonim ashij gimiigiwaaminaan giga-ojitoonaan.*
    We'll build a dam and we'll build our house.

35. *Giga-maawajitoonaanaan ge-miijiyag ge-biboog.*
    We'll gather together what we'll need during the winter.

36. *Giga-gibahaanaan ziibii giji-michaagamig.'*
    We'll dam up the river to make a large body of water.'

37. *Okonim ijinikaade gaa-wii-ozhitooj.*
    What he is intending to build is called a dam.

38. *Gegapiich ginwezh ani-dazhiikedogenag.*
    After a while they live there a long time.

39. *Gegapiich odabinoojiizhimiwag apiich niizho-biboon gaa-dazhiikewaaj.*
    After a while they have children after two years living there.

40. *Gegapiich odinaadogwenan odikweman aha amik.*
    After a while that beaver speaks to his wife.

41. *Gegapiich oji-moonizidog.*
    Then he had a vision.

42. *Awiyagoog gadaa-dagwishinoog ogaazhigag.*
    'People will be arriving today.

43. *Giga-gwagwe-nisigonaanag igi ge-dagwishinowaaj awiyagoog.*
    They'll try to kill us, those people who will be arriving.

44. *Animoshan oga-daabajihaawaan ashij asabiin.*
    They will be using dogs and nets.

45. *Baanimaa dash biimadwehamowaaj gimiigiwaaminaan giga-maajaamin.'*
    When we hear a knocking on our dwelling, we will leave.'

46. *Gegapiich biimadwehigaadeni omiigiwaamiwaa igi amikwag.*
    Then there's a knocking on the dwelling of those beaver.

47. *'Gakina wesaa gada-nisaaganiwiwag gidabinoojiizhiminaanag,'*
    'All of our children are going to be killed,'

48. *ikidodog aha amik.*
    says the beaver.

49. *Gegapiich maajiyaabaawedogenag omiigiwaamiwaakaag.*
    So they flee from their dwelling, swimming.

50. *Gegapiich owaabamaadogwenan asabiin e-gibaabinjin ziibiikaag.*
    After a while they see a net that is blocking up the river.

51. *Mii dash ezhi-nda-waabadamowaagwen mitigoon e-ginwaakwannig.*
    So they then go looking for the stick, the long one.
52. *Ezhi-gaadaakwahaagwen ini asabiin e-gibaabikemonjin ziibiikaag.*
    In order to knock down the net that is blocking the river.
53. *Mii dash e-wiikobinaaganiwinjin.*
    So then at last they pull it away.
54. *Mii sa dash apiich gaa-ishkwaa-wiikobinaaganiwinjin,*
    So then after they had succeeded in pulling it away,
55. *gezika ezhi-bimaabaawewaaj amikwag.*
    they were able to swim away beavers and their women.
56. *Mii eshkwaa-bimaajihowaaj wiin igiwe gichi-amikwag.*
    So then they were able to survive those adult beavers.
57. *Amikoosag dash gakina gii-nisaaganiwiwag odabinoojiizhimiwaan.*
    But the little beavers were all killed, their children.
58. *Mii ekwaag ihi aadisookaan.*
    So that's the legend.

Beginning Discourse Analysis

When my students start to engage in linguistic discourse analysis, I ask them to follow a number of steps. This helps them orient themselves into this kind of analysis and gives some hints as to what it tells us about how narratives are structured and how Anishnaabe people think and perceive the world around us. Whether you are a neophyte, as are many of my students, or familiar with the basic methodology of linguistic discourse analysis, this list should provide you with some focus for the analysis which follows. The basic steps can be summarized as follows.

Step 1. Find out some of the background information pertaining to this legend and write up a paragraph or two on such things as: information about the storyteller, the community he/she comes from, and any information about the legend being told.

Step 2. Using the English translation, summarize the legend so that you understand everything in sequence, including the pertinent details.

Step 3. Using the English summary, make a detailed outline of the story.

Step 4. Now look at the legend in some detail. You should be able to answer the following questions. Call this section 'Main Divisions.'

- Does the storyteller sign-on to the audience? (if so, give examples)
- Is it similar to other stories? (To discover this you want to compare the sign-on in this legend with the sign-ons in other stories and legends.)
- Does the storyteller sign-off to the audience? (same as above)
  - Is it similar to other stories? (same as above)
- Does the storyteller make asides to the audience? (if so, where?)
  - What purpose does the aside fulfil?

Step 5. Now you are ready to look at how characters are introduced. Call this section 'Introduction of Characters.'
- How many characters are in this legend?
- Where are the characters first introduced? (Here you want to specify the character and the lines where each character is introduced.)
- Is the first character introduced the main character? (Yes or no and why you think so.)
- Identify the third person(s) and the fourth person(s) in the story. (Who's in the spotlight?)
- Where does third-fourth person switching occur? (Make a chart similar to your verb switching chart which shows the person switches.)
- How does person switching correspond with the story structure? (Compare your chart with your story outline and see if you can see any patterns.)
- Is this consistent with other stories or are there differences? (Here you want to compare this legend with other legends.)

Step 6. Now you are ready to look at some of the performative features of this legend. Title this section Performative Features of Discourse.
- Where does direct speech occur in the story? (Write down the lines where each direct speech occurs.)
  - Does direct speech occur in other stories? (Compare with your other stories and write down where direct speech occurs.)
  - At what parts in the story does direct speech occur? (Here you want to see if there is a pattern for where in the story direct speech is used – you also might want to compare any pattern you find with other stories.)
- Does the storyteller ever tell about things that *don't* happen? (This is referred to as collateral information.)
  - If you find any instances of collateral information, what purpose does it serve in the story?
- Does the storyteller use doublet constructions? (That is, saying the

same thing or almost the same thing in the story; write down where they are found.)
- How many verb tenses are used in the story? (Present, past, future, other?)
    - Does the storyteller switch tenses in the story? (Write down the story pattern from beginning to end, e.g. lines 1–12, present tense; lines 15–16, past tense; etc.)
    - What interactional work is being done when the storyteller switches verb tenses?
- Find the particles and temporals in the story and tell where they occur. (Circle each of these particles in the legend and look for patterns. What are these particles doing where they are? Check the patterns with the story outline. Do they occur at key points in the story? If so, what points? What are they *doing* where they are?)

Particle/temporal	Rough translation
mii	So
dash	then
mega	Because, of course...
gegapiich	After a while
ihi apiich	at that time
miinawaaj	again

Step 7. Other Considerations
- What is the moral of the story? (What does it teach?)
- What does this kind of analysis show you about the elegance and complexity of language and Ojibwe ways of thinking and doing things?

In the next section I want to follow the discourse analysis instructions step by step as we explore 'Amik Anishnaabewigoban.' This will help us come to an understanding of how to engage in discourse analysis and what it can tell us about the thoughts of people who are not merely speakers of an Aboriginal language but masters of it.

STEP 1: BACKGROUND INFORMATION

The legend was recorded on cassette tape during the fall of 1982. The recording was made by linguist and personal friend Rand Valentine during an evening of visiting and storytelling at our home. The legend was told by Albert Mowatt (Okinawe), a speaker of the Algonquin dialect of Ojibwe. Okinawe lives in the Algonquin community of Pikogan in northwestern Quebec. He was about sixty years young when he recounted this legend. He lived a traditional lifestyle with minimal contact with non-Native peoples and cultures until he was moved to the reserve in the mid-1950s.

STEP 2: STORY SUMMARY

The legend tells about a mythological beaver who, while in human form, marries a human. It is important to note that by mythological we are referring to a beaver with special powers of transformation (R. Valentine, 1996). As James Dumont (1992) reminds us, before humans were created, many of the land animals lived in the mythic past in what Richard Preston terms 'an evolving geography of relationships' (1986:241). The beaver-in-human-form and the woman decide to live together. Eventually he convinces the woman to move to a different area. He tells her that he will travel ahead of her and build bridges for her to cross over every river and stream that he encounters. At one river, however, the beaver forgets to build a bridge and when he goes back to find his woman, he discovers her tracks leading into the water. He went into the water and finds her there. For some unspecified reason they decide to stay and live in the water, adopting a beaver-type lifestyle. They build a dam and live in the water. In time they have children and subsequently the beaver has a vision of humans coming to kill them. The vision is soon realized and the beaver and his wife are able to escape being killed by using a stick to move nets placed in their escape path. Their children, however, are all killed.

STEP 3: STORY OUTLINE

Narrative event	Line
I. Sign-on	1
+ background information	2
II. Part I, scene one:	3–20
a. The meeting	3–4

STEP 4: MAIN DIVISIONS

Sign-ons and Sign-offs

As Amy Dahlstrom suggests, 'The first step in considering how [a] story is structured is to separate the story proper – the sequence of events recounted by the narrator – from the brief introduction and coda which frame the story' (1996:116). In '*Amik Anishnaabewigoban*,' the storyteller, Okinawe, signs on to the audience in line 1, *Mii oowe aadisokaan amik weshkaj* (This is the story of the beaver long ago). While not part of the legend itself, the sign-on helps to orient the reader to the nature of the legend about to be recounted. The storyteller signs off to the audience in line 58, *Mii ekwaag ihi aadisookaan* (So that's the legend). This orients the reader to the boundaries of the legend and provides the hearers with closure to the narrative event.

Asides

An aside in this storytelling can be found in line 37: 'What he is intending to build is called a dam.' Asides are designed by storytellers to provide information so that the hearer has a clearer picture of what is going on in the story. This particular aside seems to be doing the work of provoking the listener to realize that a transformation has taken place – from human form to animal (beaver) form. The storyteller himself emphasizes this transformation with his references to beaver-specific activities throughout the rest of the story.

Dennis Tedlock gives us some clues into the work an aside can perform for a storyteller in his analysis of Zuni storytelling. The storyteller, a Zuni elder named Andrew, was in the middle of a legend when one of the listeners, his daughter, slipped into the next room to make some coffee. In the story Andrew was just telling about how one of the story characters had taken a female character 'into the next room.' At this point, Andrew chuckled and added an aside, thus breaking out of the story frame. He did this by looking at one of the listeners and said, 'Wouldn't it be funny if Jane [his daughter] were that girl?' The listeners burst into laughter and his daughter could be heard giggling from the kitchen where she was making coffee. As Tedlock describes it, 'With one stroke Andrew had erased not only the temporal and spatial distance of the story, but the personal distance as well' (1988:84). According to Tedlock, Andrew got straight back into the story as if nothing had happened.

STEP 5: INTRODUCTION OF CHARACTERS

There appear to be two main characters in this legend. It gets a bit tricky here as we also encounter two minor characters or players near the end of the legend: the beaver children and the people who come to kill them. As we saw in chapter 3, Algonquian languages such as Ojibwe, Cree, and Algonquin regularly use verbal morphology to distinguish the third person ('proximate') from the second, third, or fourth person ('obviative'). The verbal morphology in Ojibwe is enough to indicate to the listeners who is in focus in the recounted action, who is doing what to whom or, in theatrical terms, who is in the spotlight. Note the charting of character focus in this narrative:

Main character	Story lines
male beaver	1–7
female beaver	8–10
male beaver	11–57
little beavers	58

As can be seen, the spotlight stays on one character for long stretches and is marked within the text itself by long stretches of the same character as the proximate actor and another as the obviative actor. Full noun phrases are rarely necessary and, when used, are appropriately marked. Amik is the proximate actor in lines 1–7; then the spotlight switches to his woman when she becomes the proximate actor in line 8 and Amik is obviative. A long stretch follows where it appears from the verbal morphology that Amik is back in the spotlight (lines 11–57). Certainly the proximate focus shifting is an important structuring device available to Ojibwe storytellers for moving the spotlight from one character to another.

Dahlstrom provides us with some clues for understanding the relationship between focus shifting and obviation: 'In clauses involving more than one third person argument, the third person most central to the discourse is singled out as *proximate* and referred to by unmarked third person forms, while the more peripheral third persons are referred to by marked *obviative* forms.' She claims that the use of the proximate third person may correspond with a number of interactional goals, including demonstrating speaker empathy and showing speaker point of view. She concludes: 'This range of discourse functions available to the speaker makes the grammatical opposition of obviation an especially interesting area for ethnopoetic investigation' (1996:121).

There remain a few questions about our analysis of characters here. One question has to do with whether the little beavers are truly in the spotlight or if the epilogue portion of the narrative has turned the spotlight off at this point. Such a question raises the importance of comparison with other stories and legends. Ideally, the discovery and description of discourse features in Ojibwe legends and stories would require comparison with discourse features found in as many other legends and stories as possible. We will revisit this issue when we begin to make comparisons with a few other legends and stories in the next chapter.

STEP 6: PERFORMATIVE FEATURES OF DISCOURSE

The performative discourse features found within this legend include direct discourse, tense switching, doublet constructions, and character focus (as determined by the proximate-obviative verbal morphology). By performative features I am referring to a storyteller's creativity in using what is available in the language to tell a compelling and coherent story.

Direct Discourse

One of the devices available to storytellers in any language is the use of direct speech – that is, reporting to listeners what came out of the mouth of various story characters either verbatim, paraphrased, reconstructed, or even putting words into a character's mouth. Direct discourse can be used for a variety of interactional purposes in a storytelling. First, it helps to bring the listener into the real action of the story as opposed to a storyteller merely reporting the storyline. Secondly, direct discourse can be used to set up the storyline by highlighting key sections and situating the storyteller's own involvement. Lisa Valentine reports that the use of direct speech is common in Severn Ojibwe storytelling. In her analysis of the Severn Ojibwe legend *'Mii Tahsh Wenci-oshaawisic Pahpashki'* (1995: chapter 9), for example, she finds that sections of direct discourse account for almost a quarter of the utterances in that particular telling of the story. As she notes, 'The presence of direct discourse is often the best cue that a story is being performed rather than a storyline being reported' (1995:201). With these comments in mind, note the following uses of direct discourse found in *'Amik Anishnaabewigoban'*:

front:	12–15, 31–6
back:	24, 47–8
both:	6–7, 8–10
no marking:	17–20, 42–5

By *front* I mean that the direct discourse was marked directly in front of the quote, as in lines 12–15. (The beaver said, 'We're not going to live here ... We'll dam up the water.' So then he's leaving.) In this instance it can be seen quite clearly that the direct discourse is marked in front only.

By *back* I mean that the direct discourse was marked directly following the quote, as in lines 47–8. ('All of our children are going to be killed,' says the beaver.) By *both* I mean that the direct discourse was marked both before the quote and in back as in lines 6–7. (And he said to her, 'Let's live together,' he says to her.) One of the functions of direct discourse is to make sure that the hearer understands that a character is speaking. It is interesting to note, too, that the storyteller can draw the listener's attention to reported speech by marking it both immediately prior to and again immediately following it, as we find in lines 6–7 and 8–10. One of the uses of marking direct discourse both in front and in back early on in the story, as we see happening in this instance, is to signal that the storyteller is not merely going to report the storyline, but is *performing* the story using a variety of performative devices.

Verb Tense Switching

It appears from our analysis of this legend that the tense switching is doing some important interactional work for the storyteller. As we saw in chapter 5, through such switching the narrator is able to focus on the immediacy of the situation being described and to make the action more vivid through the use of switching from the past to the present tense. The tense structure in this narrative follows the following pattern:

present	1
past	2–6
present	7–9
past	10
present	11
past	12–15
present	16–40
past	41–5
present	46–53
past	54–7
present	58

Note that the tense usage in instances of direct discourse is omitted in our analysis of the organization of the tense switching in the legend itself. Also, many of the examples of the use of the historical present in this text are similar to its standard usage in English when a narrative gets to the peak or the exciting part. It is important to note, too, that the verb tense switching in this legend occurs more frequently at the beginning and ending of the narration and that the switching occurs as the story builds to a climax. In most of the instances demonstrating a shift from past to present tense we also found a doublet construction (discussed more fully in the next section) where, at the very least, the verb stem is repeated.

The association of the tense shifting and doublet construction is widespread in this legend and the doublet construction can be used independently of the tense shifting in order to heighten the drama and to separate narrative units. In contrast, the main purpose of the tense shifting is to make the narrative action more vivid to the hearer. We noted earlier that the tense switching in 'Amik Anishnaabewigoban' can also do the work of focusing the listener's attention on the urgency of the situation being recounted.

Doublet Constructions

The doublet construction is used throughout the legend as a means of adding force to certain parts of the narrative and as a local structuring device. It is used to highlight information to which the storyteller wishes the listener to pay particular attention. Doublet constructions in the legend under analysis are found as follows.

Lines	5–6	21–5
	6–7	
	8–10	42–3
	19–20	50–2

Analysing doublet constructions can get a bit tricky. It is important to distinguish between actual doublets and the repetition of a certain word or phrase with no prior connection. Doublets are also occasionally found in direct discourse but occur most frequently in the narrative sections. They appear to be most noticeable at crucial points in the story and thus may be considered to be instrumental in the structuring of the narrative. As with other features of discourse found in naturally occurring legends and stories by monolingual speakers of Algonquian languages, doublet constructions attest to the verbal artistry and creativity of these speakers.

Particles and Other Discourse Markers

Algonquian languages such as Ojibwe are rich in what linguists refer to as particles. These are tricky little things in Algonquian languages and they drive non-Native linguists nuts. Most linguists have been weaned on Indo-European languages, and it is difficult to grasp the notion that non-Indo-European languages, such as Ojibwe, just don't work the same way as Indo-European ones. As for the nature of particles in Ojibwe, Lisa Valentine notes: 'The Ojibwe speaker has recourse to numerous, untranslatable particles (called "discourse particles"), the precise nature of which is difficult to pinpoint' (1995:205).

I want to take a look at two frequently-occurring discourse markers. We examine *mii* and *gegapiich* in the order of their appearance in the narrative.

Particle	Line	Particle	Line
Gegapiich	3	*Gegapiich*	30
Gegapiich	4	*Gegapiich*	38
Mii	5	*Gegapiich*	39
Gegapiich	6	*Gegapiich*	40
Mii	8	*Gegapiich*	41
Mii	11	*Gegapiich*	46
Gegapiich	16	*Gegapiich*	49
Mii	21	*Gegapiich*	50
Gegapiich	22	*Mii*	51
Gegapiich	25	*Mii*	54
Gegapiich	27	*Mii*	56
Gegapiich	28	*Mii*	58

Of the many discourse particles found in Algonquin narratives, *mii* seems to be one of the most used to advance the action. It is usually found at the beginning of a sentence. In the above chart, we see that *mii* is used heavily at the end of the narrative without alternation with any other discourse particle. This contrasts sharply with the beginning, where *mii* alternates frequently with *Gegapiich*. The entire middle section contains no instances of *mii* but long stretches where *Gegapiich* is used exclusively to move the narrative along. What we see happening in this story from the Algonquin dialect of Ojibwe supports the findings of Lisa Valentine for the Severn dialect of Ojibwe, that the particle *mii* marks the advancement of the storyline. She writes: '*Mii* generally begins new sections [of the narrative], and it is also used to mark sentences or entire sections which are sequentially misaligned with the rest of the discourse' (1995:205).

After Okinawe's introduction to the story in line 1, the narrative begins with the introduction of the main characters in the context of meeting in lines 2–4. The introductory section provides the background to the story. Line 5 begins the story interaction which seems to be quite highly structured. The line begins with the first instance of the particle *mii*, which marks progress in the storyline. The first three sections of Scene I are separated by *mii* while the fourth and final part of Scene I begins with a time particle (*Gegapiich*). Scene II also begins with *mii* but then *Gegapiich* takes over for a lengthy portion of the main part of the narrative in lines 22–50. The *mii* particle comes in again at the end of Part II, scene two and continues through the epilogue and the closing with no use of the time particle *Gegapiich*. This alternation provides the storyteller and hearer with a device for separating the various sections of the narrative, for advancing the action, and for moving from one time segment to another. Again, it is clear that the narrative is highly structured by use of discourse particles.

Taken together with our analysis of character focus, doublet constructions, and tense switching, we can make the following claim: the discourse features which are of greatest importance in structuring the narrative (or dividing the narrative into different sections) are, in order of their importance, particles, tense shifting, and character focus. The most important feature in marking cohesion or togetherness within a section is the doublet construction. We are able to see that particles in Algonquian languages such as Ojibwe function to define a principle of regulation and the distribution of particles interacts with plot dynamics to help structure the legend being recounted.

We move now to the next section to see how word internal constructions also play a major role in how storytellers in the Algonquian tradition structure their stories and legends.

Word Internal Constructions

In this section we want to take a look at the morphemes *-go-*, *-dog-*, *-gwen-*, and *-ban* to see how these units of meaning are used to help structure narratives. A morpheme is defined as the smallest meaningful elements into which words can be analysed. The claim that Lisa Valentine makes for the Severn dialect of Ojibwe also holds true for the Algonquin dialect: the ability to generate and employ these subtle morphemes in narratives is considered to be one of the signs of a good story-teller. The occurrences of these morphemes in '*Amik Anishnaabewigoban*' are as follows.

Morpheme	Line
-*go*-	2, 3, 5, 6, 10, 12, 23
-*ban*-	2, 3, 5, 6, 10, 12
-*dog*-	16, 22, 24, 25, 27, 30, 31, 38, 40, 41, 48, 49, 50
-*gwen*-	21, 23, 27, 40, 51, 52

When examining Ojibwe narratives we find that the morpheme -*go*- is only used in certain kinds of narratives. The most common context is in legends and myths, which are understood to have taken place in the remote past. That is, when the storyteller wants to let the hearer know that the recounted event took place in the remote past, -*go*- is used as a marker in a number of verbs. In this instance, the first line of the legend under analysis says '*Amik Anishnaabewigoban*,' (The Beaver was once in human form). The verb morphology is as follows: *aanishnaabe* (person) + *wi* (he/she is) + *go* (remote past) + *ban* (past participle). Thus we see that -*go*- is used only in the context of legends and old stories. In speaking with the elders about this grammatical feature, I understand that it is doing the work of informing the listener that the story takes place long ago when humans and other-than-humans interacted freely with each other. The dubitative forms -*dog*- and -*gwen*- (the former found in independent verb constructions and the latter in conjunct constructions) can be used in a variety of conversational and narrative settings and, as such, are not restricted to legends and old stories. Their use is normal, however, in remote past stories. The same can be said for -*ban*-, where its use is not restricted to a certain genre of discourse.

STEP 7: OTHER CONSIDERATIONS

This step offers an invitation to cultural members in particular, and other interested readers, to begin to make interpretive statements about the moral of the story, what kinds of things it may be teaching, and a rationale for coming to certain conclusions. I asked a number of Ojibwe speakers to address the question of the moral of this particular story and what lessons it is designed to teach. Here are some of the lessons that

Ojibwe students came up with.

We must be able to adapt to our environment in order to reach our goals in life; however, in so doing we should not forget those around us, our loved ones, or we will suffer negative consequences.

When we make a commitment to someone, it is important to respect who that person is so that our goals can be accomplished in consideration for other people.

We must take care of whatever we have done in the past because it has a way of sneaking up on us. Our dreams are important to pay attention to because they are messages from the Creator, sometimes giving us warning about what can happen.

The beaver was able to adapt to his environment but he forgot to take care of his partner and almost lost her. There's an important lesson there for us.

Pay attention to your dreams!

Conclusion

The analysis of '*Amik Anishnaabewigoban*' provides many insights into the structuring devices used by speakers of Algonquian languages to create, produce, and arrange a narrative. For the teller of '*Amik Anishnaabewigoban*,' the most important ones are particle phrasing, tense shifting, proximate/obviative shifts, and direct discourse. The ability to use such devices without thinking about them attests to the teller's expertise and reputation as a storyteller and, more important, shows him to be a fluent speaker brought up in a particular cultural milieu. From this brief analysis of the legend, we can see that the teller creates a compelling performance, rich in discourse features and useful for the amusement and instruction of his audience. Essential to the discussion of Aboriginal world views and spiritual traditions is the concepts of legend and myth. They are considered to embody the sacred truths of a people. In his book *The Power of Myth*, Joseph Campbell writes about what he considers to be the basic functions of indigenous legends and myths:

What human beings have in common is revealed in stories ... stories of our search for truth, for meaning, for significance. We all need to tell our story and understand our story. We all need to understand death and to cope with death, and we all need help in our passages from birth to life and then to death. We need to ... understand the mysterious, to find out who we are. (1988:5)

11

'Why the Lynx Has Short Intestines': Collateral Information in Ojibwe Storytelling

In our first winter in Pikogan we were invited to go to the bush with a family who were becoming our friends. Their bush camp was accessible by road, but only a four-wheel drive could get through the snow on the bush road. Even then, we had to make a couple of trips to transport both families and all of our stuff. It was a wonderful time for us. Our first winter living with Anishnaabe people and spending Christmas in the bush! There were thirteen of us all crowded into a tent, young babies and not-so-young adults all together. Our hosts had brought a small stove-pipe stove with them and the tent was quite cozy and warm inside even though it was minus 30 celsius outside. Alfred, Henry, and I set some rabbit snares and trekked around the bush looking for whatever game might be encountered in the dead of winter. On Christmas Eve we brought a small fir tree into the tent to give it that 'Christmas Spirit.' We had all brought some small presents with us and we nestled them up under the tree. Then we all snuggled into our blankets and sleeping bags and went to sleep.

My next memory is of a bright flame coming from inside the tent! My first thoughts were to grab as many kids as I could and get out of there before we were engulfed in flames. What had happened was that someone had got up in the wee hours of the morning to keep the fire going. When he discovered that it was no longer burning, he piled some wood into the stove, grabbed some lighter fluid, sprayed the wood with the fluid, and then lit the stove with a match.[1] Unbeknownst to him, some of the lighter fluid had spilled on the ground around the Christmas tree, and when he tried to light the wood the tree caught fire. At first, he tried to stamp out the fire with his bare feet, but changed his mind about that method after just a couple of stomps.

Thinking quickly, he grabbed one of the heavy blankets (actually, *my* blanket!), and proceeded to smother the flames. It all happened so fast that some of the younger kids didn't even wake up. When everything was under control we examined our presents for fire damage. Sure enough, most of the presents under the tree had been scorched or warped beyond recognition. Still, we were all thankful the situation hadn't escalated and that everyone was all right.

We all laughed and joked about it during the day and it became quite a funny story when we all got back to the reserve. One interesting thing about the telling of the story (and I heard it told countless times) is the emphasis on what *didn't* happen. Most versions I heard (and told myself) included standard lines such as: 'The tent didn't catch on fire,' 'No one was hurt,' and, 'We didn't have to leave the tent.' The more I thought about the structure of the various versions of that story that was told and retold, the more I began monitoring my own and others' stories for a similar structure. I began to realize that it was quite common for people to tell about what didn't happen in the midst of telling a story about something that did happen. But why would someone tell about something that *didn't* happen while telling a story about what *did*? That basic question eventually led me into the kinds of considerations that we will explore in this chapter.

This feature of storytelling is not an Ojibwe-exclusive discourse structure. As research on conversational storytelling in a variety of contexts and languages informs us, one kind of thing that happens to narratives told in live discourse is that the listeners may transform them, in an effort to figure out the sense of what they have been told (Sharrock and Turner, 1978; Bal, 1985; Barnes, 1992). In effect, when a story gets told in everyday conversation, those listening may have to do some figuring out to get the sense of it, to understand what went on and why it was told. Further, when stories are told in naturally occurring contexts, some of the information included may not necessarily be part of the course-of-action in the narrative. Most discourse linguists refer to this kind of information as *background* (Grimes, 1975; Hatim, 1990; Silverman, 1993). Much of this background is used to clarify a story and to explain other information in the story, much as we were doing when relating the Christmas fire episode to people back at Pikogan. These explanations or accounts often involve things that the storyteller feels need to be clarified in order to avoid any misunderstanding.

This chapter examines instances where storytellers tell about things that did not happen (termed *collateral* information in the linguistic discourse literature) as they recounted their stories. First we will look at a linguistic discourse analysis treatment of collateral as found in the linguistic literature relating to narrative. Then we will examine the same phenomenon from the perspective of conversation analysis. In so doing, I do not merely extend a linguistic discourse analysis treatment of the issues, but show how the issues get transformed in theoretically interesting ways. Finally, we will examine how collateral information functions in Ojibwe storytelling and compare that with the way collateral works in English.

A Linguistic Treatment of Collateral

One of the integrative themes of this book is that the discipline of linguistics has much to offer the student of live discourse. Some issues arising in sociolinguistics, for example, find parallels in linguistic discourse analysis (LDA). Its treatment of collateral information in discourse is one of those issues. Joseph Grimes, in *The Thread of Discourse*, was one of the first linguists to describe collateral information in narratives from a linguistic discourse perspective. Grimes notes that the main function of collateral information is to set off what actually happens in a narrative with what might have happened.

One example he uses is from a Saramaccan narrative about a canoe trip that ended when the canoe capsized in the rapids. One part of the story is as follows: 'The canoe overturned. The father didn't die, the mother didn't die, the children didn't die. Instead, they all escaped to land.' Grimes writes: 'By telling what did not happen to the participants, [the storyteller] throws their escape into relief' (1975:64). He then attempts to describe a roster of the grammatical forms associated with collateral information.

Adversatives are a form of negation in Grimes's roster that imply parallel but disjoint action. His example, 'They brought pickles but we brought mustard,' implies, 'They did not bring mustard and we did not bring pickles.' Adversatives can also imply that the speaker assumes the hearer to have inferred something that is plausible but that did not in fact happen. His example, 'We arrived late but were received immediately,' implies, 'I, the speaker, think that you, the hearer, must expect that if we were to arrive late the logical thing would be for our reception to be postponed. Contrary to your expectation, we were received immediately' (Grimes, 1975:65).

It should be noted that questions in English are often used to indicate collateral information and can be treated with regard to the information they presuppose vis-à-vis what they inquire about. Grimes writes:

When did John get here? presupposes that John did get here, so that the area of uncertainty is restricted to the time of his arrival. When did you stop beating your wife? is more complex; it assumes that you have a wife, that there was a time when you beat her, and that there was a time after which you no longer beat her. The question is directed toward ascertaining that time. The presuppositions in a question are almost like conditions laid down by the speaker for the hearer to give an acceptable answer. If the hearer accepts the presuppositions, then he can give the missing information that is required; if not, he is in a bind. (1975:66)

According to Grimes, then, collateral information relates non-events to events and, by providing a range of non-events that might take place, heightens the significance of what actually happens. Furthermore, collateral information has the effect of anticipation of what is likely to happen in a narrative when the alternatives are spelled out in advance. Grimes notes that, in this respect, 'collateral information is not very different from foreshadowing' (1975:65).

In *The Grammar of Discourse* (1983), Longacre begins to build upon Grimes's notion of collateral information. He divides narratives into seven parts with regard to notional (deep) structure: exposition – where background information of time, place and participants is given; inciting moment – when the planned and predictable is broken up in some manner; developing conflict – in which the situation intensifies, or deteriorates, depending on one's viewpoint; climax – where everything comes to a head; dénouement – a crucial event happens which makes resolution possible; final suspense – which works out the details of the resolution; and conclusion – which brings the story to some sort of end. Each part of discourse corresponds with narrative surface structures, e.g. inciting moment (deep structure) with pre-peak episode (surface structure). Not all narratives contain all seven parts, but Longacre claims that a well-developed narrative is likely to have most or all of them, since each part contributes to the success of the narrative.

In describing main-line versus supportive material in discourse, Longacre makes the claim that 'it is impossible to make structural distinctions among discourse types without taking [supportive material] into account' (1983:14). He cites Grimes as having already described the types of information in which a distinction is made between events and non-events (collateral). The example of collateral information which he uses in discussing supportive material is a passage from Mark Twain.

In a minute a third slave was struggling in the air. It was dreadful. I turned away my head for a moment, and when I turned back I missed the King! They were blindfolding him! I was paralyzed; I couldn't move, I was choking, my tongue was petrified. They finished blindfolding him, they led him under the rope. I couldn't shake off that clinging impotence. But when I saw them put the noose around his neck, then everything let go in me and I made a spring to the rescue – and as I made it I shot one more glance abroad – by George! here they came, a- tilting! – five hundred mailed and belted knights on bicycles! (Cited in Longacre, 1983:16)

Longacre notes that in this paragraph some course-of-action events (what happened) are reported along with some supportive material (non-events). After delineating the main-line material in the discourse (events), he describes the other clauses in the paragraph which have a supportive function. These clauses are excluded from the course-of-action analysis, even though this information supports the course-of-action. He then comments on one clause which contains collateral information – 'I couldn't shake off that clinging impotence' – by saying that 'Grimes calls this collateral' (1983:16).

Larry Jones (1983) discusses the use of collateral in his examination of author comments or asides in narrative discourse. He contends that by these comments and asides, one is able to discover and describe many of the assumptions the author made concerning his or her intended reader and the topic of the discourse. Wilbur Pickering (1979) treats collateral under the heading of *prominence*. He begins by saying that 'we can only perceive something if it stands out from its background' (1979:40), and that there seems to be a problem of terminology in linguistics with regard to prominence. Some linguists use the terms 'topic,' 'focus,' 'theme,' and 'emphasis' quite broadly, which leads to areas of overlap and confusion. He uses the term 'prominence' to refer to any device which gives certain events, participants, or objects more significance than others in the same context (1979:41).

In LDA it is recognized that the feature of *strategy* is also important. Strategy, according to Pickering, reflects 'a basic characteristic of communication and of most human behavior: it has a purpose' (1979:70). This comment relates to an assumption made by most discourse linguists: namely, that a speaker or author ought to try to be meaningful in his or her communication. Writers such as Grice (1975), Gordon and Lakoff (1975), and Sadock (1978), have been concerned with the notion of conversational implicature, that is, the way hearers conclude a lot of implicit information on the basis of what a speaker says. George Huttar (1982) gives the following example to illustrate a treatment of conversational implicature.

A: I'm out of gas.
B: There's a garage around the corner.

Huttar argues that, because garages are thought by members of A's and B's culture to be places where you can get gas when you need it, the above pair of utterances hang together. Strategy relates to collateral information in discourse about what did not happen, where its use is influenced by such factors as the speaker's judgment as to what knowledge his or her hearers share, the topic of the narrative, and what the speaker is trying to communicate. These considerations encourage discourse linguists to examine the ethnographic dimension in LDA, an area which has been painfully missing from these studies (Moerman, 1988; Valentine, 1995). Even when attempting to embrace the ethnographic dimension, discourse linguists are usually bound by edited texts. Written, edited texts have recognized conventions that distinguish them from live discourse. Thus, in written texts there will necessarily be a different distribution between the two. For example, Jan Renkema (1993) suggests that the written text shows clearer organization than the oral text. This is because the author has had time to plan the development of the story which results in the lack of hesitation words and abnormal ordering of words and sentences due to afterthought.

Certainly there is an ethnography of writing as surely as there is an ethnography of speaking, and LDA has tended to neglect this consideration when analysing written texts (Moerman, 1988; Poole, 1990; Hopper, 1991). The discourse linguist Pickering early on formulated this problem in linguistic discourse analysis: 'While I insist that situation and culture are part of the prior context upon which given information [in narrative] may be based, I freely confess that I do not know how to handle it.'

And this is the crux of the matter in LDA and its treatment of a feature such as collateral; there has been a recognition of the lack of the contextual factor, but no understanding of how to handle it. Pickering concludes: 'I am entering a plea that more linguists recognize both the legitimacy and necessity of grappling with the role of situation and culture in discourse analysis' (1979:170).

A Conversation Analysis Treatment of Collateral Information

In linguistic discourse analysis there seems to be a notion that narratives can be analysed as if they were self-contained speech units (Lee, 1992; Cortazzi, 1994). Missing in the discourse literature is a consideration of why people would want to generate a narrative in the first place. This is not a small matter, for without such a consideration the discourse analyst lacks a theory of conversation to make the ethnographic connection between the social function of telling about past experiences with the purpose(s) of members engaged in conversational interaction (Poole, 1990; Tedlock and Mannheim, 1995). Certainly narratives in live discourse cannot be analysed adequately without taking into account the fit between the generated narrative and the discourse in which it is embedded.

In conversation analysis, our understanding of narrative structures is expanded by making the connection between narratives and the surrounding discourse via the use of social identities and membership categories. The issue of social identity is, I believe, important in discourse analysis. Any one person can have a number of social identities that can be applicable at any one time. For example, someone could be identified as a wife, lawyer, the lady next door, neighbour, or whatever, and the relatedness between identity categories that go together (e.g., employer-employee) is a major interactional resource in the construction and sustaining of social order. In relation to narratives told in live discourse, they are more than mere displays of verbal skill. Rather, narratives can be used in a number of interactional ways, such as presenting oneself as a certain kind of person, offering advice, seeking a solution to a personal problem, and so on.

In examining stories in English it becomes noticeable that in many narratives the storyteller not only tells about the events which happen, but those that did not. As my point of departure, I want to return to the Louise and Ken story which we examined in an earlier chapter.

Louise: One night (1.0) I was with this guy that I liked a real lot, and uhh (3.0) we had come back from the show, we had gone to the Ash Grove for a while 'n we were gonna park. An' I can't stand a car, 'n he has a small car.

Ken: Mm hm.
Louise: So we walked to the back, 'n we just went into the back house
             'n we stayed there half the night (1.0) we didn't go to bed with
             each other but, it was so comfortable 'n so nice.
Ken: Mm hm.
Louise: Y'know? there's everything perfect.

Note, first, that Louise brings the listener, Ken, to a point of decision
in the course-of-action sequence, at which point possibilities are investigated which set apart what actually happened from what might have
happened. She does this twice in the narrative, ' 'n we were gonna park,'
and 'we didn't go to bed with each other.' Further, we can see from the
transcript how including this collateral information may predict actions
that might or might not take place later on in the narrative. As linguistic
discourse studies have shown, at a point in a narrative where the storyteller includes collateral information, the fact that what did not happen
is mentioned makes what happened stand out. In this story, Louise
would be telling a different kind of story if she had not included collateral information in her narrative. The following is Louise's story without the collateral information.

Louise: One night I was with this guy that I liked a real lot, an uhh we
             had come back from the show, we had gone to the Ash Grove
             for a while, so we walked back to the house, an' we just stayed
             in the back house half the night. It was so comfortable 'n so
             nice.

By including collateral information, a storyteller may relate non-
events to course-of-action events, the provision of such non-event alternatives heightening some significant aspect of what happened. And we
can see that the narrative sounds quite different without those alternatives. Comparing the real version of the story with the hypothetical one
above, Louise comes across as two different persons. Further, it is not
like providing ground for merely not doing something, for example, 'We
were going to walk to the Cubs game, but it was raining so we ended up
taking the bus.' Some other kind of work is getting done for the storyteller, and one way to get at what that work is can be accomplished by
examining how it functions in other contexts.
       Let us first suppose that in this story Louise had not included the col-
lateral information. Then it would be open to the listeners to conclude

that storytellers are the kind of people who would normally do what they were telling about. Louise, for example, could be viewed as the kind of teenager who would normally use an unchaperoned house in order to engage in sexual activities. Both Louise and Ken are seventeen years old. In this instance, however, with the inclusion of what didn't happen, Louise builds a defensive design into her story. That is, Louise can anticipate that Ken might think of her as the kind of girl who might normally participate in an adult sexual situation. After all, that's what makes the story risky in the first place – that the normal place for teenagers to negotiate sex (a car), was abandoned in favour of an adult place. Thus Louise makes sure she attends to the defensive design of her story in order to inform Ken that what happened was spontaneous and unplanned and not something she would normally do. Further, the sexual aspect of the activity is somewhat minimized in that she was with 'this guy that I liked a real lot.' That is perhaps a lot different than describing him as 'a guy I know' or 'a friend' or 'this guy,' which might make Ken think that she was not particularly choosy about who she engages in sexual situations with. As it is, the way Louise positions what didn't happen, she makes it clear to Ken that she would normally use the normal place for teenagers to negotiate sex, in a parked car, but that due to extenuating circumstances this one time she happened to have abandoned the normal place for teenagers and opted for an adult place. By telling about what didn't happen, then, she informs Ken that alternatives were assessed, thus allowing him to interpret her actions as being something she would not normally do. This work gets done by orienting to local teenage standards.

Furthermore, we can see in this story that Louise tells about another activity that didn't happen, another piece of collateral information. Having told about going to the back house, she goes on to say, 'we didn't go to bed with each other,' information which Louise feels needs to be made explicit. If Louise had not included this, Ken might have thought, 'If she would do that, what else would she do?' In effect, Louise knows that what she is telling about may be considered to be somewhat abnormal behaviour for a teenager. Thus, she embeds in her recounting of what happened two instances of collateral information, that is, what didn't happen.

What we have, then, are some technical resources put into operation in order to isolate a particular occurrence of abnormal behaviour by teenage standards. These resources provide Ken with a sharp specification of what kinds of terms Louise has for such a project. They also lend credibility to Louise's defensive design to her narrative in that, by telling about what didn't happen, she can perhaps ward off any negative inferences Ken might draw from the specific event that she is describing. With the above analysis in mind, we now turn to an analysis of the use of collateral information in Ojibwe storytelling.

Collateral Information in Ojibwe Storytelling

In Algonquian languages such as Ojibwe, we can see how collateral information in a non-English narrative might be treated. In the following narrative, note the three instances of collateral information.

'Mooz Aadisokaan' (Story about a Moose)

1. *Abitibi zaagahigan nigii-oji-nisaa nimoozom.*
   Abitibi Lake is where I killed my moose.
2. *E-bimibizowaagiban jimaanikaag nibaapam e-wiijiiwag.*
   I was canoeing with my father.
3. *Oniijaanii niitam nigii-waabamaa.*
   I was the first to see the female moose.
4. *Mii dash gaawin nidooji-gwagwe-baashkizawaasi, ozaa gichi zagaakwaaban.*
   I didn't even try to shoot right away because of the branches.
5. *E-aabanaabiyaag gaa-bimijigabawij gichi-yaabe.*
   When I looked back there was a big buck at her side.
6. *Aabidin eta nigii-baashkizawaa.*
   I only shot him once.
7. *Gaawin waawaaj midaasozid gii-oji-ipatosii.*
   He didn't even run ten feet.
8. *Bagii dash gii-gwazigwani giji-boozihaayaag jiimaanikaag, gaa-ishkwaa-bagojiinaakeyaag e-mochi-niizhiyaag.*
   He was a bit heavy to load into the canoe even after we cut him up because there were just two of us.
9. *Apiich dash wedi gaa-ishkwaa-giiweyaag wedi miigiwaamikaag, gichi-mamagahan e-giiwebizowaag.*
   When we arrived back at the camp, there were big waves on the lake while we were canoeing.
10. *Mii sa dash gaa-oji-ojibizowaag wedi gaa-izhi-dazhiikeyaag.*
    So then we drove back to our camp.
11. *Mii gaa-inasaayaag nimoozominaan.*
    We had to leave the moose (in the canoe).

12. *Gabe-dibik jiimaanikaag gii-abi.*
    He was in the canoe all night.

13. *E-gizhebawashig dash e-wii-bi-giiweyaag megwaaj e-boodaasowaag moo-
    zogaashkaag weji-bi-agwaabizowaaj.*
    In the morning we wanted to go home, but while we were loading
    the moose, the game wardens drove by.

14. *Deshiwaag goj, 'Gaawin maajiikegon, kidakoninom,' nidigomin.*
    Right away they said, 'Don't move, you're under arrest,' we were told.

15. *'Gaawin gidinendaagozisii giji-nisaj mooz.'*
    'You're not allowed to kill a moose.'

16. *Nigii-gwagwe-wiidamawaa ohomaa e-izhi-anookiiyaag ashij dash nind-
    inendaagozinan giji-nisag nimoozom.*
    I tried to tell them that we trapped there, and that I am allowed to
    kill a moose.

17. *Gaa megaa dash owii-debwetasiin.*
    Of course he didn't want to believe me.

18. *Mii dash gakina baashkiziganan ogii-odaapinaanan, boodaajigan, ashij
    waasakonenjigan, gakina ogii-boozitoonaawaa odaabaanikaag.*
    So then they took all of the guns, the moose call and the flashlights,
    they loaded everything into their vehicle.

19. *Baanimaa dash nigii-giiwebizomin miinawaaj gaa-izhi-bagojiinaakeyaag
    giji-waabadahag aadi gaa-izhi-nisaayaag mooz nibaapaam niinawid.*
    Then we had to go back to where we had cut up the moose to see
    where my father and I had killed the moose.

20. *Ogii-boozitoonaawaan okaadan, gakina gegoon.*
    They loaded the legs, everything.

21. *Gaawin gegoon odooji-ishkonasiinaawaa.*
    They didn't leave anything behind.

22. *Mii gaa-izhi-maajidoowaajin.*
    Then they took it all away.

23. *Cochrane baanimaa nigii-izhiwinigoog.*
    They had to take me to Cochrane.

24. *Gaawin nidooji-gibaahogosii.*
    They didn't lock me up.

25. *Gegaad nigii-gibahogoo baanimaa egaa dash nigi-ozhibiihodizonan giji-
    zaagahamaan.*
    I was almost locked up, then I had to sign something so I could leave.

26. *Mii dash gaa-niizhogajigwagag gaa-ikidoj, 'Aabitawiseg niga-bi-aanim-
    wemin.'*
    So then on Tuesday he said, 'I'm going to call on Wednesday.'

27. *Ge-apichi-tibaakonigoowaanen gekwaan giji-gooki-giiwe-miinigowaanen nimoozom.*
They said they would make a decision whether to sentence me or give me back my moose.

28. *Mii dash gaa-aabitawisenig gii-bi-aanimwe ashij dash nigii-aabajihaaban Cochrane anishinaabe dibaakonigewinni.*
So then he called on Wednesday and by then I had hired an Indian lawyer.

29. *Mii aha gaa-miikidag.*
So then he worked on it.

30. *E-aabitawisenig gii-bi-dewesijige moozogaashkaa.*
On Wednesday the game warden called.

31. *'Giga-biinajiwinaa gimoozom wedi zaagahiganikaag.*
'You can come pick up your moose at the lake.

32. *Nigii-izhiwinaanaan gaa-odinaawaajin.'*
We took him back to where he came from.'

33. *Mii dash gaa-nda-waabamag nimoozom.*
So then I went to look for my moose.

34. *Niwaabamaag igi moozogaashkaag, gaawin waawaaj nidayamihigosiig.*
I saw those game wardens [there], they wouldn't even talk to me.

35. *Megaa gaa-apiichi-agajihidizowaaj.*
Because, of course, they were ashamed of themselves.

36. *Mii eta.*
That's it.

In the first instance of collateral information (line 4), the storyteller gives an account for why he didn't immediately try to shoot the moose he saw in the forest, *Mii dash gaawin nidooji-gwagwe-baashkizawaasii, ozaa gichi zagaakwaaban* (I didn't try to shoot right away because of the branches). In line 17, we find another utterance containing collateral information, *Gaa megaa dash owii-debwetasiin* (Of course he didn't want to believe me). Then in line 24 we find a third instance of collateral information in the narrative, *Gaawin nidooji-gibaahogosii* (He didn't lock me up). In Ojibwe, as in English, utterances in stories which are constructed with negatives almost always contain collateral information. One reason for this, a reason which places emphasis on the function of collateral as viewed from a discourse linguist's perspective, is that collateral information can be useful as a *highlighting device*. In Ojibwe, as in other languages, events that are reported in storytelling as having not taken place have significance only in relation to what actually does happen in a narrative. Collateral information in Ojibwe narratives contributes to a high-lighting effect by focusing the attention of the listeners on what else might happen in the place of what did not happen.

In reading the above story note that the sorts of relationships between telling about what happened and telling about what didn't happen are analytically interesting. We can see that someone involved in telling a narrative in live discourse may or may not choose to tell about what did not happen. In the case of the former, we might ask why someone in the midst of telling a story would tell about something that did not happen. How can there be a place in a story for something that did not happen? After all, live discourse is full of people telling about what they did or what happened to them. These preliminary questions lead us to deeper issues, one being how storytellers in Ojibwe may employ alternative activity assessment procedures.

ALTERNATIVE ACTIVITY ASSESSMENT PROCEDURES

Up to this point I have suggested that it is not unusual to find instances of narratives in live discourse in which the storyteller includes collateral information and tells about something that did not take place. A deeper issue, however, is that not only why what didn't happen is told about in some instances, but how this recounting is positioned in the narratives as alternative to what did happen, so that this collateral information is presented as a *rejected* alternative. One way of getting to the heart of the matter is by exploring how people make sense out of observable sights in which other people are apparently active; that is, how do people go about making sense of a witnessed activity? In order to begin to answer this question I want to revisit one of the legends that we explored earlier in chapter 5.

First, I want to discuss a structure which the sociologist Sheldon Twer characterized many years ago as 'assessing alternatives.' These positions are structured by the 'instead of,' as in 'instead of A, then B,' A being filled by a class of possible activities and B being filled by a class of activities which may be seen as alternatives to those in A. Not only do they stand as alternative activities but they can also stand together. That is, it seems reasonable to suggest that the A and B activities chosen by storytellers show how things can be classified together, that names of activities can be classified as a group, one feature being that they can stand as alternatives in the 'instead of A, then B' structure. One feature of conversation upon which this structure is grounded is that people hold certain expectations about what happens when people are engaged in conversational interaction. One of those expectations is that people are constantly figuring out what is going on and responding according to what they are 'hearing' or 'seeing' in any interactional context.

The point here is that people who describe their activities in conversational interaction, such as happens in most storytelling situations, have criteria for choosing one action rather than another, or one action as an alternative to another. Furthermore, actions can be made to belong where they occur in descriptions. Twer was one of the first to refer to these positions of descriptions as 'action spots' and suggested that people describing their activities can know, find, or suggest provisions for that activity's occurrence. These action spots are characteristically filled by things that have happened. What we are attempting to analyse here are the facilities Ojibwe storytellers use for describing an activity and at least partially knowing what the description will tell, how it will inform, and what it will mean to the listeners. In that our interest in this chapter is particularly concerned with occasions in which people talk about behavioural episodes, there is a natural relation to narratives in live discourse as one such occasion. I suggest that the analysis of such descriptions permits a formulation of a set of features of behaviour that people apparently use when they try to make sense of such descriptions. With these comments in mind, let us return to an excerpt from the legend of 'The Lynx and the Marten.'

5. *Gegapiich ogii-inaan owiijiiwaaganan waabishtaan, 'Giin giga-babaami-nizhawaag amikwag.*
   After a while the lynx said to his friend the marten, 'You make the beavers run around.
6. *Gadaa-bidaahamoogij.*
   They will be caught in the net.
7. *Niin niga-gaaniwenimaa gidasabinaan.'*
   Me, I will watch our net.'
8. *Gegapiich bidaahanaadog waabishtaan amikwan.*
   After a while the marten catches a beaver.
9. *Ezhi-jaagizhegwaagonedaabiigwen odamikoman waabishtaan.*
   The marten must be hiding his beaver.
10. *Gaawin owiidamawaasiwan owiijiiwaaganan.*
    He doesn't tell his friend.
11. *Bizhiw megaa dash owiijiiwaan aha waabishtaan e-anokiiwaaj.*
    Of course the lynx always goes with the marten to hunt.

We want to pay some attention here to how the storyteller builds into the legend a variation of the alternative activity assessment structure. Note, first, that, intuitively, other choices of activities for A, what did not happen, would not make the same kind of sense as, in this instance, the marten sharing the beaver he caught with his friend the lynx. That is, the choice of sharing the beaver he caught with the lynx is not merely chosen at random but is chosen as an alternative to what ended up getting done, which was hiding the beaver from the lynx and not telling him. Implied here is the notion that when someone uses such a structure there exists some kind of criterion for choosing one activity as an alternative to another. For example, to answer the question, 'What is the marten doing?' the notion of doing, which is invoked in the above examples from live discourse, provides us with materials for beginning to search for a solution to the problem I formulated earlier. How so?

In this legend we can see that one alternative activity is accepted and another rejected and that a structure similar to the 'instead of A, then B' is being employed, albeit with an additional constraint. Not only are alternatives assessed at the time of the event but they are *reported* as assessed at the time of the telling. It is important to keep in mind, though, that just because an event may be seen as an alternative to another, that does not necessarily imply that the other is alternative to it. That is, while the storyteller reports that the marten hid the beaver from the lynx as alternative to sharing the beaver, if the marten *had* shared the beaver with the lynx, it would indeed have been odd to report that this activity was done as an alternative to hiding the beaver from his friend. After all, what is the story about and how would it be a different story if the storyteller had told about how the lynx and marten went hunting together, the marten caught a beaver, shared it with his friend the lynx and they both lived happily ever after? Then it becomes the kind of story one might see on *Sesame Street* or *Barney the Dinosaur*. And this is the crux of the matter. Contained within this observation is a potential solution to the formulated problem, and with it we will be able to begin to technicalize some of the interactional work which gets done when a storyteller includes collateral information in his or her narrative.

We can begin to justify this observation by consulting Sharrock and Turner. They write: 'We assume nevertheless the possibility of [listener] transforms constrain tellers and that they may employ devices intended to constrain the reworkings that their tellings may undergo' (1978:187).

We are seeking to locate and describe one of those devices a storyteller can use in directing the listener to make sense of what happened in the narrative and what the story is about. In this story, for example, by telling about what didn't happen ('He doesn't tell his friend' in line 10), the storyteller instructs the listener that there was a rejected alternative to what happened. Had the storyteller not included this alternative activity assessment, the listener has no available resources for interpreting what happened as something that is not normal behaviour on this particular occasion. On the contrary, with the storyteller's deployment of the alternative activity assessment device, the listener is clearly instructed to interpret what happened as something distinctly unusual and not merely a mundane course-of-action story.

ACTIVITY ASSESSMENT AS AN INTERACTIONAL RESOURCE

Thus far I have noted that storytellers sometimes include collateral information in their narratives, telling about what didn't happen as alternative to something that did happen. However, the other, if it happens, would not necessarily be presented as an alternative to the first. In the legend under analysis, the storyteller presents sharing the beaver with the lynx as a rejected alternative and hiding the beaver from the lynx as an alternative which fills the action spot in his narrative. Our question becomes: What interactional work is getting done by the storytellers' alternative activity assessments?

In the legend 'The Lynx and the Marten,' the marten ended up doing what he did by being diverted, for whatever reason, from an expected course of activity, the category-bound activity of hunting together. Hunting together is a natural course of activity as we can gather from the story itself in line 11, *Bizhiw megaa dash owiijiiwaan aha waabishtaan e-anokiiwaaj* (Of course the lynx always goes with the marten to hunt). What he ultimately did (hiding the beaver from the lynx) was something that came about by virtue of some other agenda, in this case the desire to play a trick on the lynx or wanting to keep the beaver all to himself, or whatever. A natural course of activity was expected as the story unfolds, and that project gets changed in the course-of-action. The project of hunting together and sharing what was caught had already been oriented to in lines 1 and 2, *Bizhiw ashij waabishtaan babaa-anokii-waagoban* (The lynx and the marten were hunting around,) *Amikwan babaa-anoojiihaawaagoban* (They were hunting for beavers). One feature of the storyteller's inclusion of the activity assessment is its spontaneous nature. There is a deviousness in the marten's actions as reported

by the storyteller's use of the alternative activity assessment, a deviousness linked with the spontaneous nature of what the marten ended up
doing.

By using the assessing alternatives structure, then, a storyteller can
instruct those listening to the story that what happened occurred as an
alternative to what didn't happen. The structure provides for the listeners to see that alternatives were assessed. As I noted earlier, it would,
after all, be quite a different story if the story unfolded as a mundane
reporting of the lynx and the marten going hunting for beavers, catching
one and eating it together. As it is, the storyteller instructs the listeners
to see that one alternative was rejected and another accepted. By
employing this structure the storyteller makes clear that it was not a
common occurrence for the marten to hide the beaver from the lynx nor
to play a devious trick on him. That what happened ought not to be seen
as normal can be seen in line 11, *Bizhiw megaa dash owiijiiwaan aha
waabishtaan e-anokiiwaaj* (Of course the lynx always goes with the marten
to hunt).[2]

In a general sense I have confined my interests to one possible feature
of narratives: the assessment of alternative activities in a specified environment as part of a storyteller's design. The general procedure for
building a design into the sequence of a story provides for the hearer to
see the rejected alternative as a normal activity and the accepted alternative as the abnormal one. It follows, therefore, that if you hear a story
containing an assessment of alternative activities, then you must hear
that assessment as constituting part of the storyteller's design.

Differences between Conversation Analysis and Linguistic Discourse Analysis

One further subject remains to be explored here. In this chapter I want to
travel full circle and show how the use of conversation analysis (CA)
can make a methodological contribution to linguistic discourse analysis
(LDA) and re-emphasize what CA can tell us about Ojibwe-specific
ways of thinking, interacting, and perceiving the world around us. I
want to do this by examining how LDA attends to dialogue and compare that with how CA addresses the same phenomenon in a way which
offers LDA some ways of looking at naturally occurring talk and interaction which have been neglected. In so doing, I will demonstrate how a
conversational analysis methodology raises interesting issues which
LDA currently neglects.

A LINGUISTIC DISCOURSE ANALYSIS TREATMENT OF DIALOGUE

As I mentioned earlier, there is a recognition in LDA that valuable contributions might be found in other disciplinary perspectives (Button
and Lee, 1987; Lee, 1992; Cortazzi, 1994; Fleming, 1995). Linguists are
perhaps more aware than those in other disciplines of the need to integrate. In fact, a number of invitations have been extended from the linguistic community to other disciplines. Longacre, for example, ends
the chapter on repartee with the following comment: 'All that we have
written here needs eventually to be supplemented by and compared
with the current research into the nature of live conversation' (1983:75).
Jones, too, writes about the need for a broader linguistic vision which
encompasses the social sciences: 'One of the new frontiers of linguistics,
discourse analysis, is in fact a part of a larger frontier, the study of how
people think and how they express their thoughts ... In exploring
this new territory, the discourse linguist ... who chooses to remain close
to his own linguistic border will be, I believe, infinitely the poorer'
(1983:137).

The LDA view of sequencing in discourse, for example, has traditionally been viewed as sentences strung together in much the same way
that clauses within sentences can be joined with various kinds of con-
nectives (Crystal, 1987; Poole, 1990; Cortazzi, 1994). In a linguistic
treatment of repartee (dialogue), however, the need for an ethnographic
dimension (including features of culture and situation in the analysis) is
painfully apparent. In LDA, attention is paid to response structures –
that is, question-answer. However, as Grimes notes, 'The content of the
second part is dependent upon the content of the first part to a greater
extent. How to express this interlocking seems to be beyond us'
(1975:212). As an example of what I think Grimes is referring to, in the
linguistic literature there is a treatment of the hearer rejection option in
dialogue; that option can surely be extended to narrative responses. But
little attention is paid to how hearer rejection works or the different
ways it can be accomplished. Response types are identified and cata-
logued, but the related issues of how they are generated in live discourse, what they look like, and how they work in conversational
interaction are neglected. In live discourse, for example, the links
between utterances cannot necessarily be paraphrased as connections,
and sequences which discourse analysts may judge as being ill-formed
when taken in isolation actually occur quite frequently. Recall the following example from chapter 4:

A: I have a fourteen-year-old son.
B: Well, that's all right.
A: I also have a dog.
B: Oh, I'm sorry.

Such remarks and responses seem strange when taken in isolation, but quite natural when taken in the context of the actual conversation in which A is raising a series of possible disqualifications for apartment rental with the landlord, B (Sacks, 1992). Thus an LDA treatment of sequencing which suggests the existence of ill-formed sequences may be seriously questioned.

Longacre was one of the first discourse linguists to address the treatment of simple repartee which illustrates the kinds of issues now being studied by linguists interested in the analysis of discourse structures (Poole, 1990; Lee, 1992; Cortazzi, 1994). In his discussion of dialogue, Longacre notes that the surface structure of a language contains a basic dialogue paragraph which may be characterized as beginning with an *initiating utterance* (IU). The initiating utterance encodes what Longacre refers to as three notional units. These units are *question* (Q), *proposal* (Pro), and *remark* (Rem). Question signifies a solicitation of information.

A request may be made by examining ... presuppositions of the request, i.e. we may say *Have you a match?* when we mean *Please give me a match.* Or we may say *Is there any more salad down there at that end of the table?* when we really mean *Pass me the salad.* All of these really are notional proposals rather than notional questions. (1983:48)

Longacre's use of the term proposal includes such things as advice, suggestion, invitation, threat, command, and so on. In the surface structure of language, a proposal may have a declarative, imperative, or interrogative structure. The proposal is a call to action rather than a request for information. Remark, then, indicates that a speaker is making a comment or a declaration. It may be used, for example, as a request for an evaluation from the other conversationalist(s) to see if they agree or disagree with the observation of the first speaker.

Longacre claims that a simple dialogue concludes with another surface structure unit, which he refers to as the *resolving utterance* (RU). This is usually generated by a second speaker rather than by the first, and encodes three units of notional structure: *answer* (A), *response* (Res), and *evaluation* (Ev). Answer resolves the structure initiated as a question, response resolves the structure initiated as a proposal, and evaluation resolves the structure initiated as a remark: 'The three underlying structures correspond to the three underlying structures which encode within the initiating utterance. This gives us three pairs of utterances: question-answer, proposal-response, remark-evaluation' (1983:49).

Longacre's analysis leads him to conclude that we are able to posit three simple dialogues in most languages, as follows:

1. A: What time is it? (IU, Q)
    B: It's four o'clock. (RU, A)
2. A: Come over here. (IU, Pro)
    B: Okay, I'm coming. (RU, Res)
3. A: The whole matter is absurd. (IU, Rem)
    B: Yes, indeed. (RU, Ev)

In addition, Longacre claims that simple dialogue may contain a *terminating utterance* (TU) which encodes two different kinds of deep or notional structures: *acquiescence* (Acq) and *rejection* (Rej). His analysis is designed to be relevant to response options in a variety of dialogue settings, and he claims as much in his discussion of complex repartee: 'A complex dialogue results when the second speaker does not ... accept the dialogue on the terms suggested by the first speaker. On the contrary, the second speaker wants to ... moderate the force of the first speaker's utterance; he wants in some way to blunt its point' (1983:51).

A second speaker can accomplish this by using what Longacre terms a *continuing utterance* (CU), which appears between the initiating utterance and the resolving utterance. The continuing utterance encodes three deep structures: *counter-question*, *counter-proposal*, and *counter-remark*. This structure can occur as a chain of continuing utterances of indeterminate length. Longacre claims that a dialogue can also involve the interplay of units of different sizes, including *narrative*. But surely there is more to hearer responses in naturally occurring conversational interaction than acceptance, rejection, and continuing utterances. It is at this point, I believe, that CA has much to offer the discourse linguist.

A CONVERSATION ANALYSIS TREATMENT OF DIALOGUE

For the discourse linguist there is an interest in tying features of a discourse type to distinctions already made in linguistics. That is to say, the linguist interested in the study of both spoken and written texts seeks to discover and describe the functions of various syntactic constructions (such as the functions of modifiers and particular sentence types), and considers such discovery and description as a key task of discourse analysis (Jones, 1983; Longacre, 1983; Crystal, 1987; Cortazzi, 1994). There is, however, a deeper issue involved, and it is at this point that CA may be seen as a valuable tool for the discourse linguist. Rather than seeking to tie discourse features to already existing categories in linguistics, as when Jones ties first-mention character references to existing syntactic features such as definite and indefinite articles, possessive pronouns, and so forth, CA goes about the discovery task differently. CA starts with interactional issues and categories, then examines what possibilities can be embodied by definite articles, possessive pronouns, proper names, or whatever. So then, for some purposes, definite articles and proper names may be interchangeable, but before such a claim can be made we have to first understand their interactional function. If we begin discourse analysis with existing linguistic features as our basic categories, we neglect the basic notion that speaker decisions can be embodied in more ways than one. CA starts with interactional properties, such as what a speaker assumes a hearer already knows. For example, in narrative discourse one might say, 'So this guy who lives across the street came to help me out,' or 'So Tony came over to help me out,' depending on what the narrator understands the listener to know. But we do not have the opportunity to discover these kinds of discourse features if we start with syntactic categories as our master categories.

While there certainly exists a hearer design to written texts as well as to conversational discourse, there is a puzzling equivocality in the linguistic literature in relation to this issue. Recall Longacre's claim that 'all that we have written here needs eventually to be supplemented by ... the current research into the nature of live conversation' (1983:75). On the one hand, it seems that the discourse linguist is saying, in effect, 'We'll analyse the data using linguistic categories, and you analyse the data using interactional categories, then we'll integrate the two.' But, as Sacks (1992) has shown, both aspects are intricately connected. For example, in written materials a category such as genre may be important. If one were to pick up a book of fables and open it to any page and read 'Fox went down to the house,' one would take a different meaning from that sentence than if it were a sentence in a detective novel. As a sentence in a fable, 'Fox' is understood by almost any reader as an animal and not, for example, 'Mr Fox the mailman,' or whatever. If one were to open a detective novel to any page and read 'The inspector nodded approvingly,' one would know that 'The inspector' is certainly not a food inspector but a police investigator. How is it known? By our common-sense understanding of what we call genre. Thus a category such as genre is important in the analysis of written texts. The discourse linguist also invokes the category of genre, but its use usually refers to the discipline's own analytical typology, distinguishing parables and riddles from ordinary narratives. In CA, the use of genre refers to a discourse form which hearers recognize and select and to a set of expectations which a storyteller can employ in order to make a narrative intelligible. As Roy Turner argued years ago, utterances cannot 'be treated as reports or descriptions without reference to the interactional location of the utterance in question' (1976:173).

In a CA treatment of responses to what another is saying in naturally occurring dialogue, one kind of system that connects hearer responses with what the speaker is saying is characterized by Pomerantz as chained actions. She characterizes an action chain as a type of organization in which two related action, Action 1 and Action 2, are linked. Thus the performance of Action 1 provides for the possibility of the performance of Action 2 as an appropriate next action.

Pomerantz draws a distinction between chained actions and Sacks and Schegloff's 'adjacency pair' structure: 'With "action chains" what is being proposed is that an Action 2, or "second pair-part," is not a *should* but a *may* for recipient, that is, an option among several specifiable options' (Pomerantz 1978:110). In an action chain, the second pair-part is not obligatory but optional, whereas in the adjacency-pair structure the second pair-part ought to be realized. Pomerantz considers the second pair-part of an action chain to be one of a number of possibilities.

There is a retrospective-prospective feature of the action chain which marks a difference between the action chain structure and the adjacency-pair structure. With the former, it is the production of an Action 1 which provides for the formulation of an Action 2. One consideration I am exploring is the possibility of preferences among potential Action 2s. Although these initial observations in themselves tell us little about the relationships between hearer responses and possible response types, we may begin to justify these claims by investigation of the conversational materials presented earlier.

Linguistic discourse analysis assumes that there is a set of rules governing the sequential organization of what is being said in any conversational dialogue. This assumption makes the claim that it is paired utterances – that is, questions and answers, offers and acceptances (or rejections) – which motivates the generation of sequencing rules. I would suggest, however, that live discourse is generally not constituted of pairs, and that rules that bind pairs are not of a syntactic nature but of a contextual nature. We find that questions can be followed by partial answers, statements of ignorance, rejections of the presuppositions of the question, silence, or whatever. In CA, for example, what makes some utterance after a question heard as an answer to the question depends not merely on the nature of the utterance itself, but also on the fact that it occurs after a question within a particular context. What I understand as response, then, is a complex action identified by sequential location and topical coherence in relation to a previous action.

Generally, LDA is an attempt to extend the techniques and analytical categories in descriptive linguistics to the analysis of units beyond the sentence. The basic procedures employed are: the isolation of a set of basic categories or units of discourse for analysis; the discovery and description of a roster, as nearly complete as possible, of the factors that may reasonably be expected to contribute to the function of the discourse; and the formulation of a set of rules related to the function of individual discourse types. Other features of LDA include: the tendency to take one or two written texts and give an in-depth analysis of all of the features in that type of text; and an appeal to intuition about, for example, what is a coherent or well-formed discourse and what is not (Wardhaugh, 1993; Silverman, 1993).

In LDA, then, there seems to be a notion that discourse can be analysed as self-contained speech units. Lacking in the discourse literature on narrative, for example, is a consideration of how a narrative is generated and terminated. This is not a small matter, for without such a consideration the discourse linguist lacks a theory of conversation that would lead one to make the ethnographic connection between the social function of telling about past experiences and the purposes of people engaged in conversational interaction. For the discourse linguist there is an interest in tying features of a discourse type to distinctions already made in linguistics. That is to say, the linguist interested in the study of discourse seeks to discover and describe the functions of various syntactic constructions (such as modifiers and particular sentence types), and considers this a key task of discourse analysis (Jones, 1983; Longacre, 1983; Renkema, 1993).

There are, of course, overlaps between CA and LDA, and it is important to keep in kind when discussing methodological differences between the two approaches that CA is concerned primarily with interaction and LDA with linguistic structures. As Button and Lee suggest, 'Discourse analysis is concerned to provide a corrective to a tradition of linguistic analysis which has ... been too prone to treat the sentence as an isolated object of analysis without regard for the location of sentences within a sequence of sentences or in terms of its relation to the uses to which language can be put' (1987:304).

The bottom line, however, is that CA and LDA look at language from different perspectives and it is difficult, as Button and Lee (1987) suggest, to 'do everything at once nor go at things in very different ways simultaneously.' I leave the final word on the matter, at least for now, to Sherzer:

Since discourse is an embodiment, a filter, a creator and transmitter of culture, then in order to study culture we must study the actual forms of discourse produced and performed ... the myths, legends, stories, verbal duels and conversations that constitute a society's verbal life. But discourse is also an embodiment of language. Grammar provides a set of potentials. Since these potentials are actualized in discourse, they can only be studied in discourse. (1987:306)

Conclusion

We examined collateral information in narrative discourse as treated in linguistic discourse analysis followed by a conversation analysis treatment. In the linguistic discourse treatment, it seems that narratives are analysed as self-contained units rather than as activities embedded in a natural context – that is, live conversation. In the CA treatment of collateral, I make use of social identities and membership categories which testify to the fact that narratives are social activities, and the analysis stresses their social nature.

One of the contributions of this chapter to our understanding of Ojibwe discourse and how it works in the contexts of legends relates to the integration of CA with the linguistic study of collateral information in Ojibwe discourse. I am claiming that there are discovery procedures in conversation analysis which can be effectively applied to the study of Ojibwe discourse. These methodological procedures, characterized below, illuminate the issues with which this discussion began.

First, we located and described instances from live discourse where an Ojibwe storyteller tells not only about the events which transpired but also about what did not transpire. When a storyteller tells about what didn't happen in the telling sequence (collateral), we isolated those instances where collateral information acts as an assessment of alternative activities. We noted some similarities and differences between a narrator's assessment of alternative activities and the 'instead of A, then B' structure. In building upon that structure, I claimed that Ojibwe storytellers telling legends in live discourse often account for why one activity was chosen over another activity. These accounts are reflected in storytellers' descriptions of what did and did not take place, and including these kinds of structures inform the listeners about what the story is teaching and why it is being told. Furthermore, by indicating various devices available to Ojibwe storytellers for making assessments of alternative activities, a methodology is offered for identifying activity assessments in narrative discourse in Ojibwe. The methodology offers a starting point in the analysis of collateral information and categories useful in the formal analysis of Ojibwe narratives.

This chapter also offers several contributions to the larger study of discourse, particularly the isolation of alternative assessment activity procedures as a group for special study. These procedures provide the discourse analyst with a useful category for formal analysis. They also help in understanding how storytellers can structure their stories so as to inform the listeners as to the importance of the story and what is being taught through the legend; that is, what the moral of the story is.

Finally, rather than seeking to tie discourse features to already existing categories in linguistics, conversation analysis begins with interactional issues and social categories, and then examines what possibilities can be embodied by linguistic categories. If we begin our analysis with existing linguistic features as our basic analytical categories, we neglect the notion that speaker/hearer decisions can be embodied in more than one way. CA begins with what a speaker assumes a hearer knows and thus is able to embody his or her decisions in a variety of ways.

PART FOUR
CONCLUSION

12

'Last Call': Some Practical Uses of Discourse Analysis

This final chapter is designed to tie together the various strands of the book: conversation analysis, discourse analysis, Ojibwe ethnography of speaking, culture-specific ethnomethods and interaction patterns, and how all of these relate to understanding Ojibwe ways of thinking and doing things in the contemporary context. I have attempted to show how one might use existing methods and techniques to this end as a way of contributing to the bridge-building literature in a practical and accessible manner. Ultimately, *'You're So Fat!'* seeks to capture the essence of Anishnaabe experience via how Anishnaabe people talk about that experience. Theirs is a life that is saturated with a wisdom, humour, and joyfulness that is painfully missing from existing books about Aboriginal people. The 'Living Voice' is at the heart and soul of the book – listening to the Native voice with the invitation to join in on a journey of discovery and exploration, a journey for Natives in the process of recovering traditional teachings, for non-Natives seeking to better understand Native ways of thinking and perceiving the world. For linguists, anthropologists, sociologists, and others in the academic realm interested in exploring issues in conversation analysis, linguistic discourse analysis, the ethnography of speaking, ethnomethodology and anthropological linguistics, *'You're So Fat!'* may provide a springboard for that exploration.

Aboriginal Languages in the Contemporary Context

I want to relate the kind of analysis we have been exploring to the crucial concerns of teaching Aboriginal languages, language and identity, revitalization, and preservation. In other words, what are the benefits of engaging in this kind of analysis for First Nations people, in particular educators, language teachers, and community members, interested in learning more about their languages? How can this analysis be used in appropriate interaction and second language teaching?

As John Steckley notes, most of us understand that language can be either the key to meaningful communication between people or an impenetrable barrier between people – at times even among those who may speak the same language. He writes:

In these days of resurgence in ethnic pride and identity, many are realizing the importance of first languages or 'mother tongues' of the peoples of the world through which communication is attained and in which world views, philosophies, histories, identities and relationships are generated and sustained. Most of us already have a sense that language is neither merely a means of interpersonal communication and influence, nor is it merely a carrier of culture [ways of thinking and doing things]. When we really think about it, language itself is content; a referent for attitudes, relationships, loyalties and animosities, an indicator of social status, a marker of situations and identities, and much, much more. (1994a:27)

Why study Aboriginal languages in a contemporary context? Because they are key to the survival and growing strength of the nations who have spoken them for centuries. There is a close link between language and the identity necessary for that survival and growth. As we saw in chapter 3, language provides identity roots to both individuals and nations in concrete, tangible ways. For First Nations peoples, language is the original and most natural way of transmitting traditional stories and the wisdom of generations of elders. To understand the uniqueness, beauty, insight, and power of an Aboriginal language, it is not enough to merely know its structure. You have to hear it in its social context, in the places in which it belongs. As Basil Johnston suggests, 'Language is crucial. If scholars are to increase their knowledge and if they are to add depth and width to their studies, they must study a Native language. It is not enough to know a few words or even some phrases ... Without a knowledge of the language, scholars can never take for granted the accuracy of an interpretation ... let alone a single word' (1991:11).

Perhaps the most important point to keep in mind is that language is meant to be used in natural settings for a variety of interactional purposes. We do hundreds of things each day and much of what we do is accomplished via language: telling stories, joking, apologizing, conversing, teasing, negotiating, repairing broken friendships, greetings, leave-takings, and so on. All of these activities are important in their own right and related directly to language-in-use.

Understanding a language enables us to understand a people better. Every culture has specific ways of interacting in a variety of different contexts, and an understanding of how these activities are accomplished gives us a glimpse into peoples' heads and hearts. In this book we have addressed a number of questions. How tightly is one's identity tied to one's language? What interactional differences can we see between people of Aboriginal descent and European-based people? Does our mother tongue influence the way we view the world around us? How can we best find out about and come to an understanding of Ojibwe-specific ways of speaking, thinking, and interacting?

Benefits for Native Educators, Language Teachers, and Language Learners

The various methodological approaches to exploring language I have presented have contributed greatly to the multi-faceted domains of inquiry within the complex field known as discourse analysis. Of particular importance to Native educators and language teachers is how discourse analysis in its many forms can be of benefit in the classroom. Discourse analysis is not designed to be a teaching method, per se. But it does offer Aboriginal language teachers, educators, ethnographers, applied linguists, and virtually anyone interested in culture-specific ways of thinking and doing things a fundamentally different way of looking at language. More important, it provides the resources for coming to a deeper understanding of what people can do with language. What we found in introducing some basic concepts of discourse analysis to Aboriginal language teachers, for example, is that its methods and techniques can be applied in practical ways in the teaching and revitalizing of Aboriginal languages. We found teachers were better able to understand and teach appropriate ways of using the language in naturally occurring settings, transmit how the language works beyond the level of the sentence, and explore the relationship between language and identity, world view, and culture-specific ways of thinking and doing things.

In my experience in teaching some of the principles of discourse analysis to Aboriginal language instructors, I noticed that most of these teachers, while not necessarily trained in the field of linguistics, have intuitive understandings of what constitutes successful language teaching and language acquisition. The value of learning the principles of discourse analysis, then, has to do with the insight gained into how spoken language is structured beyond the level of the sentence and how talk follows orderly patterns in a wide variety of interactional settings. Invariably, the language instructor has a better idea of how to teach the language as something real and useful in everyday life. One of the principal aims of 'You're So Fat!' is to introduce you to some of those insights.

In a more general sense, for educators working with Aboriginal students, studies in discourse analysis can be of tremendous benefit in understanding culture-specific ways of thinking and interacting. Understanding these culture-specific ways, especially for non-Native teachers working with Aboriginal students, can enhance the learning experience for these students. Identifying the discourse patterns characteristic of Native interaction can help to alleviate the interactional expectations of mainstream classrooms (Wild, Nalonechny, and St-Jacques, 1978; Scollon and Scollon, 1981; Rhodes, 1979, 1988; Spielmann, 1993a). As Scollon and Scollon found, for example, Athabaskan children are expected to display knowledge verbally in the mainstream educational system classroom. As such, they are confronted with a culturally alien context. Scollon and Scollon's discourse analysis of Athabaskan interaction patterns demonstrates that the overt 'displaying of what one knows' and being put in the spotlight in group situations represent discontinuous discourse practices for Athabaskan students. Wild, Nalonechny, and St-Jacques were among the first to suggest the importance of understanding Native-specific ways of thinking, learning and interacting as related to the mainstream educational system by exploring the culture-specific concepts of 'wait-time' (the length of time expectation between the posing of a question and the subsequent response to the question), forms of address (particularly between teachers and students), and silence (which is often misinterpreted as displaying ignorance or lack of intelligence).

In my own experience teaching at a band-run school, working with Aboriginal teachers, and teaching Aboriginal students at the post-secondary level, I have found that studies in discourse analysis help me as an educator to respect culture-specific communicative practices. It is difficult, for example, and culturally incongruent, for Aboriginal students to display knowledge in a manner consistent with the expectations of mainstream schools. Discourse studies can lead to better understandings and increased respect for Aboriginal-specific ways of learning and enhance the educational experience for both Aboriginal students and non-Aboriginal teachers. The learning experience in the Canadian educational system still strikes me as restrictive. While discourse studies are most often carried out without specific reference to pedagogical goals, they can be extremely useful both for teachers and curriculum designers who are concerned with making the educational experience meaningful in a multicultural society such as Canada. Discourse analysis can provide a foundation for understanding teaching/learning differences which is empirically grounded and goes beyond mere intuition.

Teachers, curriculum developers, and educators at all levels will have to come to their own conclusions as to whether their approaches to teaching and learning need revisiting in light of what studies in discourse analysis are telling us. Some of these findings suggest that Aboriginal teachers tend to proceed in the classroom in a slower and more deliberate manner; there is more of a shared sense of pacing between Aboriginal teachers and students than between non-Aboriginal teachers and students. In addition, there is a tendency to avoid putting the spotlight on individual students in Aboriginal classrooms, which includes not calling on individual students by name to display their knowledge or respond to specific questions. Whether or not individual teachers and educators respond to these studies is their business, but there is no doubt that discourse studies represent a significant body of evidence that culture-specific ways of thinking and doing things can enhance the educational experience for Aboriginal students and both Aboriginal and non-Aboriginal teachers. For example, the role of culture in organizing the kinds of interactional sequences that may influence classroom interaction and the relevance of that role to teaching can no longer be ignored. Our understanding of the learning process – from the perspectives of both the teacher and the student – has much to gain from discourse studies.

As for those attempting to learn to speak an Aboriginal language with a certain degree of conversational fluency, understanding discourse features and patterns can be of tremendous benefit. Learning to speak any language can be challenging and I gained a great deal in my own learning of the Algonquin dialect of Ojibwe by taking a discourse approach. I found a discourse model of language learning to be the quickest and most efficient means of achieving conversational fluency. The discourse (or text-based) method of language learning begins with the recording of short texts of various genres by mother-tongue speakers of the language, preferably elders. The various genres that I began with were stories, first-person narratives, third-person narratives, how to do something (for example, setting a rabbit snare), and short conversations. Most of my early language-learning texts were recorded when I was visiting elders in their homes or they were visiting in our home. The real benefit of the discourse-based language-learning approach is that one starts right from the beginning to learn language as it is used in everyday talk.[1] As Harriet Hill suggests, 'Languages encode different cultural realities, different perceptions of the universe, and sometimes almost different universes (fields and spirits versus subways and malls). Reality is classed into different categories, different modes of interaction are employed, and different structures are used' (1990:5).

I would like to end with an example from my experience with Aboriginal language teachers in the Algonquin community of Winneway. After spending time together in two courses dealing with discourse analysis in relation to Aboriginal language teaching, the whole nature of what we were trying to do in the program began to change. The teachers said they were now better able to explain to second-language learners how the language is used in real talk and interaction. Thus the focus of the program changed from one of learning grammar along with isolated words and phrases to one of learning to talk: to tell stories, to generate short conversations, to ask questions of the elders – in other words, to use the language in everyday life. In addition, a discourse-centred approach to language teaching and learning places a focus on the richness and complexity of the thinking that underlies language use and what language and language-in-use can teach us about culture-specific ways.

Conclusion

'You're So Fat!' merely scratches the surface of what exploring language and language-in-use can tell us about how people think and do things through talk. It is based on the underlying principle that the maintaining of one's Native language is tantamount to maintaining one's culture. I believe that language is the heart and soul of a culture. If a person loses his or her language, lost also are the ideas and culture-specific ways of relating to each other. Aboriginal peoples need their languages to preserve thoughts and ideas that can only best be expressed in their language of origin.

Equally important, language provides direct contact with the wisdom and teaching of the elders. If a person has his or her language and identity, it can go a long way in preventing assimilation into another culture and in preserving tradition-specific ways of relating to others, be they human or other-than-human persons. The philosophy, world view, spirituality, and culture-specific ways of thinking and doing things of a people are built right into the very structure of their language. It is a route to seeing history and an alternative way of reconstructing a more accurate and representative picture of history. As our Department of Native Studies at the University of Sudbury motto so succinctly puts it:

One cannot know where one is going lest one knows where one comes from.

Chi-banai

Notes

1: Introduction and Overview

1 There are a number of different versions of the meaning and derivation of Anishnaabe. Eddie Benton-Banai (1979:3) breaks the word down to mean 'From whence the male species was lowered' (*ani*, from whence, *nishnaa*, lowered, *abe*, male species). The elders I asked at Pikogan offered a variety of ethno-explanations unassociated with the actual etymology of the word. A number of elders told me that *Anishnaabe* means First People. Others thought the term was one given them by the Creator and had no real etymology to it. One elder offered the explanation that the word could be broken down into two components: *aanishaa* (roughly translated as just for fun) and *naabe* (man). The important thing to keep in mind, especially for non-cultural members, is that *Anishnaabe* is the term that people use to identify themselves, and that acknowledging and using the term is a show of respect for Anishnaabe people.

2 Gumperz and Hymes (1972) still contains about the best description of what Harold Garfinkel means when he refers to people's ethnomethods. They write: 'Here is the fundamental contention of Garfinkel's work: that the orderliness, rationality, accountability of everyday life is, as he puts it, a contingent, ongoing accomplishment, a kind of "work," or "doing."'

The term ethnomethodology is based on a relatively simple concept. When a botanist studies the local plants utilized by a particular people, she is engaging in ethnobotany. Similarly, an ethnomusicologist is one who studies the particular musical patterns, rhythms, and instruments of a particular people. The study of ethnomethods is the study of the methods people use in their everyday lives to do a countless number of things, from carrying on conversations to walking down a crowded city sidewalk. The primary focus here is on Ojibwe-specific ethnomethods: how Ojibwe people do things both in and through talk (although the study of a people's ethnomethods is certainly not limited to language and talk).

3 The linguist Kenneth Pike (1964) coined the terms 'etic' and 'emic' to refer to surface-structure and deep-structure descriptions of linguistic and behavioural phenomena. In anthropological terms, etic descriptions and understandings can be best grasped as cultural outsider understandings of ways of thinking and doing things, while emic descriptions and understandings capture cultural insider understandings. If I were asked to describe a cricket match, for example, I would describe it in etic terms: 'It's kind of like baseball, one player tries to throw a ball past a batter and hit three stakes in the ground. When the batter hits the ball he tries to run back and forth between two places,' etc. In other words, since I don't understand the game, I can only try to describe it in terms of its constituent parts. But for the game of baseball, I would be able to provide an accurate and comprehensive cultural member's (emic) description of the game, with all of its nuances, intricacies, and with a cultural insider's understanding. In ethnographic research, the non-cultural member tries to move along the continuum of understanding from etic to emic; from a cultural outsider's understanding to a cultural insider's understanding of whatever way of thinking or doing is being explored.

4 Russell Means, one of the co-founders of the American Indian Movement (AIM), gives us a clue to the frustration experienced by many Aboriginal people in relation to the crucial issue of 'appropriation of voice' when he writes:

My culture, the Lakota culture, has an oral tradition and so I ordinarily reject writing. It is one of the white world's ways of destroying the cultures of non-European peoples, the imposing of an abstraction over the spoken relationship of a people.

So what you read here is not what I've written. It's what I've said and someone else has written down. I will allow this, because it seems that the only way to communicate with the white world is through the dead, dry leaves of a book. I don't really care whether my words reach whites or not. They've already demonstrated through their history that they can't hear, can't see, they can only read (of course, there are exceptions, but the exceptions only prove the rule). I'm more concerned with Indian people, students and others, who have begun to be absorbed into the white world through universities and other institutions. ('The Same Old Song,' 1983:19)

Whether one agrees or disagrees with Means's position is not as important as understanding the sense of frustration that he expresses, a frustration that is apparent in much Native-produced literature today. Why is there such a sense of frustration? Certainly the issue of 'appropriation of voice' is at the heart of the matter. Who speaks for cultural authenticity? Native-White relations and 'studies' of Indian people have been explored at length in the mainstream disciplines of sociology, anthropology, psychology and linguistics, among others. But are not Aboriginal peoples themselves in the best position to speak for cultural authenticity and to present accurate portrayals of self-identification?

5 Linda Akan writes of this awkwardness from a Native perspective:

> A non-Native friend of mine once told me that, after trying to be Native and feeling uncomfortable with herself, she finally came to the realization that she had her own 'tribe.' It was fine and desirable for her to walk alongside a Cree woman and learn from her, but it was not desirable for her either to walk in front of the woman or to follow behind in her footsteps. My friend had her own experience and cultural teachings to give her a sense of dignity and respect. In my experience in education I have noticed that it is often the *Mooneyahquay* or 'whitewoman' who reaches out and extends a hand of genuine friendship to First Nations people in her belief that we have something of value to share with the western cultures. (1992:312)

> I firmly believe that First Nations people do have much of value to share with non-Native Canadians, and *'You're So Fat!'* is designed to provide a forum for doing exactly that. Zorica Benkovic, a true *Mooneyahquay,* reflects a similar vision in her study of Key North, a job placement training centre for Native women. She writes:

> As I continued to become more at ease with the stories that were told to me, I proceeded to grapple with my role as a white woman researching what Native women were experiencing ... I had formulated a kind of 'partnership' between the women and myself. I eventually came to accept my role as a non-Native researcher not as someone who was researching 'for' or 'on behalf of' First Nations peoples, but as someone who was working along side them toward the same goal – empowerment. (1997:25–26)

6 I try to follow the lead of my Native friends and colleagues when using terms to refer to Native people. It is much simpler when speaking Ojibwe or Algonquin because everyone uses Anishnaabe when referring to themselves and others in the Algonquian tradition. It gets much more complicated in English where a plethora of terms abound. Most Anishnaabe people I know use a variety of terms to describe themselves: Native, First Nation, Aboriginal, indigenous, and, depending on the context, Indian. Some prefer one term and others prefer different ones. I usually use Native, Aboriginal, and ·

First Nation because those are the terms I most often hear my Native friends and colleagues using.

7 I met Drew Hayden Taylor three years ago when the Department of Native Studies at the University of Sudbury brought him in to do some workshops on Native arts and theatre. I had been using some of his writings in my Native Studies classes for years, and hanging out with him for a couple of days only confirmed to me his keen eye for observation and a dead-on intuition and Native sensibility in relation to cultural differences between Native people and non-Natives. Since that time we have had him back for more workshops and he continues to amaze me with his humour-tinged observations on life from a distinctly Anishnaabe perspective.

8 I include Native people here because of my experience as an educator in the discipline of Native Studies. Many Aboriginal students take our courses in order to recapture and regain a sense of Aboriginal identity. Our program emphasizes the importance of learning and preserving Aboriginal languages (our focus is on Ojibwe and Cree), and the importance of language in terms of Aboriginal identity and the rebuilding of Aboriginal self-esteem. Many Native people are in the process of finding out about Aboriginal history, philosophy, spirituality, and ways of governance.

2: Value Differences between Natives and Non-Natives

1 Some of these themes may be specific to the community of Pikogan. In my experience, however, the themes presented here appear to be indigenous themes, most of which are corroborated in studies by both Aboriginal and non-Aboriginal researchers, educators, and scholars.

2 In their study of notions of competence in the Ojibwe community of Big Trout Lake in northwestern Ontario, Jo Anne Bennet and John Berry offer support for this claim. They write:

Adult restriction of children's interactions ... is kept to the barest minimum ... [and] seldom interfere with their children's exploratory drives. They learn about their world first-hand, from direct and personal engagement with it and the world is explored without fear of adult disapproval. Knowledge comes from immediate first-hand involvement. It is not filtered through the experience or the approval of adults ... A direct result of this kind of early interaction with the physical world is the development of a remarkable (to outsiders) degree of independence and self-sufficiency in young children. (1990:43–4)

3 Bennet and Berry provide us with some insight into this principle from another Ojibwe context: 'In Big Trout Lake a high value is placed on leaving

people alone, on not butting into others' affairs. It is rude to make suggestions to people about what they ought or ought not to be doing ... Rather, people are left alone to heed warnings as they will and the consequences of not paying attention often form the basis of humorous stories remembered and told long afterwards' (1990:45).

4 You will notice this book makes only casual reference to what is commonly called Native spirituality. In my opinion, it is extremely difficult, if not impossible, for non-indigenous people to share the deeply entrenched sense of what it means. Most Anishnaabe people I know don't use that phrase. Instead, I mostly hear people talking about a way of life, or a relationship with the Creator. The Native-produced book, *A Gathering of Wisdoms*, tells us: 'Spirituality pervades every aspect of Indian life in ways difficult to grasp for most non-Indians ... Spirituality is not treated as a separate or discrete part of life ... It is understood to be a fundamental reality of all life and all people, inseparable, connected to physical reality, bodily events, interpersonal relations, individual destiny, mental processes and emotional well-being. (1991:126–7).

3: Language as a Window on a People

1 I was fortunate to live in an Aboriginal community where the language is extremely strong and still pretty much the everyday language of communication. In getting to know Anishnaabe people in the Sudbury area, most of whom are not proficient in their Aboriginal language, I am often asked, 'How did you learn to speak an Aboriginal language?' and 'What would you suggest to someone who wanted to learn to speak their language fluently?' It is a cry from the heart for many Aboriginal people. I usually answer by saying something along these lines: 'Taking a course in Ojibwe (or whatever language) can teach you a lot about the language, and is helpful for those wishing to become conversationally fluent. But to really learn how to communicate in the language, I urge you to seriously think about taking a year out of your life, moving to a northern Aboriginal community where the language is still spoken on an everyday basis, and immerse yourself in that setting.' Needless to say, few people can just pick up and move north for a year. But anyone able to do that would not only return home fluent in the language, but would also look back on that year for the rest of their lives as one of the most significant things they had ever done.

2 Rupert Ross writes about the more egalitarian relationship between men and women in Ojibwe culture as compared to Euro-Canadian practices and observes a phenomenon I noticed many times over the years which seemed

confusing to me. When men and women are going somewhere together, often times the man is walking quite far in front of the woman. Ross asked one of the elders about this.

> She began by asking me to remember where those old people had spent their lives, to imagine walking down a narrow trail through the bush with my own family. She asked me to think about who I would prefer to have out in front ... to be the first to face whatever dangers the bush presented. In one way, she said, it could be compared to wartime. 'Where,' she asked, 'do you put your generals? Are they out in front or are they in the rear, where they have time to see and plan and react?' Viewed in that way, things appeared to be the opposite of what I had first supposed. Instead of occupying an inferior position, the woman was seen as the organizer and director, while the man out in front was counted on for his capacity to take action under her direction. (1996:52)

3 The distinction between what is commonly called animate and inanimate in Algonquian languages is a difficult one to grasp for non-cultural members. It goes much deeper than the terms usually used to describe them: living and non-living. Darnell sheds some light on this distinction when she writes: 'The inanimate is a residual (grammatical and conceptual) category for that which has no claim to power, self-awareness or capacity for action. Human persons are included in the category of living beings, but its prototypes are to be found in the spirit world rather than the human. Living beings are united by their ability to function in the world of power' (1993:99).

4 This is not meant to imply that some languages are superior to others. There are some who still believe that primitive languages exist; languages with simple grammars, few sounds, and limited vocabularies. Nothing could be further from the truth. Linguists agree that there are no such things as primitive languages. Crystal sums up the situation:

> Every culture which has been investigated, no matter how 'primitive' it may appear to be in cultural terms, has a fully developed language, with a complexity comparable to those of so-called 'civilized' nations ... All languages have a complex grammar; there may be relative simplicity in one respect (e.g., no word-endings), but there seems to always be relative complexity in another (e.g. word-position) ... There is no evidence that any people are 'handicapped' by their language. (1987:6–7)

While some languages can often do different things in more or less better ways than others, every language has its relative strengths and weaknesses. No linguistic or anthropological studies thus far have demonstrated that any one language is inherently superior to another in terms of complexity or abstraction.

5 The first two quotes come from the Assembly of First Nation's *Handbook on Language and Literacy* (1992:3–4). The third quote was told to me by Mr Albert Mowatt of Pikogan and I translated it into English.

6 The Royal Commission on Aboriginal Peoples presented its report to the Canadian government in November 1996. There are many references to Native languages throughout the five-volume report, including a number of recommendations. Following are some of the key recommendations:

1. That Aboriginal language education be assigned priority in Aboriginal, provincial and territorial education systems to complement and support language preservation efforts in local communities (Vol. 3:468).

2. That Canada's post-secondary institutions recognize Aboriginal languages on a basis equal to other modern languages (Vol. 3:512).

3. That federal, provincial, and territorial governments recognize promptly that determining Aboriginal language status and use is a core power in Aboriginal self-government, and that these governments affirm and support Aboriginal nations and their communities in using and promoting their languages and declaring them official languages within their nations, territories and communities where they choose to do so (Vol. 3:617).

4. That each Aboriginal nation consult with its constituent communities to establish priorities and policies with respect to Aboriginal language conservation, revitalization and documentation (Vol. 3:618).

5. That the federal government make a commitment to endow an Aboriginal Languages Foundation for the purpose of supporting Aboriginal initiatives in the conservation, revitalization, and documentation of Aboriginal languages (Vol. 3:620).

6. That the federal government recognize the special status of Aboriginal-language broadcasting explicitly in federal legislation (Vol. 3:634).

7. That the federal government recognize Aboriginal people's contribution to Canada through much greater use of Aboriginal place names, languages, ceremonies, and exhibits and by honouring Aboriginal meeting places and historic sites (Vol. 4:109).

7 I wish to thank Gordon Polson of the Algonquin First Nation for telling me about the works of Ngugi Wa Thiong'o. He learned of Ngugi while completing his MA in Canadian Studies at Carleton University and we had many long conversations relating Ngugi's ideas to the status of First Nations languages in Canada. When we presented a paper exploring some of those ideas at the 4th Biennial International Native American Studies Conference at Sault Ste Marie, Michigan, in May 1991, Gordon said something that I believe reflects a common attitude among many First Nations people in relation to the issue of linguistic hegemony:

I feel as though I represent my own people as a mass of contradictions. For here I am making claims for the liberation of Native languages and I am drawing from the written word (in English no less!) and I think and speak in English. The absurdity of the situation would be humorous if it wasn't so goddammed sad. Thus the contradiction. I am constrained to put across my ideas in a foreign language which, while I have been forced to adopt it, will never be the language of my heart. So, while my people will continue to use foreign languages, English and French, as we write and talk about the liberation of Native languages in Canada, and will continue to do so for a long time to come, the real strength and depth of our identity as a distinct people will ultimately depend on our ability to revitalize and reinstate the idiom of our cultures in our own languages.

4: An Introduction to Conversation Analysis

1 I have benefited greatly over the years from talking with my close friend Dr Rand Valentine, professor of Amerindian linguistics at the University of Wisconsin. He suggested that these interactional patterns are firmly rooted in the structure of the Ojibwe language itself, particularly in relation to a sense of 'beginning to do' or 'beginning to be.' He writes:

   A striking feature of Ojibwe semantics is the systematic ambiguity between the achievement of a state or action expressed by a verb and the process of changing to or commencing that state or action. This aspect of Ojibwe grammar was first pointed out by Truman Michelson in his introduction to the posthumously published texts of William Jones (Jones 1917–19). It is enough in English to say that 'he commenced his work,' or that 'he started to grow in stature'; but it is common in Ojibwe to say that 'he began to commence his work,' or that 'he began to start to grow in stature' (p. xii). Were this aspect of Ojibwe semantics to be carried over into English, it would find a striking dissonance in the use and interpretation of English achievement verbs such as 'finish' and 'quit,' where successful attainment is so central to the truth-conditions of English usage, but where, in Ojibwe, there might be more truth-conditional ambiguity between 'beginning to finish' and 'finish,' and 'beginning to quit,' and 'quit.' Ojibwe, then, encompasses even the acts of mental resolution antecedent to the act. (Rand Valentine, personal communication, 1997)

2 A word on the use of transcripts when engaging in CA and other discourse-centred approaches to language-in-use. In an ideal situation, 'You're So Fat!' would not merely be a book filled with transcripts from naturally occurring talk, but would include a videotape of all the interactional situations

included in the book. That, of course, is virtually an impossible scenario, aside from the considerations involved when a video camera is present in any interactional setting (unless it is hidden, which is generally agreed to be unethical). So we are stuck with using transcripts of tape-recorded talk. But that should not be too unsettling for the analyst or the reader. As Michael Moerman writes:

> Transcripts represent, or render, events that occurred in the real world; they provide an inexhaustible resource for your own, and future, interests. My descriptions, analyses, arguments and claims are based on the transcriptional evidence they cite. You can therefore evaluate them ... The specific features the transcripts reveal are features of the natural world in which the talk has actually occurred. Since the work of transcribing and analyzing is often dull and frustrating, it helps to know that we are mining real ore. (1988:12–13)

3 Garfinkel assumes that the social world is constantly being created by people and that this continuous creation is not a problem for them. That is to say, through their use of taken-for-granted, commonsense knowledge about how the world works and how people can manage their affairs in acceptable ways, members of a society can be seen to be creating the society. He writes that his studies are 'directed to the tasks of learning how people's actual, ordinary activities consist of methods to make practical actions, practical circumstances, commonsense knowledge of social structures, and practical sociological reasoning analyzable; and of discovering the formal properties of commonplace, practical commonsense actions "from within" actual settings as ongoing accomplishments of those settings' (1967:viii).

4 Garfinkel's program suggests that everywhere one looks one can see people going about their ordinary business, performing familiar, unremarkable activities, and that these activities are the very crux of the social world. In that the ability of people to perform these activities successfully in collaboration with others makes the social world possible, one ought to take these practical actions and examine them for how they are accomplished.

5 Simply put, the concern of the conversation analyst is with the methods people use to carry out the activities of everyday life and the practices by which they convey to others that their activities are rational and ordinary. The crux of the matter is that people do many things by talking about them (Turner, 1970).

6 Sacks et al. write in relation to turn-taking, for example:

> While understanding of other turn's talk are displayed to coparticipants, they are available as well to professional analysts, who are thereby afforded a proof criterion ... for the analysis of what a turn's talk is occu-

pied with. Since it is the parties' understandings of prior turn's talk that is relevant to their construction of next turns, it is *their* understandings that are wanted for analysis. The display of those understandings in the talk in subsequent turns affords a resource for the analysis of prior turns, and a proof procedure for the professional analyses of prior turns, resources intrinsic to the data themselves. (1974:45)

7 From the beginning, Garfinkel's major concern was to focus on the 'background expectancies' of situations which makes interaction possible and which makes social reality an ongoing accomplishment. People do hundreds of things every day, and these things are viewed by Garfinkel as practical accomplishments which deserve as much attention by social scientists as more extraordinary phenomena.

8 This points to a major difference between conversation analysis and linguistic discourse analysis from a sociolinguistic perspective. Gumperz writes: 'We must draw a basic distinction between meaning ... and interpretation, i.e. the situated assessment of intent' (1982:207). Surely we can agree with Gumperz that the content of meaning is situational, that meaning is generated in a situation and is reflexively reinforced in talk.

9 Very few studies using the methods of CA have been carried out on non-Indo-European languages such as Ojibwe. Most studies focus on English-speaking North America conversational phenomena (cf Moerman, 1988). However, a few studies are now beginning to make their way into the literature using CA on non-Indo-European languages and cultures, and Michael Moerman is certainly at the forefront of this movement. While Lisa Valentine's ethographic study of Severn Ojibwe (1995) is not CA-based per se, her discourse-centred approach to understanding culture provides a firm foundation for anyone attempting to apply CA methods to non-Indo-European languages and cultures.

10 As Zimmerman and Boden claim, 'Social structure is not something "out there" independent of members' activities ... Rather, they are the practical accomplishments of members of society. [People] can and must make their actions available and reasonable to each other and, in so doing, the everyday organization of experiences *produces* and *reproduces* the patterned ... qualities we have come to call "social structure"' (1991:19).

11 Few interested in discourse in its broad definition (language-in-use) would disagree with the notion that people interpret what other people say in light of the context in which it is said.

12 In his article 'The Search for an Integrational Account of Language,' Roy Fleming helps us to come to terms with this:
One might say, then, that, for the conversation analyst, context is all; that

context is a temporal, interactional, and local construct; and that conversational acts and their embedding context are reciprocally related ... In other words, an interactional event cannot be understood except by reference to its context ... At the same time, every action contributes to the terms by which the next action is understood. Thus, an utterance in a conversation is 'shaped' by the context in which it occurs; simultaneously, it 'renews' the context by which future utterances will be interpreted. (1995:86)

13 Many of the community elders at Pikogan and Winneway were quite used to being tape-recorded or videotaped. A common practice in Pikogan was for the elders and other community members to gather together on a Sunday afternoon at the band-run school for a session of storytelling, joke-telling, teaching, and conversing. These sessions would be videotaped by various community people in order to have the elders speaking the language and telling stories and giving teachings on tape for future generations. The community radio station, too, offered many opportunities to record and listen to the Aboriginal language being spoken. Finally, visiting in the homes of the elders and having them visit us in our home provided many opportunities for tape-recording naturally occurring talk, always with the permission of the elders involved.

14 Implied here is a notion of what constitutes 'culture.' There seem to be two basic approaches to understanding culture which are reflected in the approaches taken by ethnosemantics and ethnomethodology. The goal of ethnomethodology is essentially the same as ethnosemantics; that is, to explicate culture where culture is knowledge, 'whatever it is one has to know or believe in order to operate in a manner acceptable to a society's members' (Eglin, 1976). James Spradley defines culture as the 'acquired knowledge that people use to interpret experience and generate social behavior' (1979:5). In contrast, I tend to look at culture as a set of methods for doing things, and I take it that a person's knowledge of his or her culture is methodological rather than merely substantive, or 'knowledge how' rather than merely 'knowledge about,' and where the 'how' is interpretational. The idea is not new and is not mine (cf. Garfinkel, 1967; Eglin, 1976; Turner, 1978), but I am beginning to see the value of the view that people know their culture as methods of interpreting its objects where those methods *are* cultural knowledge.

15 A friend at Pikogan told me of a conversation with someone from the community who needed some money. It went like this (my friend is B in this conversation):

A1:   *Gidayawadog midaaswaabig.*
      You must have ten dollars.

B1:   *Ehe, anish dash ninadawendan noogom dawate.*
      Yeah, but I need it for the weekend.

A2:   *Midaaswaabig ninoodese.*
      I'm short ten dollars.

B2:   *Gaawin ni-gichi shooniyamisii.*
      I don't have much money.

A3:   *Midaaswaabig eta.*
      Just ten dollars

B3:   Okay.

While he did end up lending A some money, my friend told me that he wished A had let the matter drop after his first response in B1. He told me, 'I had to lend him the money. He wouldn't take no for an answer and he asked me *three times.*'

5: Interactional Resources in Ojibwe Storytelling

1 By story I mean, following Sacks, the telling of some event. Ryave suggests that this should be taken to mean the telling of some event or events in more than one utterance. The distinction is not crucial to this paper. Ryave writes:
   When I speak of the 'telling of a story in conversation,' I have in mind not only the utterances of the storyteller, but also the comments made in the course of a story presentation by those who are the recipients of the story. The fact that this sort of work goes on can affect the in-progress unfolding of some relating of an event, and consequently the very sense that a series of utterances might obtain. This is a distinguishing characteristic of stories told in conversation as opposed to, for example, stories told in performance situations. This not only differentiates our concerns and interests in storytelling from students of, for example, folklore, but it affirms the sense in which storytelling in conversation is an interactionally collaborative achievement. (1978:131)

2 Holly Gardner and I (1979) take a detailed look at how people in the midst of telling stories can discover that the tense being used may not be able to set the listener up for what the storyteller plans to say later in the story. When this happens, we have instances where the storyteller actually changes tense in the middle of a word. In our article, we present a tape-recorded transcript where a storyteller discontinues the use of a past tense because to use it at that point in the story may inhibit the way she wants to tell the story a few seconds later. These instances provide us with clues as to the subtlety and intricacy of the verb tense apparatus.

3 The idea of 'story recipient processing' is important here because of the

structure of the telling of this story. It seems to work something like this: the story is being told to people who, most likely, have never heard it before and have little or no idea what it's going to be about. Consequently, the telling must be 'processed' bit by bit by the listeners. Following a lead by Goffman (1974), we propose that for a storytelling to be successful, the listeners must in some way be ignorant of what is to be told and should be somewhat interested in finding out. Goffman writes:

> The listeners must put themselves in the hands of the teller and suspend the fact that the teller knows what is to occur and that the individuals in the story, including the teller in his 'I' form, will have come to know and therefore must (in some sense) now know. Interestingly, listeners can appreciate that a speaker has told the same tale several times before, without discrediting the teller's spontaneous involvement in his task, his savouring the unfolding of his own storytelling. It is only if the listeners themselves have already heard the story ... that the savouring by the teller will seem false and inappropriate. (1974:507)

4 Goffman writes: 'No wonder, then, the teller's license to suddenly switch from the past tense to present tense, as in "Then he refused to back the car up. I get in mine. I give him a push. Then he really got sore"' (1974:508–9).

6: Humour, Laughter, and Teasing in Ojibwe Storytelling

1 This underscores an important part of what we are trying to do in the discipline of Native Studies. Most of our courses contain a mixture of Native and non-Native students. I try to get across to my students that they are not being evaluated on how much they buy into the Native perspective that I present in the classroom. What I strive for is open and honest dialogue and an understanding of the Native perspective on a variety of issues. I attempt to create a climate of openness so that we can explore together, both Native and non-Native, this oft-neglected yet fundamentally important part of Canadian history and the contemporary Canadian scene. I usually draw two analogies to illustrate what we are trying to accomplish. If one were to take a course in marxist anthropology, for example, it is hoped that one would not be evaluated on the extent to which one accepts the tenets of marxism. One should, however, be prepared to be evaluated on how well one understands those tenets. In the discipline of Native Studies, we try to take the same approach. The analogy I use to illustrate this is the controversial issue of abortion. Almost everyone has a personal position on this issue, and the Native perspective is very clear. There is linguistic, ethnographic, and observational evidence that makes it quite clear that abortion is not recognized as a viable

option in most First Nations traditions. For Algonquin people, for example, the term coined by the elders to refer to abortion is translated as 'to kill a child.' The point here is that I don't care what any individual student believes about abortion; it's none of my business. What I am interested in, and what I evaluate my students on, is not whether they agree with the Native perspective on anything, but that they can understand and articulate what the Native perspective is on a variety of issues.

2 This distinction will be used to account for a common feature of both stories; they seem to build up a puzzle that is solved through a punchline/solution structure. Then, even after the punchline/solution, tellers often continue the story for a couple of utterances. I propose that the utterances that follow the punchline/solution are not intended to merely pad or explain the punchline, but are components of the second structure that is built into the funny stories.

7: Conversation Analysis

1 Jo Anne Bennet, in her analysis of changing concepts of self in northern Ontario Aboriginal communities, provides us with what I consider to be an accurate rationale underlying the contemporary relationship between elders and the younger generation in many Aboriginal communities:

The elders ... whose traditional role was to provide direction to the young, have grown old in their expectation that in the years of their age they would be listened to with respect ... that they would serve as guides to the young people. In these expectations they have been disappointed ... Today the elders are experts on very little that is important to the future of the young. The advice of the elders is seldom sought, yet the young feel a dismal lack of direction. Both sides are bewildered and hurt. (1992:13–14)

2 Some people have expressed concern about using this particular story since it makes reference to 'those who drink' and what happens because of it. In response, I defer to the elders who taught me. They always spoke from the heart and said what was on their minds. They never pulled any punches or tried to soften their vision of reality. Alcohol and drug abuse in the community are part of that reality and the elders are active in trying to instill traditional values and ways of thinking into the hearts and minds of the next generation in order to nudge people along the path of healing and wellness. These kinds of stories, and there are many of them, are not meant to be heard merely as stories, but as teachings about how to live right.

3 I hear this portion of the story as constituting a 'complaint' or 'doing complaining,' not because there are any obvious syntactic or semantic features

which identify it as such, but because the talk is directed to the recurrent kinds of troubles or bad things that persons can find themselves involved in (or inheriting) which naturally seem to go together with this particular categorial identification. Further, while there is a boundedness to the activity of complaining (as there is to any conversational activity), there is no *a priori* reason that I can think of that any conversational activity should be expected to require so many words or utterances to perform.

4 While it is true that some people may not be considered competent members by others through mental disability or whatever, there still exist different categories other than competent for such people – mentally ill or whatever – which inform our understandings of what is taking place in conversational interaction.

8: An Introduction to Linguistic Discourse Analysis

1 Lisa Valentine writes: 'One of the challenges of writing a book about discourse has been to clarify just what the terms "discourse" and "discourse analysis" mean at any given point in a discussion. One way to elucidate the terms that I am using is to give a brief overview of key analytic methodologies that inform this work' (1995:8).

She then lists what she considers to be six major schools of discourse analysis within linguistics and linguistic anthropology. Rather than reproduce her chart here, I refer you to pp. 8–9 of Valentine's book. Briefly, she lists: (1) *Text analysis*, which focuses on 'topic, comment, and text-internal relationships' (p. 8); (2) *Conversation analysis*, which seeks to discover and describe 'interactional routines found in conversational genres' (p. 8); (3) *Sociolinguistic research*, which is intent on discovering 'reasons for linguistic variation within a speech community; that is, to account for language change synchronically' (p. 9); (4) *Discourse as a social-interactional resource*, which focuses on a wide variety of communicative strategies not limited to spoken language (p. 9); (5) *Form-content parallelism*, which is concerned with exploring 'ways in which a variety of formal features interact to provide culturally specified, rhetorical structuring of texts' (p. 9); and (6) *Ethnopoetics*, which 'focuses on artistic genres' and 'structuring devices' (p. 9). There are a number of overlapping concerns between these discourse approaches, and this book is intended to display some of the links between them. While *'You're So Fat!'* focuses on the methodologies found in conversation analysis and text analysis, we can see certain elements in two other of Valentine's approaches: discourse as a social-interactional resource and form-content parallelism.

2 As Longacre stated, 'It seems to me there is more at stake than simply the fact that a discourse perspective is needed to round out linguistic analysis on any level, and that this is an area of growing interest within the field of discourse analysis' (1990).

3 In listening to legends, stories, and teachings over the years I recall many times not really understanding the essence of a story or teaching. Other times I found a particular story or teaching to be quite strange from my non-Native perspective. Parts of this teaching fell into that category and I had to ask Okinawe for clarification on a couple of items.

9: Using Discourse Analysis to Understand Ojibwe Cosmology

1 I wish to express my deepest gratitude to Mary Ann Corbiere of the Department of Native Studies, University of Sudbury, for her contribution to this chapter. Ms Corbiere graciously took the time to speak with some of the elders from the community of Wikwemikong and the comparative component of this chapter would not have been possible without her assistance. I would also like to thank Anna and Albert Mowatt of Pikogan for their patience and generosity in sharing their insights and dreams with me for so many years. Further, great thanks are due the elders from Wikwemikong: Kate Assinewai, Madeline Enosse, Violet Naokwegijig, and Mary Corbiere, and the elder from Sagamok, Annie Owl McGregor, for taking the time to share their valuable insights. I would also like to thank Barry Ace of the Department of Native Studies at the University of Sudbury for interviewing Mrs McGregor on my behalf. Finally, I wish to acknowledge the influence of Gordon Polson, a member of the Algonquin First Nation, on my own thinking and transformation of self while living with his people.

2 By ethnography of speaking I am referring to the study of linguistic genres and their culture-specific use and distribution. According to Lisa Valentine, 'The ethnography of speaking is not a field or a discipline; rather it is a perspective, an orientation towards the relationships among language, culture, and society' (1995:4). This chapter follows the general ethnography of speaking tradition by systematically studying a community's language use within its cultural context.

3 This perspective receives support from the existing literature relating to the Algonquian evaluation of the bear as the most intelligent other-than-human person. The bear as being spiritually powerful is well known and has been discussed by Hallowell (1926), Speck (1935), and Skinner (1911), among others. In *Legends of My People the Great Ojibway*, Norval Morriseau writes about

some of the beliefs of his people concerning the bear. He writes, for example, that his people held this animal to be very sacred: 'Legend states that the bear was at one time in the early history of the Ojibway a human, or had human form. Then it turned into an animal ... If Indians meet a bear, they address it as "Our Grandfather to all of us, the great Ojibway," and start to talk to it.'

He also gives us a clue as to the significance of bear dreams when he writes: 'My grandfather on my father's side at the time of his fasting year had a great medicine dream of a bear. The bear said to him in his dream, "My son, I will be a guardian to you and give you some special power ... You will have power to do good. I will also give you good luck, but you must respect me in my present form and never kill me"' (1965:45).

4 Jennifer Brown and Robert Brightman, citing Densmore (1928) and Landes (1968), write: 'Among some Southwestern Ojibwa ... [the] bear was identified as [one of the] the spirit guardians of shamans' (1988:175). As for the connection between dreaming about a bear and its association with warnings, Brown and Brightman quote from one of George Nelson's unpublished journals of 1825: 'The Bear is a rough beast and makes a devil of a racket,' implying a cultural outsider's view of what may constitute a cultural member's understanding of one feature of a warning. While Mrs Mowatt characterizes bear visitors in dream states as *Gimasagwaabadaan* ('It was an unlucky dream'), certainly dreaming about a bear is beneficial in the sense that, as Mrs Mowatt emphasizes, if one pays attention to the details of a bear dream, one may be able to avoid the possible misfortune of which the bear visitor warns. But here I am on shaky ground.

5 While I refer to bear-dream accounts in this chapter as Algonquin-specific, I recognize that they do appear as warnings in other Algonquian traditions. In speaking with a member of another Algonquian tradition, I was informed that bear dreams and bears as dream visitors are common and also signify, as in Algonquin, warnings about future misfortune (Schuyler Webster, Mennominee Nation, personal communication, 1992). I use the term 'Algonquin-specific' only in the comparative sense between the Algonquin and Odawa dialects of Ojibwe. There is, however, one feature of bear dreams which does seem to be specific to the Algonquin tradition; that is, if you pay attention to the details of one's dream about a bear, you may avoid potential misfortune. I have not, as yet, heard of techniques for avoiding this misfortune in other Algonquian traditions.

6 The way the story was told, I wasn't sure if the visitor appeared in a dream or while the one giving the account was in a conscious state. The details of the story itself lead me to believe that it was a dream experience.

10: Discourse Analysis of a Traditional Anishnaabe Legend

1 According to the late Joseph Campbell, for indigenous people, legends and myths define their special relationship with the land and their role within creation. They were not only shaped *by* the land; they were created *for* the land. This belief that Aboriginal people were placed on the Turtle Island (North America) is essential to myth – the special place for the Red Colour of People. The idea of being created for the land and being placed on the land is a vital component of Anishnaabe identity. I have heard elders talk many times of how Anishnaabe people are inseparable from the land. Inextricably reinforced by the notion that Anishnaabe people were created for the land is the affirmation that they originated here. The belief is that they did not migrate from another continent, nor originate from any other peoples. This is affirmed again and again in the legends and myths from the people themselves. When we come to consider the contemporary claims of origin and identity from *Anishnaabe* people themselves, this affirmation becomes central to the Native perspective on these issues.

2 Rand Valentine writes:
   Mode is a term used by Algonquianists to designate a set of suffixes which categorize aspectual and evidential parameters of a predication. There are four modes: plain, dubitative, preterite and preterite dubitative. The dubitative mode is most commonly seen in *aadizookaanan*, traditional tales. Plain is simply the absence of any of the other modes, and is not itself indicated with an audible formative. (1996:390)

11: Collateral Information in Ojibwe Storytelling

1 One elder to whom I told this story commented: 'Sounds like he was trying to start a fire the traditional way.' The irony was not lost on my friend who tried to start the fire with lighter fluid when I told him what the elder said.

2 This is not altogether true. In Algonquin-specific stories in which the lynx is a character, he is always cast as the one who is deceived, tricked, and made fun of. I tend to view the lynx in Algonquin legends as the Wile. E. Coyote of the Anishnaabe world.

12: Some Practical Uses of Discourse Analysis

1 My experience working with Aboriginal language teachers in the Algonquin community of Winneway, as well as my own language learning experience, has made me a firm believer in this approach to language learning. Such an

approach is not new. William M. Clements, in his book *Native American Verbal Art*, writes: 'Many Native American communities are using texts as the basis for language instruction. And one motive ... has been to provide a record for the people themselves. Robin Ridington has suggested an analogy between a tape-recording of an oral expression and a documentary photograph' (1996:208).

References

Akan, Linda. 1992. *Pimosatamowin sikaw kakeequaywin*: Walking and talking – a Saulteaux elder's view of native education. *Canadian Journal of Native Education*, 19, no. 2:191–214.

Assembly of First Nations. 1993. *Declaration on Aboriginal Languages*. Pamphlet.

Atkinson, J.M., and J.C. Heritage, eds. 1984. *Structures in Social Action: Studies in Conversation Analysis*. Cambridge: Cambridge University Press.

Awasis Agency of Northern Manitoba. 1997. *First Nations Family Justice*. Thompson, Manitoba: Awasis Agency of Northern Manitoba.

Bal, M. 1985. *Narratology: Introduction to the Theory of Narrative*. Toronto: University of Toronto Press.

Barnes, Trevor J. 1992. *Writing Worlds: Discourse, Text, and Metaphor in the Representation of Landscape*. London: Routledge.

Basso, Keith. 1979. *Portraits of the 'Whiteman': Linguistic Play and Cultural Symbols among the Western Apache*. Cambridge: Cambridge University Press.

– 1983. 'Stalking with stories': Names, places and moral narratives among the Western Apache. In *Text, Play and Story: The Construction and Reconstruction of Self and Society*, 19–55. Proceedings of the American Ethnological Society.

Beach, Wayne A. 1991. Searching for universal features of conversation. *Research on Language and Social Interaction* 24:351–68.

Beck, Peggy, Anna Walters, and Nia Francisco. 1993. *The Sacred: Ways of Knowledge, Sources of Life*. Tsaile, Arizona: Navajo Community College Press.

Benkovic, Zorica. 1997. 'Break Out of Your Shell!': An Evaluation of KeyNorth Office Services and Training. MA thesis, Laurentian University, Sudbury, Ontario.

Bennet, Jo Anne. 1992. Changing concepts of self in northern Ontario communities and some implications for the future. In William Cowan, ed. *Papers of the Twenty-Third Algonquian Conference*, 12–21. Ottawa: Carleton University Press.

Bennet, Jo Anne, and John W. Berry. 1990. Notions of competence in people of northern Ontario. In William Cowan, ed., *Papers of the Twenty-First Algonquian Conference*, 36–50. Ottawa: Carleton University Press.

Benton-Banai, Edward. 1979. *The Mishomis Book: The Voice of the Ojibway.* Saint Paul: Indian Country Press.

Bilmes, Jack. 1988. The concept of preference in conversation analysis. *Language in Society* 17:161–81.

Blass, Regina. 1990. *Relevance Relations in Discourse.* Cambridge: Cambridge University Press.

Blondin, George. 1989. Dene history is key to defining rights. *Native Press*, 27 January, p 15.

Bloomfield, Leonard. 1933. *Language.* New York: Holt, Rinehart and Winston.

– 1934. *Plains Cree Texts.* American Ethnological Society Publication 16. New York: G.E. Stechert.

Brant, Clare C. 1990. Native ethics and rules of behaviour. *Canadian Journal of Psychiatry* 35:534–9.

Brizinski, Peggy. 1993. *Knots in a String.* Saskatoon: University of Saskatchewan Press.

Brown, Jennifer S., and Robert Brightman. 1988. *The Orders of the Dreamed: George Nelson on Cree and Northern Ojibwa Religion and Myth, 1823.* Winnipeg: University of Manitoba Press.

Bruchac, Joseph. 1990. Striking the pole: American Indian humor. *Parabola* 12, no. 4:22–9.

Bunge, Robert. 1987. Language: the psyche of a people. In *Our Languages, Our Survival*, 13–20. University of South Dakota.

Burman, E., and I. Parker. 1993. *Discourse Analytic Research, Repertoires and Readings of Texts in Action.* London: Routledge.

Button, Graham, and John R.E. Lee. 1987. *Talk and Social Organisation.* Philadelphia: Multilingual Matters Ltd.

Campbell, Joseph. 1988. *The Power of Myth.* New York: Doubleday.

Canada, Royal Commission on Aboriginal Peoples. 1996. *Report of the Royal Commission on Aboriginal Peoples.* 5 vols. Ottawa: Canada Communications Group.

Chafe, Wallace. 1994. *Discourse, Consciousness, and Time: The Flow and Displacement of Conscious Experience in Speaking and Writing.* Chicago: University of Chicago Press.

Christensen, Rosemary Ackley. 1993. Ojibwe language: a competence exchange model for administrative curriculum makers and first language speakers. In Thomas E. Schirer and Susan M. Branstner, eds., *Native American Values: Survival and Renewal*, 30–46. Sault Ste. Marie, Michigan: Lake Superior State University Press.

Clements, William M. 1996. *Native American Verbal Art: Texts and Contexts*. Tucson: University of Arizona Press.

Corbiere, Mary Ann. 1997. Teaching native languages so they will survive. In Thomas E. Shirer and Susan Branstner, eds., *Celebration of Indigenous Thought and Expression*, 218–30. Sault Ste Marie, Michigan: Lake Superior State University Press.

Cortazzi, Martin. 1994. Narrative analysis: state of the art. *Language Teaching*, 27:157–70.

Coulthard, Malcolm. 1977. *An Introduction to Discourse Analysis*. London: Longman Group Ltd.

Cruikshank, Julie. 1991. *Life Lived Like a Story: Life Stories of Three Yukon Native Elders*. Vancouver: University of British Columbia Press.

Crystal, David, ed. *The Cambridge Encyclopedia of Language*. Cambridge University Press, 1987.

Dahlstrom, Amy. 1996. Narrative structure of a Fox text. In John D. Nichols and Arden C. Ogg eds., *Nikotwâsik iskwâhtêm, pâskihtêpayih! Studies in Honour of H.C. Wolfart*, 113–62. Memoir 13, Algonquian and Iroquoian Linguistics.

Darnell, Regna. 1991. Thirty-Nine postulates of Plains Cree conversation, 'power,' and interaction: a culture-specific model. In William Cowan, ed., *Papers of the Twenty-Second Algonquian Conference*, 89–102. Ottawa: Carleton University Press.

– 1993. Functions of English in Southwestern Ontario Native Discourse. In William Cowan, ed., *Papers of the Twenty-Fourth Algonquian Conference*, 81–96. Ottawa: Carleton University Press.

– 1996. What are texts for these days? In John D. Nichols and Arden C. Ogg, eds., *Nikotwâsik iskwâhtêm, pâskihtêpayih! Studies in Honour of H.C. Wolfart*, 163–70. Memoir 13, Algonquian and Iroquoian Linguistics.

Darnell, Regna, and Michael Foster. 1988. *Native North American Interactional Patterns*. Ottawa: Canadian Museum of Civilization.

Deloria, Vine, Jr. 1970. *Custer Died for Your Sins: An Indian Manifesto*. New York: Avon.

Densmore, F. 1928. Uses of plants by the Chippewa Indians. *Annual Report of the Bureau of American Ethnology* 44:275–397.

Drew, Paul. 1984. Speakers' reportings in invitation sequences. In J.M Atkinson and J.C. Heritage, eds., *Structures of Social Action: Studies in Conversation Analysis*, 129–51. Cambridge: Cambridge University Press.

– 1987. Pro-faced receipts of teases. *Linguistics* 25, no. 1:219–53.

Dumont, James. 1992. Journey to daylight land: Through Ojibway eyes. In David R. Miller et al., eds., *The First Ones: Readings in Indian/Native Studies*, 75–80. Saskatchewan Indian Federated College Press.

– 1993. Justice and Aboriginal people. In *Aboriginal Peoples and the Justice System*,

Report of the National Round Table on Aboriginal Justice Issues, 44–61. Toronto: Canada Communication Group.

– 1994. Culture, behaviour and the identity of the native person. NATI 2105 course manual, Department of Native Studies, University of Sudbury.

Eglin, Peter. 1976. Culture as method: Location as an interactional device. Paper presented at the Third Annual Symposium of Symbols and Symbol Processes. Las Vegas, Nevada, 30–31 March.

Erasmus, George. 1989. Solutions we favour for change. In *Drumbeat: Anger and Renewal in Indian Country* 295–302. Toronto: Summerhill Press and the Assembly of First Nations.

Ezzo, David. 1988. Female status in the Northeast. In William Cowan, ed., *Papers of the Nineteenth Algonquian Conference*, 49–62. Ottawa: Carleton University Press.

Finnegan, Ruth. 1992. *Oral Traditions and the Verbal Arts*. New York: Routledge.

Fleming, David. 1995. The search for an interactional account of language. *Language Sciences* 17, no. 1:73–98.

Foster, Michael K. 1982. Canada's first languages. *Language and Society* 7 (Winter/Spring): 7–14.

Fox, Mary Lou. 1991. MCTV news report, Sudbury, Ontario.

Freedle, R., ed. 1979. *New Directions in Discourse Processing*. Norwood, NJ: Ablex.

Freire, Paulo. 1970. *Pedagogy of the Oppressed*. New York: Seabury Press.

Gardner, Holly. 1982. Narrative analysis and models of interaction. *Papers in Linguistics* 15, nos. 3–4:191–204.

Gardner, Holly, and Roger Spielmann. 1980. Funny stories and conversational structures. *Papers in Linguistics* 13:179–200.

Garfinkel, Harold. 1967. *Studies in Ethnomethodology.* Englewood Cliffs, NJ : Prentice-Hall.

Gavin, Kenneth J. 1980. Story structure in the recall of simple stories by children and adults. Ph.D. dissertation. Northwestern University, Evanston, Illinois.

Geertz, Clifford. 1987. *Works and Lives: The Anthropologist as Author*. Stanford: Stanford University Press.

Goddard, Ives, ed. 1996. *Handbook of North American Indians*, vol. 17: Languages. Washington: Smithsonian Institution.

Goffman, Erving. 1959. *The Presentation of Self in Everyday Life*. New York: Doubleday Anchor Books.

– 1967. *Interaction Ritual*. New York: Doubleday Anchor Books.

– 1974. *Frame Analysis*. New York: Harper and Row.

– 1981. *Forms of Talk*. Philadelphia: University of Pennsylvania Press.

Gordon, David, and George Lakoff. 1971. Conversational postulates. *Papers from the Seventh Regional Meeting Chicago Linguistic Society,* 63–84. Chicago: Chicago Linguistic Society.

Grice, H.P. 1975. Logic and conversation. In Peter Cole and Jerry Morgan, eds., *Speech Acts,* 41–58. New York: Academic Press.

Grimes, Joseph E. 1975. *The Thread of Discourse.* The Hague: Mouton.

Gumperz, John. 1982. *Discourse Strategies.* Cambridge: Cambridge University Press.

Gumperz, John, and Dell Hymes. 1972. Introduction to 'Remarks on Ethnomethodology.' In John Gumperz and Dell Hymes eds., *Directions in Sociolinguistics: The Ethnography of Communication,* 301–9. New York: Holt, Rinehart and Winston.

Hallowell, Irving A. 1926. Bear ceremonialism in the northern hemisphere. *American Anthropologist* 28:1–175.

– 1975. Ojibwe ontology, behavior and world view. In Dennis and Barbara Tooker, eds., *Teachings from the American Earth,* 148–71. New York: Liveright Press.

Hatim, B. 1990. *Discourse and the Translator.* London: Longman.

Hill, Harriet. 1990. Text-based language learning. *Notes on Linguistics* 50:4–8.

Hopper, Robert. 1989. Sequential ambiguity in telephone openings: 'What are you doin'?' *Communication Monographs* 56, no. 3:240–53.

– 1991. Ethnography and conversation analysis. In *Research on Language and Social Interaction* 24:161–70.

Huttar, George. 1980. Metaphorical speech acts. *Poetics* 9:383–401.

– 1982. Linguistic pragmatics. *Notes on Linguistics* 23:26–31.

Hymes, Dell. 1981. *'In Vain I Tried to Tell You': Essays in Native American Ethnopoetics.* Philadelphia: University of Pennsylvania Press.

Jefferson, Gail. 1972. Side sequences. In David Sudnow, ed., *Studies in Social Interaction,* 294–338. New York: Free Press.

– 1978. Sequential aspects of storytelling in conversation. In James Schenkein, ed., *Studies in the Organization of Conversational Interaction,* 219–48. New York: Academic Press.

– 1979. A technique for inviting laughter and its subsequent acceptance/declination. In George Psathas, ed., *Everyday Language,* 97–122. New York: Irvington.

– 1984. On the organization of laughter in talk about troubles. In J.M. Atkinson and J.C. Heritage, eds., *Structures of Social Action: Studies in Conversation Analysis,* 347–69. Cambridge: Cambridge University Press.

Johnston, Basil. 1991. One generation from extinction. In W.H. New, ed., *Native Writers and Canadian Writing,* 10–15. Vancouver: University of British Columbia Press.

Jones, Larry. 1983. *Pragmatic Aspects of English Test Structure.* Dallas, Texas: Summer Institute of Linguistics.

Jones, William. 1919. *Ojibwa Texts*. In Truman Michelson, ed., *American Ethnological Society Publications* 7.1, Leiden/New York; 7.2, New York.

Keeshig-Tobias, Lenore. 1990. White lies. *Saturday Night*, October, pp. 67–8.

Kinkade, M. Dale, and Anthony Mattina. 1996. Discourse. In Ives Goddard, ed., *Handbook of North American Indians*. Vol. 17: Languages, 244–74. Washington: Smithsonian Institution.

Kirkness, Verna J. 1989. Aboriginal languages in Canada: From confusion to certainty. *Journal of Indigenous Studies* 1:97–103.

Krajewski, Bruce. 1992. *Traveling with Hermes: Hermeneutics and Rhetoric*. Amherst: University of Massachusetts Press.

Landes, Ruth. 1968. *Ojibway Religion*. Madison: University of Wisconsin Press.

Leavitt, Robert M. 1992. Confronting language ambivalence and language death. In David R. Miller, ed., *The First Ones: Readings in Indian/Native Studies*, 6–8. Saskatchewan Indian Federated College Press.

Lee, David. 1992. *Competing Discourses: Perspective and Ideology in Language*. Essex: Longman.

Levinson, Stephen C. 1983. *Pragmatics*. Cambridge: Cambridge University Press.

Lincoln, Kenneth Jr. 1993. *Indi'n Humor: Bicultural Play in Native America*. New York: Oxford University Press.

Longacre, Robert E. 1983. *The Grammar of Discourse*. New York: Plenum Press.

– 1990. Introduction to *Occasional Papers in Translation and Textlinguistics* 4, no. 2:1–17.

Mandelbaum, Jenny. 1991. Beyond mundane reason: Conversation analysis and context. In *Research on Language and Social Interaction* 24:333–50.

Mawhiney, Anne-Marie, ed. 1993. *Rebirth: Political, Economic and Social Development in First Nations*. Toronto: Dundurn Press.

McNickel, D. 1973. *Native American Tribalism: Indian Survival and Renewals*. New York: Oxford University Press.

Medicine, Bea. 1983. Warrior women – sex role alternatives of Plains Indian women. In Patricia Albers and Bea Medicine, eds., *The Hidden Half: Studies of Plains Indian Women*, 213–28. Lanham: University Press of America.

Miller, J.R. 1989. *Skyscrapers Hide the Heavens: A History of Indian-White Relations in Canada*. Toronto: University of Toronto Press.

Moerman, Michael. 1988. *Talking Culture: Conversation Analysis and Ethnography*. Philadelphia: University of Pennsylvania Press.

– 1991. Exploring talk and interaction. In *Research on Language and Social Interaction* 24:173–87.

– 1992. Life after C.A.: An ethnographer's autobiography. In Watson and Seiler, eds., *Text in Context: Contributions to Ethnomethodology*, 20–34. Newbury Park, California: Sage Publications.

Mohatt, G., and F. Erickson. 1981. Cultural differences in teaching styles in an Odawa school: A sociolinguistic approach. In H. T. Trueba, G.P. Guthrie, and K.H. Au, eds., *Culture and the Bilingual Classroom: Studies in Classroom Ethnography,* 105–19. Rowley, Mass.: Newbury House.

Morriseau, Norval. 1965. *Legends of My People the Great Ojibway.* Toronto: McGraw-Hill Ryerson.

Morrison, R. Bruce, and C. Rodney Wilson. 1986. *Native People: The Canadian Experience.* Toronto: McClelland and Stewart.

Nelson, Christine. 1994. Ethnomethodological positions on the use of ethnographic data in conversation analytic research. *Journal of Contemporary Ethnography* 23:307–29.

Ngugi, wa Thiong'o. 1986. *Decolonizing the Mind.* London: James Currey.

Nichols, John. 1988. *An Ojibwe Text Anthology.* London, Ont.: Centre for Research and Teaching of Canadian Native Languages, University of Western Ontario.

Nichols, John D., and Arden C. Ogg, eds. 1996. *Nikowâsik iskwâhtêm, pâskihtêpayih! Studies in Honour of H.C. Wolfart.* Memoir 13, Algonquian and Iroquoian Linguistics.

Norrick, Neal R. 1994. Involvement and joking in conversation. *Journal of Pragmatics* 22:409–30.

Norton, Ruth, ed. 1990. *Towards Linguistic Justice for First Nations.* Ottawa: Assembly of First Nations.

– 1992. *Towards Rebirth of First Nations Languages.* Ottawa: Assembly of First Nations Press.

– 1993. Aboriginal languages and literacy. *An Information Handbook by the Education Secretariat.* Assembly of First Nations.

Philips, Susan. 1983. *The Invisible Culture: Communication in Classroom and Community on the Warm Springs Indian Reservation.* New York: Longman.

Pickering, Wilbur. 1979. *A Framework for Discourse Analysis.* Arlington, Texas: SIL and University of Texas Press.

Polson, Gordon, and Roger Spielmann. 1990. 'Once there were two brothers ...': religious tension in one Algonquin community. In William Cowan, ed., *Papers of the Twentieth Algonquian Conference,* 303–12. Ottawa: Carleton University Press.

Pomedli, Michael M. 1992. Orality in early Greek and Cree traditions. In William Cowan, ed., *Papers of the Twenty-Third Algonquian Conference,* 334–43. Ottawa: Carelton University Press.

Pomerantz, Anita. 1978. Compliment responses: Notes on the co-operation of multiple constraints. In James Schenkein, ed., *Studies in the Organization of Conversational Interaction,* 79–112. New York: Academic Press.

– 1984. Agreeing and disagreeing with assessments: Some features of pre-ferred/dispreferred turn shapes. In J.M. Atkinson and J.C. Heritage, eds., *Structures in Social Action: Studies in Conversation Analysis*, 57–101. Cambridge: Cambridge University Press.

Poole, Deborah. 1990. Discourse analysis in ethnographic research. *Annual Review of Applied Linguistics* 11:42–56.

Powell, J.V. 1989. Review of *Talking Culture: Ethnography and Conversation Analysis* by Michael Moerman. *Anthropologica* 26:31–2.

Preston, Richard. 1986. Twentieth-century transformations of the West Coast Cree. In William Cowan, ed., *Actes du Dix-Septiéme Congrès des Algonquinistes*, 239–52. Ottawa: Carleton University Press.

Renkema, Jan. 1993. *Discourse Studies: An Introductory Textbook*. Philadelphia: John Benjamins Publishing Company.

Rhodes, Richard. 1988. Ojibwe politeness and social structure. In William Cowan ed., *Papers of the Nineteenth Algonquian Conference*, 165–74. Ottawa: Carleton University Press.

– 1979. Some aspects of Ojibwe discourse. In William Cowan, ed., *Papers of the Tenth Algonquian Conference*, 102–17. Ottawa: Carleton University Press.

Ross, Rupert. 1996. *Returning to the Teachings*. Toronto: Penguin Books.

– 1992. *Dancing with a Ghost: Exploring Indian Reality*. Ottawa: Octopus.

Russell, Kevin. 1996. Does obviation mark point of view? In John D. Nichols and Arden C. Ogg eds., *Nikotwâsik iskwâhtêm, pâskihtêpayih! Studies in Honour of H.C. Wolfart*, 367–82. Memoir 13, Algonquian and Iroquoian Linguistics.

Ryave, Alan. 1978. On the achievement of a series of stories. In James Schenkein, ed., *Studies in the Organization of Conversational Interaction*, 113–32. New York: Academic Press.

Ryave, Alan, and James Schenkein. 1974. Notes on the art of walking. In Roy Turner, ed., *Ethnomethodology*, 265–74. Markham, Ontario: Penguin.

Sacks, Harvey. 1970, 1971, 1972. Transcripts of unpublished lectures. School of Social Science, University of California at Irvine.

– 1978. Some technical considerations of a dirty joke. In James Schenkein, ed., *Studies in the Organization of Conversational Interaction*, 249–70. New York: Academic Press.

– 1992. *Lectures in Conversation*. 2 vols. Oxford: Basil Blackwell.

Sacks, Harvey, and Emanuel Schegloff. 1974. Two preferences in the organization of reference to persons in conversation and their interaction. In N. H. Avison and R. J. Wilson, eds., *Ethnomethodology, Labelling Theory and Deviant Behaviour*, 289–327. London: Routledge and Kegan Paul.

Sacks, Harvey, Emanuel Schegloff, and Gail Jefferson. 1978. A simplest systematics for the organization of turn-taking for conversation. In James Schenkein, ed., *Studies in the Organization of Conversational Interaction*, 7–54. New York: Academic Press.

Sadock, Jerrold. 1974. *Towards a Linguistic Theory of Speech Acts*. New York: Academic Press.

Schegloff, Emanual A. 1987. Analyzing single episodes of interaction: An exercise in conversation analysis. *Social Psychology Quarterly* 50:101–14.

Schenkein, James. 1978. Identity negotiations in conversation. In James Schenkein, ed., *Studies in the Organization of Conversational Interaction*, 57–78. New York: Academic Press.

Scollon, Ron, and Suzanne Scollon. 1981. *Narrative, Literacy and Face in Interethnic Communication*. Norwood, NJ: Ablex Publishing.

Sharrock, Wes, and Roy Turner. 1978. On a conversational environment for equivocality. In James Schenkein, ed., *Studies in the Organization of Conversational Interaction*, 173–98. New York: Academic Press.

Sherzer, Joel. 1983. *Kuna Ways of Speaking: An Ethnographic Perspective*. Austin: University of Texas Press.

– 1987. A discourse-centered approach to language and culture. *American Anthropologist* 89:295–309.

Silverman, David. 1993. *Interpreting Qualitative Data: Methods for Analyzing Talk, Text and Interaction*. London: Sage Publications.

Spielmann, Roger. 1980. Performative utterances as indexical expressions. *Journal of Linguistics* 16:89–93.

– 1986. Linguistic discourse analysis and conversation analysis. *Journal of Literary Semantics* 15:98–127.

– 1987. Preference and sequential organization in Algonquin. In William Cowan, ed. *Papers of the Eighteenth Algonquian Conference*, 321–34. Ottawa: Carleton University Press.

– 1988a. Response preferences in narrative discourse. *Semiotica* 71:93–123.

– 1988b. Laughing together in Algonquin conversation. In William Cowan, ed., *Papers of the Nineteenth Algonquian Conference*, 201–12. Ottawa: Carleton University Press.

Spielmann, Roger 1993a. 'You're so fat!': Value conflicts in Native/non-Native collaborative research. In Anne-Marie Mawhiney, ed., *Rebirth: Political, Economic and Social Development in First Nations*, 3–14. Toronto: Dundurn Press.

– 1993b. 'Makwa Nibawaanaa': Analyse de Récit Algonquin concernant les Rêves sur les Ours. In Daniel Clément, ed., *Recherche Amérindienne au Québec* 23, no. 2–3:109–23.

Spielmann, Roger, and Holly Gardner. 1979. Verb tense organization as an interactional resource in conversational storytelling. *Papers in Linguistics: International Journal of Human Communication* 12, no. 3:293–330.

Spielmann, Roger, and Bertha Chief. 1986. Requesting and rejecting in Algonquin: notes on a conversation. In William Cowan, ed., *Actes du Dix-Septième Congrès des Algonquinistes*. 313–25. Ottawa: Carleton University Press.

Spinder, George, and Louise Spinder. 1984. *Dreamer with Power*. Prospect Heights: Waveland Press.

Steckley, John. 1994a. Relatedness in languages. Notes prepared for the *NATI 2005EZ* manual, Department of Native Studies, University of Sudbury.

– 1994b. Verbs and nouns. Notes prepared for the *NATI 2005EZ* manual, Department of Native Studies, University of Sudbury.

– 1994c. Pronominal morphemes in Inuktitut, Huron and Cree. Notes prepared for the *NATI 2005EZ* manual, Department of Native Studies, University of Sudbury.

– 1994d. More than eight million words: Huron language productivity. Notes prepared for the *NATI 2005EZ* manual, Department of Native Studies, University of Sudbury.

– 1994e. Oneness and twoness: Huron grammar and philosophy. Notes prepared for the *NATI 2005EZ* manual, Department of Native Studies, University of Sudbury.

Tannen, Deborah. 1989. *Talking Voices: Repetition, Dialogue, and Imagery in Conversational Discourse*. Cambridge: Cambridge University Press.

– ed. 1988. *Linguistics in Context: Connecting Observation and Understanding*. Norwood, NJ: Ablex Publishing.

Taylor, Drew Hayden. 1996. *Funny, You Don't Look Like One: Observations from a Blue-Eyed Ojibway*. Penticton, BC: Theytus Books.

Tedlock, Dennis. 1988. Ethnography as interaction: The storyteller, the audience, the fieldworker and the machine. In Regna Darnell and Michael K. Foster, eds., *Native North American Interaction Patterns*, 80–94. Ottawa: Canadian Museum of Civilization.

Tedlock, Dennis, and Bruce Mannheim, eds. 1995. *The Dialogic Emergence of Culture*. Chicago: University of Illinois Press.

Todorov, Tzvetan. 1990. *Genres in Discourse*. Cambridge: Cambridge University Press.

Tonkin, Elizabeth. 1992. *Narrating Our Pasts: The Social Construction of Oral History*. Cambridge: Cambridge University Press.

Turner, Roy. 1972. Some formal properties of therapy talk. In David Sudnow, ed., *Studies in Social Interaction*, 367–96. New York: Free Press.

– 1974. *Ethnomethodology*. Markham, Ontario: Penguin.

– 1976. Utterance positioning as an interactional resource. *Semiotica* 17:233–54.

Twer, Sheldon. 1972. Tactics for determining persons' resources for depicting, contriving, and describing behavioural episodes. In David Sudnow, ed., *Understanding Everyday Life*, 233–54. New York: Free Press.

Valentine, Lisa Philips. 1992. Wemihshoohsh and the burned shoes. Unpublished ms.

– 1994. Code switching and language leveling: Use of multiple codes in a Severn Ojibwe community. *International Journal of American Linguistics* 60, no. 4:315–41.

– 1995. *Making It Their Own: Severn Ojibwe Communicative Practices*. Toronto: Univeristy of Toronto Press.

– 1996. Metanarration in Severn Ojibwe. In John D. Nichols and Arden C. Ogg, eds. *Nikotwâsik iskwâhtêm, pâskihtêpayih! Studies in Honour of H.C. Wolfart*, 429–60. Memoir 13, Algonquian and Iroquoian Linguistics.

Valentine, Rand. 1996. *Amik Anicinaabewigoban*: Rhetorical structures in Albert Mowatt's telling of an Algonquin tale. In John D. Nichols and Arden C. Ogg, eds., *Nikotwâsik iskwâhtêm, pâskihtêpayih! Studies in Honour of H.C. Wolfart*, 387–428. Memoir 13, Algonquian and Iroquoian Linguistics.

Van Dijk, Teun. 1997. *Discourse Studies: A Multidisciplinary Introduction*. Vols. 1 and 2. Amsterdam: University of Amsterdam.

Wardhaugh, Ronald. 1993. *An Introduction Sociolinguistics*. Oxford: Basil Blackwell.

Watson, Graham. 1992. The understanding of language use in everyday life: Is there a common ground? In Watson and Seiler, eds., *Text in Context: Contributions to Ethnomethodology*, 1–19. Newbury Park, California: Sage Publications.

Watson, Graham, and Robert M. Seiler. 1992. *Text in Context: Contributions to Ethnomethodology*. Newbury Park, California: Sage Publications.

Wild, Joy, Carole Nalonechny, and Bernard St-Jacques. 1978. Sociolinguistic aspects of native indian speech. *Sociolinguistics* 11:34–6.

Wolfson, Nessa. 1979. 'The Conversational Historical Present in American English Narrative.' Ph.D. dissertation, University of Pennsylvania.

Wooton, Anthony J. 1981. The management of grantings and rejections in request sequences. *Semiotica* 37:59–89.

Zimmerman, Don, and D. Boden. 1991. Structure-in-action: an introduction. In D. Boden and Don Zimmerman, eds., *Talk and Social Structure: Studies in Ethnomethodology and Conversation Analysis*, 3–21. Berkeley: University of California Press.

Index